IN COMMAND

...200 things I wish I'd known before I was Captain.

by: Captain Michael Lloyd FNI

A Witherby Seamanship Publication

First published 2007
Reprinted 2008

ISBN-13: 978 1 85609 353 8

British Library Cataloguing in Publication Data

Lloyd, Conrad Michael
In Command : 200 things I wish I'd known before I was captain
1. Ship captains - Miscellanea
2. Ship handling - Miscellanea
3. 623.8'824

ISBN-13: 978 1 85609 353 8

© Witherby Seamanship International Ltd 2008

All rights reserved. No part of this publication may be reproduced, stored in a retrieval system, or transmitted in any form or by any means, electronic, mechanical, photocopying, recording or otherwise, without the prior permission of the publishers.

Notice of Terms of Use

While the advice given in this book (In Command) has been developed using the best information currently available, it is intended purely as guidance to be used at the user's own risk. Witherby Seamanship International does not accept any responsibility for the accuracy of any information or advice given in the document or any omission from the document or for any consequence whatsoever resulting directly or indirectly from compliance with or adoption of guidance contained in the document even if caused by failure to exercise reasonable care.

This publication has been prepared to deal with the subject of Command. This should not however, be taken to mean that this publication deals comprehensively with all of the issues that will need to be addressed or even, where a particular issue is addressed, that this publication sets out the only definitive view for all situations.

The opinions expressed are those of the author only and are not necessarily to be taken as the policies or views of any organisation with which he has any connection.

Published by:

Witherby Seamanship International Ltd.
4 Dunlop Square, Deans Estate, Livingston,
West Lothian, EH54 8SB

Tel : +44 (0) 1506 463 227
Fax : +44 (0) 1506 468 999
Email: info@emailws.com
www.witherbyseamanship.com

Foreword

A number of years ago I took a temporary job ashore that was entirely unrelated to seafaring. It was as a junior civil servant, which was quite a change after 25 years at sea with 10 of them in command.

Shortly after taking the position I attended a course on management skills and the relationships between senior management. I found it to be excellent and wished that such guidance had been available before I assumed command.

For the first time in the profession, Captain Lloyd's book presents such guidance for both aspiring young officers and newly appointed Captains.

A newly appointed Master will feel richer for having studied it and my own experience leads me to the conclusion that all who are connected with shipping, especially those who interact with the Master, should read this book.

The rocks and shoals a ship's Captain has to avoid are not always out at sea. They are often found amongst those you have to deal with in all areas of your responsibilities.

It is more preferable by far to keep a happy and comfortable relationship with your employers, but this is not always easy and is as dependent on your competence and professionalism as much as theirs.

Let us hope that a commonsense approach can be found, worldwide, on sensible levels of ship operation in line with acceptable profits.

It's a bit like wishing for World Peace!

Michael Lloyd's book goes a long way to helping us with this goal.

Captain Edward Martin Scott, RD FNI RNR**

Captain Edward Martin Scott, RD FNI RNR**

In May 1959, Martin's seagoing career commenced with a year of pre-sea training at the School of Navigation, Warsash, Southampton. He was apprenticed to the Royal Mail Line in 1960, trading in passenger and cargo ships to South America, the West Indies and North America. On gaining his Master's certificate in 1970 he joined what was then British Rail Shipping and International Services Division at Weymouth in Dorset.

Promotion to Master came in 1975, and he commanded most units of the Sealink fleet of passenger RoRo vessels, serving the southwest coast of England to the Channel Isles and France until the division's closure in 1986.

A variety of commands followed, including Sea Container's 650 passenger cruise ferry Orient Express, sailing to Italy, Greece, Turkey, West Africa, the Canary Isles and Madeira, and the Trinity House research vessel Trinity Explorer during its 1990 season in the Arctic Ocean. When Holland America Line appointed British officers to its Windstar fleet of sailing cruise ships in 1992, he was selected for command, sailing in French Polynesia, Central America, West Indies, and the Mediterranean, until his retirement in 2004.

A full career in the Royal Naval Reserve ended in 1997 after 37 years' service. Appointed a Midshipman in 1960, he was promoted to Commander in 1981 and Captain in 1991. He has served in many Naval units including minelayers, frigates, assault vessels and aircraft carriers and took part in several exercises to Northern Norway and the Mediterranean with the United Kingdom Amphibious Task Force.

Martin is a Founder Member and Fellow of the Nautical Institute and was President 2000-2002. He is also a Younger Brother of Trinity House.

He succeeded Princess Anne, the Princess Royal, as Master of the Honourable Company of Master Mariners in 2007.

The Honourable Company of Master Mariners

The Honourable Company of Master Mariners is a City of London Livery Company with membership open to British and Commonwealth Master Mariners from the Merchant and Royal Navies.

The objectives are:

- To provide a central body representative of the Senior Officers of the Merchant Navy for the purpose of developing and promoting, in the interests of the Commonwealth, the traditions and efficiency of the British Merchant Navy, to encourage and maintain a high and honourable standard of ability and professional conduct in its Officers.

- To promote and maintain efficient and friendly co-operation between the Merchant Navy, the Royal Navy and all other nautical organisations and societies.

- To constitute a body of experienced seamen, who will be available to act as members of, or to give evidence before, any Royal Commissions, Courts of Enquiry, Committees, or Boards of any description, or governing, examining or other bodies, official or otherwise, and who will be available for advice and consultation on all questions concerning or affecting the Merchant Navy, or judicial, commercial, scientific, educational or technical matters relating thereto.

- To provide facilities for the discussion, study and promulgation of matters concerning or affecting the Merchant Navy, or sea-craft, navigation or nautical science.

- To provide a central consultative body of practical seamen, who will be available for information and advice on all matters connected with the safety and preservation of ships, passengers, seamen and cargo.

- To provide in whole or in part for the maintenance of any necessitous Master Mariners, Navigating Officers, and their dependants through charitable funds.

HQS Wellington, a Grimsby class sloop moored at Victoria Embankment, is the floating livery hall of the Honourable Company of Master Mariners.

Built at Devonport in 1934, HMS Wellington served in the Pacific mainly on station in New Zealand and China before the Second World War. During the war the Wellington served primarily in the North Atlantic on convoy escort duties. She shared in the destruction of one enemy U boat and was involved in Operation Dynamo, the evacuation of troops from Dunkirk.

Redundant at the cession of hostilities she was purchased by the Honourable Company of Master Mariners and beautifully converted to serve as their Livery Hall moored at Temple Stairs, Victoria Embankment, London.

The imaginative displays of the Company's marine paintings and artefacts, gold and silver plate, ship models and newly discovered very early 18th century charts, help make the ship a Livery Hall which is admired throughout the City of London.

In 2004 HQS Wellington was awarded the prestigious Maritime Heritage Award by the World Ship Trust. In 2005 ownership of the Wellington was transferred from the Honourable Company to the Wellington Trust, a charitable trust established to ensure the preservation of this historic ship.

HQS Wellington

Michael started his career on the training Ship HMS Conway and went to sea as a Cadet with P&O.

He was promoted to master on a deep sea tow vessel at the age of 32. He then commanded a wide variety of ships including general cargo, passenger, reefer, heavy lift, container, bulk carriers, anchor handlers, supply vessels, response and rescue vessels in the north sea, oil field support vessels in Nigeria, middle trade multi-purpose vessels in the Black sea and the Baltic.

Michael served 35 years in the Royal Naval Reserve and for 10 years he represented shipmasters on the Council of Numast. He is a Fellow of the Nautical Institute and a Younger Brother of Trinity House.

Michael retired from the sea in March 2007 after 50 years seagoing and 35 years in command. He now works with Witherby Seamanship International as a Senior Advisor and Technical Author.

Contents

1 Shipping Companies 1
    1.1   The Company and Your Relationship 2
    1.2   Your Contract 6
    1.3   The Departments 7
    1.4   Charterers and Charter-Party 10

2 Joining the Ship 13
    2.1   Questions for the Leaving Master 15
    2.2   On Your Own 16

3 Relationships 19
    3.1   The Chief Engineer 22
    3.2   The Chief Officer 22
    3.3   The Catering Department 24
    3.4   The Crew 24

4 Sailing 27
    4.1   Gangway Notice Board with ETD 28
    4.2   Crew Lists Ready 29
    4.3   Other Forms 29
    4.4   Stowaway Search 29
    4.5   Draught Read 29
    4.6   Pilot Boarding 29
    4.7   Weather Reports 29
    4.8   Tide States 30
    4.9   Testing Navigation Equipment, Steering and Engines 30
    4.10 All Crew Onboard 32
    4.11 One Hour Before Sailing 32
    4.12 Draught and Stability Information 33
    4.13 Squat 33
    4.14 From the Agent 33
    4.15 Sailing 34
    4.16 The Pilot 34
    4.17 Tugs 35
    4.18 Berth Clearance 35
    4.19 Anchor 36
    4.20 Bridge Orders 36
    4.21 Lights 36
    4.22 Leaving the Harbour 37
    4.23 Disembarking the Pilot 37
    4.24 Speed 38

5 At Sea 39
    5.1   The Fairway 39
    5.2   Securing the Anchors 39
    5.3   Securing Ship 40
    5.4   Full Away 40

	5.5	Standing Orders	40
	5.6	The Night Order Book	44
	5.7	The Watches	44
	5.8	The Lookouts	45
6		**Your Ship**	**47**
	6.1	Items for Attention	48
	6.2	Engine Room	50
	6.3	Weekly Inspection	50
7		**Ship Management**	**53**
	7.1	Defects - Deck Safety	53
	7.2	Safety Training	54
	7.3	Bunkering	55
	7.4	ISM	56
8		**Discipline**	**57**
	8.1	Assault	59
	8.2	Theft	60
	8.3	Drugs	60
	8.4	Disobedience to a Direct Command	61
	8.5	Insolence and Verbal Abuse	61
9		**Safety**	**63**
	9.1	The Paperwork	64
	9.2	The Safety Committee	64
	9.3	Your Equipment	65
	9.4	The Fire Detection System	65
	9.5	Emergencies	66
	9.6	The Stations Bill/Muster List	68
	9.7	Exercises	69
	9.8	Fire	70
	9.9	The Emergency Party	71
	9.10	Radio Medical Assistance	74
10		**Difficult Circumstances**	**75**
	10.1	Port of Refuge	75
	10.2	Abandon Ship	76
	10.3	Grounding	77
	10.4	Piracy	80
	10.5	Medical Emergencies	83
11		**Collisions**	**85**
	11.1	Why Collisions Really Happen	85
	11.2	The Ideal Situation	86
	11.3	The Prevailing Situation	86
	11.4	STCW (Politics)	87
	11.5	The Financial Dimension	87
	11.6	The Human Element	89
12		**Man Overboard**	**91**

12.1	The Present Predicament	92
12.2	Preparation	93
12.3	MOB - The Plan	96
12.4	The Execution	98

13 Welfare ... 102

13.1	You and the Ship's Company	103
13.2	Social Relationships	103
13.3	Newly Joined Personnel	104
13.4	Dependants	105
13.5	Provisions	109
13.6	Bedding	110
13.7	Work Clothing	110
13.8	Alcohol	111
13.9	Bond	114
13.10	Wages	115
13.11	Medical	116
13.12	Shore Leave	118
13.13	Crew Mail	119
13.14	Cash Advances	119
13.15	Visitors	120
13.16	Uniform	120
13.17	Unions	121
13.18	Animals	122
13.19	Bullying	122
13.20	The Chaplain	123

14 Communications, Letters and Reports ... 124

14.1	Communication	124
14.2	Letters	125
14.3	Reports	126
14.4	Meetings	129

15 Surveys and Inspections ... 131

15.1	Port State Control	131
15.2	ISM Audits	132
15.3	Security Audit	134
15.4	Charterer's Inspections	135
15.5	Flag State Inspections	136
15.6	P&I Inspections	137
15.7	Class Inspections	138

16 Breakdowns ... 140

17 Helicopter Operations ... 141

18 Stowaways ... 142

19 Passengers ... 145

20 Ethics ... 147

21 Portage Accounts, Budgets and Stores ... 149

22	Ocean Routeing	151
23	**Weather Conditions and Ship Handling**	**155**
23.1	Poor Visibility	155
23.2	Weather	156
23.3	Seas	157
23.4	Taking Water	158
23.5	Heading Into the Sea	159
23.6	Running Before the Sea	160
23.7	Turning the Ship	160
23.8	Heaving To	160
23.9	Severe Weather in Port	162
23.10	Precautions	163
23.11	Cold Weather Conditions	164
23.12	Extreme Weather	166
23.13	Extreme Weather at Sea	167
23.14	The Rogue Wave	169
24	**Drydock**	**173**
24.1	Responsibilities	173
24.2	Safety	174
24.3	Security	175
24.4	Pollution	176
24.5	Fire Control	176
24.6	Shipboard Management	177
24.7	Catering	178
24.8	Crew Welfare	178
24.9	Completion	179
25	**Port Entry**	**181**
25.1	Port Planning	182
25.2	Forward Preparation	184
25.3	The Agents	185
25.4	Note of Protest	187
25.5	Ship Regulations	187
26	**Anchoring**	**190**
26.1	Regulations	191
26.2	Manoeuvrability	192
26.3	Anchorages	192
26.4	Positioning	192
26.5	Responsibilities	194
26.6	Anchorage Design	195
26.7	Anchoring Your Vessel	196
26.8	The Anchor Watch	197
27	**Arrival at the Port**	**199**
27.1	The Port Approach	199
27.2	Pilotage	200
27.3	Port Navigation	204

28	In the Port	206
28.2	Official Visitors	208
28.3	The Port	209
28.4	Cargo Management	210
28.5	Ship Management	212
28.6	Personnel	213
28.7	Port Services	213
28.8	Pollution Control	214
28.9	The Berth	214
28.10	Berth Preparation	215
28.11	The Gangway	215
28.12	The Watch in Port	216
29	You and the Law	221
30	The Final Word	225

Author's Introduction

To Command a Ship – 'To have or be in control or authority over a ship and its company'

'It is a serious relation, that in which a man stands to his ship. A ship is a creature which we have brought into this world, as if it were on purpose to keep us up to the mark. In her handling, a ship will not put up with a mere pretender'

Joseph Conrad.

This book aims to advise the newly appointed Captain and help him with many of the problems he may face in the modern world of international shipping.

The command of a merchant ship is not the act of safely navigating a ship from one port to another, nor is it dealing with the business and cargo side of the ship, although the ability to do both of these is a requirement for the position. It is about running the ship and those under you in a way that achieves maximum efficiency, to the satisfaction of those who employ you while maintaining the well being of the ship and those onboard.

The word command is used because that is what we do. It is the peak of our profession and it is as relevant today as it was in the early days of sail. The pages of nautical history are littered with examples of the skills of command. Unfortunately, they are also littered in equal measure with the failures. Command and leadership go hand in hand. Leadership is about having confidence, not necessarily in your ability but in yourself, and the ability to infuse that confidence into others. Equally important is the realisation of your own limitations, knowing when and how to use other's abilities and giving them the confidence to voice their opinions to the benefit of the command. By such simple steps good commanders are made.

Command today is far more difficult than when I first became Captain. In earlier times, most Captains commanded their ships by authority and it was this authority that gave them their unquestioned position. Supported by well trained officers, and firm regulations, they were often able to govern their ships in a remote and autocratic manner, with image and presentation often more important than any personal leadership qualities. The ship functioned under this system because the Master's authority, both with the company and with the port and shore authorities, provided enough support to the ship and those onboard that problem situations were able to be dealt with.

The modern Master may well have to deal with chronic under-manning, fatigue, poorly trained officers and crew, poorly maintained ships, a vast increase in often meaningless paperwork, disinterested ports and head offices that hold him in poor regard within their structures and often, with the ease of modern communications, try to control his ship from their desks thousands of miles away. There can sometimes be very little support for the Master on his ship, either from the senior officers onboard or the managers ashore.

For many officers, the reduced time in rank required for experience and the general lowering of standards of certification means that the training has not really been adequate for command. Promotion to the rank within one company or on short sea trades may mean some of the personnel problems found in the deep sea ships are alleviated. But, for those who wish early command, or live in nations with declining national fleets, sometimes the only place to go is where command is offered and this can often lead to uncharted waters, especially when working for manning agencies.

The growth in crewing agencies can also mean that Captains are appointed to all different types of ships, with the agency having no knowledge of where they are sending him. A young colleague was recently sent by an agency to join a Turkish owned ship with a North Korean registry. Not only was the ship in an appalling state, but all the officers' certificates were forged. This became evident not only through the incompetence of the officers, but because the ship was arrested in Singapore after calling there with engine problems that prompted the interest of Port State to come and have a look. Previously, it had been trading between countries where the flag state officials were what we will generously call 'amenable'.

Regardless of the ship you are appointed to or the company you work for, the transition from Chief Officer to Captain can be traumatic and very little will have prepared you for it. You may think you are ready but the difference between having someone to call and being the one called can be quite thought provoking. It is truly surprising that, in the Merchant Navies, very few Chief Officers will have had the opportunity of actually handling or anchoring a vessel, have dealt with port officials or even had contact with the company offices. In other words, even if you think you are prepared, it is far more likely that you are not.

This is not a book about seamanship, although a considerable number of seamanship matters are discussed, nor does it intend to specifically advise you on matters such as 'how to guide your ship in bad weather' or 'how to deal with a particular port approach or anchorage situations'. Those are subjects best left to more specialist publications. Neither does it necessarily follow to the letter the actions that the established shipping organisations might prescribe. It is intended as a discussion rather than a tutorial, suggesting and advising in a practical way and drawing on the experience of commanding ships of many differing types for many years in all parts of the world.

Sadly there appears to be a lack of command training and expertise in many of our nautical colleges, especially in the western nations. This has carried into the marine administrations of many countries with the result that even the regulations that support us and the examinations that grade us no longer seem to have the relevance they once had. Combine this with the reduction in sea time experience and the quick promotions that take place through a lack of seamen, and the newly promoted Captain can encounter many problems for which he is professionally unprepared and which he is unlikely to have encountered. This book is intended to assist that Captain as well as those who aspire to command.

All too often there are no *real* solutions to a problem. Too often, the outside influences that are supposed to assist, such as operating offices and ports and their officials, increase the problems. Sometimes we can solve a situation or it can be alleviated by our actions, at other times it is like a ball running down hill - we have to wait for it to get to the bottom before taking action and putting things back together again!

The modern Captain must walk a delicate path through all who stand in judgement of him often neither pleasing nor displeasing anyone completely. His powers are far less than the image suggests and yet his abilities, should he be allowed to use them, are greater than generally thought. Successful command of a ship will be strongly proportional to the company's support, the Captain's intelligence and leadership abilities and the abilities and support of his officers.

Captain Michael Lloyd, RD**, FNI, RNR(Rtd).
Younger Brother of Trinity House,
Member of the Honourable Company of Master Mariners.

In Command   Shipping Companies

1   Shipping Companies

The crew's perception of the shipowner's office

The type of situation found on your first command depends on many factors, the prime one being the company that owns or manages the ship. A company that owns and manages their own ship is far more likely to retain some pride of ownership and be willing to pay more for that ship to be run properly. Generally, the smaller the company, the more attention is likely to be paid to the ship and more care is likely to be taken in the selection of the officers and the command. Once trusted, the more freedom the command will have in the management of that ship. In the larger companies, the 'office' is more likely to control the command with, at the extreme end, the entire running of the ship dictated by the office with the Captain largely in the role of an observer who ensures the tramlines are followed.

1

The most difficult, interesting and challenging commands will often come from Ship Management companies. With usually a mixed bag of ships, different registration and class societies, different equipment, crews, trading patterns and with ships that often no senior management ever see, it becomes much more difficult for the company to standardise their management and so far more reliance must be put on the Masters. Through ISM there is a framework and, within this, there is a certain level of support for newly joining Masters. However, there is a downside to this independence of command as it is coupled with the management company's aim of running the ship as cheaply as possible for the owner. It must be remembered that the company is likely to have secured the management of the ship by promising this.

I remember one owner paying an unscheduled visit to his ship and being most surprised to find that the rust coated hull bore no resemblance to the touched up photo he had recently received from the ship management company. Stores immediately improved and shortly after, the ship was removed from that particular ship management company.

Regardless of the ship or trade, there are usually problem areas that are common to all. In this book, I have tried to examine the more difficult situations. While I cannot offer solutions to many of these problems, I have provided some thoughts and ideas for consideration and some suggestions based on my own reactions to similar situations.

1.1   The Company and Your Relationship

Your relationship with your ship's manager is important!

Generalisation of this relationship is difficult as so much depends on the country and nationality of the operating office and its executives. Companies fall within a wide spectrum with those at the top taking interest in the welfare of all of the people that work for them. The next group are the varied companies that operate specialist ships that require additional training, initiative in their officers, and often provide an interesting way to go to sea. Other companies operate good ships, following the rules, but with little interest in you or the crew other than that you should carry out instructions without question and go home. It can be quite depressing to work for such a company if it is not particularly interested in your initiatives, but really just want you to drive the ship. However, the pay is on time and your job (provided you follow their rules) is as secure as any at sea and you get your pension at the end. At the bottom end are the companies that operate with neither good ships nor good management. It is because of the prevalence of such companies we have the ISM code, as an attempt to enforce compliance with some standard of management and safety. The dilemma from a professional point of view is that it is within this group that your expertise can be not only recognised, but is very much wanted and well rewarded to compensate for corners cut elsewhere.

As Captain you need to be happy with the company you've joined (or that has just promoted you).

As you become Captain for a company you must decide what you want. Are you looking for excellent support from ashore, with a good officer and crew structure onboard, and will you be content with waiting for promotion and following the strict regulations such Companies will generally demand? Do you prefer to have short runs at sea and then go home frequently? Do you want the adventure of sailing to a wide variety of ports, tramping around the world on differing ships and crews with a wide variety of cargoes or would you rather enter the peripherals of the shipping industry by going into oil support ships and the wide variety of specialist ships ranging from salvage, towing and ship delivery to many other types? Provided you have the training to support your entry into these ships, which are outside the mainstream, this is where you can find the more adventurous side of life that can still exist at sea.

In Command   Shipping Companies

Do you know who actually owns your ship?

Who are the owners we so often see a reference to? They seem to range from a group of scurrilous men, whose only pleasure in life is plotting the next callous deed against the seafaring community, to upright gentlemen devoted to mankind and their mother. The truth is, of course, neither. The present shipping executive cannot operate with the same freedom that he did in the past but it would appear that the old style of pride in their ships has gone for ever. Now they are boxes carrying cargoes, floating hotels carrying holidaymakers or floating workplaces supporting industrial activities on the sea.

Companies of the past created an atmosphere of loyalty and pride through a combination of the appeal of belonging to "something" and the extra care and support they provided to families at home, albeit for a lower basic pay. However, as times became more commercially tough and these patrician style businesses started to fail, many of the loyal employees were left with redundancy money and poor pensions. Today, there is a more "honest" relationship, with companies paying for a service from its employees and both sides more easily able to walk away when the relationship is not right.

Regardless of the company you join, there are a few basic guidelines to follow. You will have a few indicators about how the company regards the Captains they employ by how you are received in your introduction. Were you introduced to the Operations Director? In general, the larger the company the more you will be seen as a commodity.

I remember being interviewed by a very large company in London. They sat me down in a space used for the garbage bins and a 23 year old began interviewing me. I walked out of the door. Another company, after 20 years in command, wanted me to complete a 5 page psychological assessment, one question being which pet animal I would choose to be with on a desert island. Obviously the tastiest, but I didn't stay for that job either.

4

In the past, Captains were treated as senior executives within a company, with all the status and perks that implies. This is no longer the case, with the Captain now only providing the paid for service of 'ship driver' and rarely consulted or treated as a senior member of the company.

Another strange fact about shipping is that, while you may be the most experienced Captain in the world, the minute you go to a new company you will start at the bottom, with little regard paid to your previously gained abilities or experience. Promotion is often obtained by staying longer than the others or by being in the right place at the right time. Rarely does any company promote completely on ability (although it is fair to say that shipping is not alone in this!).

Shipping is a traditional business. When visiting the office for the first time wear a suit, it shows respect for those who employ you and it displays you as clean and smart. A bonus is that, if they invite you to lunch, they will feel compelled not to take you to Burger King or the hot dog stand. Common sense must apply during this first visit, remember that this company is going to put their ship in the hands of you, a relatively unknown commodity.

Tact is always necessary when dealing with the office if you are to obtain their co-operation rather than antagonism, and at this stage you do not know very much about how the company operates. As Captain you will see a broader spectrum of the company's affairs than you did when you were a Chief Officer and your attitude will inevitably change. Those ashore in the departments should really be seen as your colleagues and in some companies such a relationship can certainly be developed.

Find out some basic information about the company that is about to employ you. If the ship is chartered, what kind of charter party? Who is the classification society? What are the drydocking schedules? How often is the ship visited by any department representatives? How do you escalate a problem?

| In Command | Shipping Companies |

   *In one company I had the pleasure of working for, the Deputy Chairman stated that if you had any problems, call him direct. He meant it too and this certainly kept the department managers in check! In that company, Captains leaving their ships and going on leave attended the board meeting. It was a very rare company indeed.*

If it is a management company, ask who owns the ship. Is the ship a separate company registered in some jungle hideaway or is it owned by a bunch of dentists in Switzerland? Ask if you can see the confidential files of the officers onboard. This can be very helpful, although the company may have a policy not to allow access to these. Make a list of the questions you want to know about as this is your only opportunity to find out things before you join your ship.

Take the time to understand a little about engineering when meeting the Technical Department. Superintendents attending the vessel will often be from this department and it is helpful to form a good relationship with them. A Captain who can discuss fuel quality, purifiers and knows that Sulzer is not the name of a Swiss chocolate makes a pleasant change for them.

1.2   Your Contract

Inevitably this is rather one sided and with very little mention of your own benefits or recourses to action. It is surprising that, at least for the ITF affiliated companies, that the ITF has not produced an international contract that affiliated companies must use.

If you want the job, you have to sign. But do take the time to find out about the company's medical and death benefits and repatriation regulations. This at least will assist your family and yourself if you or those close to you become seriously ill. Another aspect that you might want to discuss at this stage is the company's legal assistance initiatives in the case of your arrest, as it has become fashionable in many ports around the world to arrest the Captain for default. If you are held in jail for two years for a ship related problem not of your direct fault, will the company continue to pay you and, more importantly, will they represent you?

In recent years, time in jail has occurred far too regularly for the Ship's Captain

1.3 The Departments

A number of departments will be interested in you and you should be interested in them.

There are a number of departments that you must learn how to work with

1.3.1 Operations

Curiously, Operations is often run by people that have never been to sea, but don't let this make you leap to a judgement. One of the best Operations Managers I came across was a carpet salesman in a previous life! The operations department, which is your day-to-day overseer, should have more understanding of the reasons behind your actions than the others and must be the department that you are able to communicate with on a reasonably truthful level and to which most of your communications will be directed. 'If in doubt ask', is the generally accepted way to progress. However, they do not exist to solve all your problems and what frustrates this department is the number of Captains who are unwilling to make any decision without consulting them. However, some companies have engendered such indecisiveness through their unwillingness to recognise the Captain's senior level of management responsibility.

1.3.2 Technical

This department is run by engineers, many of whom will not rate the rank of Captain as highly as you do. With the largest budget, and knowing more about the ship than any other department, they are rightly very influential. The only problem is that their main interest is in engineering and, so as long as the engines work, then all is well. It is worth noting that the modern engineering department has more knowledge of hull problems and steelwork than the old marine departments ever did and, if your ship is a bulk or oil carrier, this can be a distinct advantage. Unfortunately, they do not have the same understanding of the bridge, deck or cargo functions and even less the catering or personnel side of the ship's operation.

1.3.3 Safety Department

This department is not popular within the company as it is seen as the department that spends money with no tangible result - it is hard to quantify the fact that 'there was not an accident' to the accountants. There is a belief that this department is independent of company pressures and can act without fear or favour, having access to the highest levels. This sounds great, but it is not the case in practice. All too often, safety departments have, as their prime directive, the protection of the company that employs them rather than the interests of those at sea, increasingly acting as internal company police forces. However, the safety department does have control of the ISM operation and this can give it some level of independence. As long as your paperwork is in order and required reports are sent in on time they are generally happy, but their audits will reflect on you and your management of a ship.

Between the Technical and Safety departments is where the old marine department responsibilities now lie, although some companies still do have marine superintendents. The general demise of the marine department means the loss of real representation in the office, which is a shame as such a department run efficiently could be very effective, especially if linked with safety. However, I have observed that there is a move back in this direction in some companies which must be seen as a positive step.

1.3.4 The Personnel Department

The Personnel Dept is the customer interface with most crew members

This is a department for which you will have mixed and fluctuating feelings when you are at sea. It is an important department that ranges from one man with a typist to a vast department. Some are well run, with the company realising the department's importance, with the personnel officer occupying a senior position within the company's structure, but this is not always the case.

One criticism often voiced with regard to personnel is that, in many cases, they have no sea experience. Personally, I have never thought this detracts from their ability to perform the job, with the proviso that this view depends on the size of the department and its authorities. If only one person performs the role then I believe sea experience is essential. With a larger department, as long as there is a proportion of the staff that have been to sea, the mix can be beneficial. If we think of this department as being the main contact with the company for the majority of our officers and ratings we can see it should be relatively approachable, with those at sea feeling themselves able to speak openly about their problems with a feeling of trust. They are in a position to give those at sea valuable advice and it should be the company's ear to the morale of a ship and the fleet in general. Unfortunately, in a number of companies, this department has degenerated into a hiring and firing agency, with little connection to those it manages.

1.3.5 Accounts

This is the department that, apart from being responsible for paying you, will be checking your portage account, clearing your expenses and, in the final analysis, deciding whether your ship is paying its way. Occasionally, in some companies, you will come face to face with them in drydock, especially if a considerable amount of work and money is involved. Increasingly, it is the accountants who will decide whether you will keep your job.

In all your dealings with the office and those who work there, remember that you are a professional and are likely to know more about ships and the sea than many of them. While the companies may prefer Captains who will do what they are told rather than think for themselves, it is your professional obligation to ensure that it is not at the expense of your ship and crew. Independence of command has become harder to find in the modern shipping scene and, if this is what you want, you will be more likely to find it in smaller companies.

When we at sea dwell on the state of affairs at sea we are likely to assume that all is well in the office but here, too, a decline has been experienced. All too often, young ex-sea staff who are untested in senior positions have replaced experienced managers and superintendents, with the rewards and expectations lowered accordingly. It is with these offices we have to have an interface with in any attempt to manage the ship, provided of course the shore office wants the ship managed. That is not as paradoxical as it sounds. If you know that you have poorly qualified personnel on the ship, then there is a tendency, especially with the ease of communications today, to try to run the ship from the office. The result of this is that the ship then takes less and less responsibility and becomes unwilling to make any decision without office approval.

1.3.6 Chartering

In an increasingly commercial world, the chartering department can have too much control over the ship, with little knowledge of the implications of their actions

These are the chaps who always write-in a speed that can only be achieved with a following hurricane and all sails set! If the company has a chartering department and is in the short sea trade business, it can at times override operations. With ships on such a trade constantly entering and leaving ports with single consignments, it is essential for the chartering department and the ship to work together. Often the ports or berths that a ship is chartered to are quite challenging and very different from deep sea ports. It is in this type of trading that severe demands can be put on a ship by people without any relevant experience and you may spend a considerable amount of time on the phone explaining why something cannot be done in the manner requested.

1.4 Charterers and Charter-Party

Charter-Party is the written contract between the charterer and ship-owner, under which a ship is let or hired for the conveyance of goods on a specified voyage or for a definite period.

| In Command | Shipping Companies |

Chartering / Ownership Options

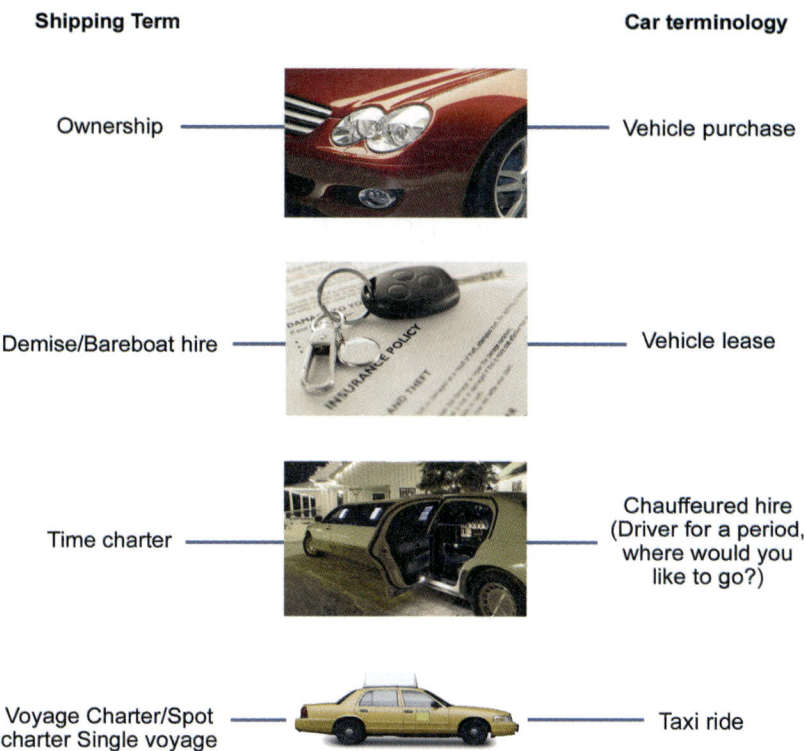

Shipping Term		Car terminology
Ownership		Vehicle purchase
Demise/Bareboat hire		Vehicle lease
Time charter		Chauffeured hire (Driver for a period, where would you like to go?)
Voyage Charter/Spot charter Single voyage		Taxi ride

It is worthwhile mentioning affreightment, which is the way the contract to carry cargo for a shipper is described. It is an agreement, between the operator and the shipper, to carry goods or give the shipper part or the whole of the cargo space on the ship, with the shipper paying the freight for this carriage.

Charterers rarely see the ship that they charter and, if they did, then probably some would not be chartered. Sometimes they commission a company to make an inspection for them but, generally, they accept the ship on the basis that the ship's certificates are up-to-date, as Flag State inspections and the ISM audit ensure that the ship is capable of carrying out their operational requirements. You should know the basics of the charter-party and any clauses that pertain to your ship. Many operators have a copy of it onboard but others choose not to show it to the Captain. If you do not have a copy onboard, you should at least know the speed your ship is chartered at (which often proves interesting) and the downtime your ship is allowed before off-hire clicks in. You might also, on a dry cargo ship, find out who is responsible for lashing and securing of the cargo.

One of the reasons that you might not have the charter-party onboard could be the mention of crew bonuses for hold cleaning, funnel insignia painting and other such work carried out on behalf of the charterer.

On a ship I worked on in the 70's, that belonged to a very well known British company, we had occasion to visit a port in Japan, where the charterer's head office was situated. They decided to visit the ship and, at the end of the visit, told us that, as we were in the port, they would give us the hold cleaning bonuses in cash rather than sending them to the company office in London. When the money was distributed to the crew there was uproar as they had been told by the company that the charterers did not pay bonuses. In actual fact the money was being sent to the office every month.

If your crew are asked to clean hatches and do other charterer's work and there is no clarified system of bonuses then, in their interests, you must find out what the bonus rates should be and ensure that they are paid.

In a company I once worked for, it was common for the Captains to deal with the sub-charters of their ships, only bringing to the attention of the office any clauses that they felt would be against the company's interest. This management approach not only assisted in expanding our knowledge of charters, it also held our interest in the commercial operation of our ship. It certainly taught us to read charter-parties very carefully.

2   Joining the Ship

This is the time to say goodbye to loved ones and family

So, now let us assume you have surmounted the hurdle of the office visit, said farewell to the loved ones or your favourite barmaid, and are now headed for your ship.

There are those who cannot go anywhere without a wife, three children and a dog. I would counsel that you take the dog and leave the rest. If this is your first time in a company, on an unfamiliar ship and first time in command, you have enough problems without towing the family along too. If you really must have them with you, bring them out later. Why do I take a strong line on this (and one I have personally followed)? As Captain, your first duty is to your ship and to your men. In an emergency, who will you look after first, your crew of your family? Case proven. Regardless of all the promises made, your wife or partner will find it impossible to avoid interfering in the ship's affairs. There will be favourites amongst the ship's personnel and this will influence you and cause discontent with your staff, hampering your ability as a Captain. It is also tough for your partner to appreciate how difficult it is to be cooped up in a steel box with all the children for several months.

There was the time when a seaman could look at a ship and the boats, and know how the ship was run and the standard of officers onboard. Unfortunately this no longer applies. The fact that the ship's sides are coated in rust can mean that the company doesn't provide the paint, that the manning is so low that there is not the crew to do the maintenance, or just that the ship is on a trade where there is not enough time to care for it. Many ports now no longer allow ships to paint alongside, on the rather suspect assumption that paint spilt into the dock will pollute the entire harbour, regardless of the cranes on the jetty leaking oil by the gallon. So, when you look at the ship from the jetty, do not pre-judge.

| In Command | Joining the Ship |

Those first few minutes onboard make a big impression

On boarding the ship, from the gangway to the Captain's cabin, you will be able to judge the ship and, if you are an experienced seaman you are likely to be 95% correct. Three minutes can tell you how things are. Is the gangway properly rigged and manned? Is the quarterdeck area clear and tidy? Is the interior clean and well lit? Does the ship smell? Is the deck clean and free of oil? A dirty ship, in common with an unhappy ship, has no place on the sea.

Don't carry your bags onboard. You are the Captain so start as you mean to go on. Have the crew take them onboard and up to the cabin. First impressions are very important. Don't join in jeans and a t-shirt. You will look like one of the crew and that is how they will regard you. In addition, the agent who may be taking you to join the ship will not be too impressed. Remember that he also reports back to the office.

| In Command | Joining the Ship |

So now you have boarded, followed your bags up to the Captain's deck and hopefully met the outgoing Master. In a well run company you will have found a clean ship with a helpful crew. The departing Captain will be waiting for you with all the handover papers to ensure your handover is smooth. He will be a most important source of information, not just about the ship but also about the company and its ways. It is vital that, prior to joining, you sit down for an hour or so and write down a list of questions to ask him.

2.1   Questions for the Leaving Master

- Portage account
  run through it with him and see his final account for handover
- ship's certificates and status
  check these against the check list. If some are ashore with the agent, make sure you have the receipt
- charts, fuel and water for the next voyage
- communications with the company
  run through the email system or any other system being used
- any bridge and engine room equipment problems and idiosyncrasies?
- any hull or structural damage and next scheduled drydocking?
- stores
  is the ship fully stored ?
- if you are unfamiliar with the port and the next scheduled port, ask about these and any problems with navigation, port facilities and officials

Trying to load stores in Swansea

- if you can check the bond, although it is probably sealed. At least see the final bond statement
- check the cash and make sure you have the safe keys and the combination
- don't forget your cabin keys
- get his assessment of the officers and key ratings, especially the Chief Officer, Chief Engineer, Watchkeepers and Cook
- probe him about the company and the way they like things done. Who are the good, the bad and the ugly? Who should be avoided and who should be leaned on?

Hopefully he will show you round the bridge and this is your opportunity to have not only the basic operation of unfamiliar bridge equipment explained to you, but also their idiosyncrasies, such as where to kick the radar when the screen goes blank or where the leaks in the deck-head are (usually directly above the electronics!). Ask about the handling of the ship. What is the power of the thrusters if you have them? Right hand or left hand propellers? If variable pitch, which way does the bow sheer when going astern? Do not believe the standard phrase that ships with variable pitch propellers do not do this, they do. If standard propellers and engines, how many movements before the air bottles need topping up and how long before you can make the next movement? There are obviously many more questions and these are just some of the more important ones. Don't forget, once the leaving Master is down the gangway, you are on your own.

2.2   On Your Own

So now you are on your ship, Master of all you survey. Well, that is the theory anyway and it sounds good with the family and general public. What you do next depends on the time you have before you sail forth on the great adventure. Any reasonable company will have made sure that you arrive in good time at the port of joining, had time to rest before and then had enough time to ensure an adequate handover and settling in period before sailing. As all at sea know, this is not always the case. Sometimes you will join a ship where there is no Captain to hand over to you, sometimes it's a pier head jump with the Pilot already on the bridge or a combination of the two.

On my first command I passed the old Captain being taken down the gangway on a stretcher and found his cabin littered with the empty bottles of Gordons Gin, his failed test pilot course and the wreckage of four months uncompleted portage accounts.

In Command	Joining the Ship

In difficult handover circumstances, at least have a brief run through of the bridge equipment from the bridge officers onboard and essential reports from the heads of departments. You can delay sailing for an hour or so to get this done. If the pressure is on, have an engine problem or something. After all, if the propeller won't turn neither the owner nor the port can do much about it! With regard to accounts not completed by the previous command, don't even try to deal with these. The company has a department ashore with people far better than you at accounts, so help keep them employed. Bundle the whole lot of papers together with all the bills and receipts you can find and send them to the office. If you get them off the ship, they cannot pester you for information.

| In Command | Joining the Ship |

Remember the company employs skilled accountants, which you are not (albeit perhaps for not having the available time!)

Hopefully the situation in which you take your first command will not be too bad. So, let's assume you had time to settle in before heading off into the blue.

Happy memories once full away on passage

3 Relationships

Get your attitude wrong and trouble will follow you on every ship

Strangely, this is the most difficult course you will have to steer in your command. You know the basics of your profession by now and should be able to scrape through your first few years without too much trauma. But get your attitude wrong and trouble will follow you on every ship. If a bad reputation builds up around you, the problems will become worse as good officers will refuse to sail with you. As Captain you command the ship, as a leader, you manage your officers and crew. Nowhere in your career will you have had any formal training in personnel. Because of this, all that you know will have been picked up along the way.

I remember in one company, a senior Master redundant from a large cruise ship company joined and half way through the voyage had to be relieved. All his problems, including personnel, were caused because he had been so remote from basic shipboard management and crew for so long. He went ashore and ran a very successful pub, which was far more suited to his professional experience and ability.

Because you will have recently been a Chief Officer, observing the Captains you have sailed with, you will have already made your mind up about the way you will conduct yourself with your officers. Your senior officers are the hinge on which your success will swing and how you handle them will be critical in obtaining their active co-operation. Let's take a quick look at some of the problems that can arise.

As Captain, you are head of the ship, not the head of the deck department. Any attempt to regard you as such must be firmly but politely corrected. The technical department ashore are often the leading culprits, and many would actively argue that 'head of deck' is what you should officially be. The reasons for this are varied but most often are caused by a failure to understand the position of command coupled with a general lowering of the standards of the Chief Officers. Under such circumstances a ship would become truly divided, with no command. An impossible situation.

In theory, the ship functions with three separate departments. The deck, headed by the Chief Officer, the engine or technical, headed by the Chief Engineer, and the catering department headed by the Chief Steward. The Captain manages the collective departments and shore management supports his authority and provides support for the ship when required. This is all based on the assumption that we still have a ship with fully professional officers and skilled ratings which unfortunately, as all of us who are in command know, we do not.

As the supportive professionalism of the junior officers onboard has declined, and as the problems to confront have increased, the Captain and Chief Engineer must work more closely together if any form of management is to be achieved. These two men, hopefully joined by a competent Chief Officer, now must form a senior management team and assist each other to perform the most important management tasks, deciding on what can safely be left out. However, it is becoming increasingly difficult for those ashore to accept that any other officer, apart from the Captain and Chief Engineer, should have responsibility.

In the past, junior officers regularly inspected equipment and signed documents, but now more and more shore agencies and shipping companies require the Master to do this, down to the most ridiculous levels. If you employ officers who are unable to be left on the bridge to navigate ships on their own in confined or busy waters, the thinking is probably correct, but it reduces the officer's rank to a meaningless title. How many companies allow the Duty Officers to lower and hoist the lifeboats without supervision by at least the Chief Officer? Yet we all regularly did this as junior officers in our youth.

Yesteryear – open lifeboat exercising!

In Command   Relationships

Companies now insist that senior officers must be onboard at all times, when in the past the duty officer was left onboard alone, perfectly happily loading different cargoes into several hatches at once with derricks, wires in a multitude of configurations and hundreds of shore labour workers onboard.

More and more companies are trying to float the idea that the Captain is the head of the deck department and not the Chief Officer, effectively removing another level of management. Already they have put the poor Chief Officer in a boiler suit for most of his life onboard, together with all the other officers, and if such a change in his department responsibility is tolerated he will be reduced to the level of a foreman.

It is so easy to say that, if you want the job to be done properly, do it yourself. However, senior officers are increasingly taking on not just the old responsibilities of the junior officers, but those of senior ratings as well. It is essential that a start is made in returning responsibilities for many tasks back to the junior officers and senior ratings, even if it means accepting that their training will have to be by their mistakes. I have much sympathy with those who say they are not there to train and even if they are, then their job is to train for the next rank rather than the one the officer is supposed to be doing. However, if an attempt is to be made to operate the ship efficiently, on-the-job training must now be considered an essential element in shipboard management.

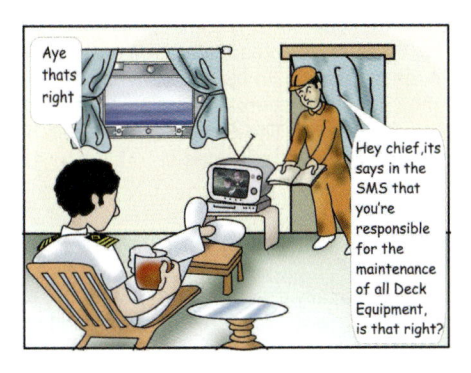

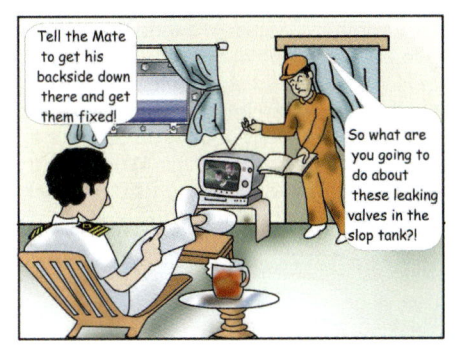

The possible permutations of department responsibilities are many and, in today's fast-changing world at sea, open to debate. Some companies make the Chief Engineer responsible for all deck department maintenance matters and for the direction of the crew and give the Chief Officer the direction of the catering department. Others choose to leave well alone. Stores are often combined, as is the workforce. Regardless of the permutations, the heads of departments must be allowed the responsibility to run their departments on a day-to-day basis, without interference but with the complete support and assistance of the Captain.

3.1   The Chief Engineer

It has often been said by deck officers that the worst thing that ever happened in the Merchant Navy was when they gave the Chief Engineer four stripes. Since that time, ship after ship has been torn apart by either Chief Engineers challenging the Captain's authority or Captains refusing to accept this Officer's expertise in his position as technical head of the ship. This can be further exacerbated by the Captain being young and in his first command, with a far older and more experienced Chief Engineer. Differences between the Captain and the Chief Engineer are immediately apparent to all onboard, with sides taken and general unhappiness with the situation arising. It is a most stupid state of affairs and yet, incredibly, not one often taken seriously by the head office. There are Chief Engineers who want to be the Captain and will not recognise the Captain as the superior officer. Equally, there are Captains who denigrate engineers and disregard the Chief Engineer's technical advice. In reality, such officers should not be at sea but often, because of their seniority, companies allow them to carry on, taking general disruption wherever they go. The Chief Engineer can be your best confidante and guide, or he can be your nemesis.

3.2   The Chief Officer

The Chief Officer is often, especially if recently promoted, the hardest worked officer on the ship. Much of what you can achieve in your command is dependant on his abilities and co-operation. At the initial stage of you joining the ship he will be busy with cargo work and all the other problems his department can throw at him. If he is experienced, you are just another Captain in a long line of them. Keep your ideas of how you want the ship to be to yourself at this stage. Initially all you want of both him and the Chief Engineer is the readiness state of their departments and to know if they have any problems that will or can interfere with the sailing of the ship and the voyage to the next destination. Hopefully, if both officers talk to each other, they will be up-to-date on matters, but do not assume this. When you try to sail the ship and the Chief Engineer says that no one told him the ETD and he has engine in bits, you will begin to get an insight into the communication situation you have inherited.

You are Captain and have a ship to play with now. Leave the Mate to the Cargo.

You are no longer the Chief Officer so do not try to do his job. There might come a time for that, but only as a final extreme due to incompetence or illness. Treat him as your right hand man and the department head he is, and keep him advised about what is coming through your desk. It is important that trust is built between you by meeting with him and consulting him on his opinions, whether you use them or not.

You must also find time to see the other bridge Watchkeepers, especially the Navigating Officer, for a review of his passage plan for the forthcoming voyage and, more importantly, the initial departure passage. In this meeting with the Watchkeepers you must properly explain what you expect of them, especially your availability to them at any time for bridge and watchkeeping matters. We live in modern times and the severe or austere approach is no longer appropriate if you expect them to feel they can call you whenever they wish.

Your expectations about when you are to be called should be clear

Any meetings should be informal and friendly. Having said that, there is and must always be a distance between you and your officers, with the exception of the Chief Engineer with whom you can hopefully achieve a more 'confidante' type of relationship. There is a good reason for this distance. While respect has to be earned, your rank automatically gives you a certain amount with which to start. While a pleasant atmosphere should prevail, you must remember that at any time you could be in the position of reprimanding them.

For your words to be taken seriously, you must be taken seriously. I suggest that, as you do not know your officers yet, you address them by their rank and they address you as Captain or Sir. In time call them by their first names if you wish, but never allow the same back, except from the Chief Engineer if your relationship allows.

3.3   The Catering Department

Reduced manning in recent times has made this department a shadow of what it once was and its composition will entirely depend on the size and trade of the ship. On some ships, especially the short sea trades, there will be only a Cook. On others there may be a Cook/Chief Steward, a Galley Boy and a Steward, with the junior officers cleaning their own cabins. If passengers are carried, then you could have a Purser or Chief Steward, which is good news as he will do the portage account.

Either way, this is the department on which you will rely for the comfort and feeding of those onboard. Most ship managing companies hate the word 'hotel' when applied to their ships, as this word contradicts their concept of crew accommodation and standards, which I believe has been copied from the Prison Service handbook on 'Guidelines for Prisoner's Accommodation' (with due reference to the Geneva Convention). The Cook is, unofficially, the most important man onboard. His job is also the most difficult. Three times a day, every day, he is judged. He is often dealing with mixed nationalities, all who have their own preferences, so he can never please all at the same time. Health onboard also depends on this man, cleanliness in food preparation, galley and storerooms. It does no harm to let him know how important to the well-being of the ship you think he is.

Tip. Never upset the Cook. Even if he is useless and you are sacking him, don't tell him until you arrive in port and his relief is coming up the gangway. There is a very simple reason, just think of the unpleasant things he can do to your food!

3.4   The Crew

Most of us are used to sailing with a multi national crew and we are hopefully free of the prejudices of land. Differing races and cultures have their good points and bad points and, as Master, it is important that you know what these are. The majority of the crew are not there by choice and would much rather be at home with their families. Depending on the company, their contracts may be much longer than yours, with some of the crew having already been a year away from home. Most will be from crewing agencies, so the company will not be too interested in them and there could be very little support from the agency itself, so they look to you. If, at the start of your command, they see a smart Captain who displays an interest in them and prefers to smile rather than frown, there will be a good base for you to build on.

Chances are you will have a multi-national crew

3.4.1 Cadets and Trainees

These young people are the Captains or Chief Engineers of the future. They are not cheap labour, regardless of how short handed the departments are. The problem is that they now have to spend so little time at sea before examination, there is not enough time to ensure they are properly prepared for future promotion. In the past, there was enough time to ensure that you could set them to various tasks until they had a full understanding of the work before moving them to the next. Now the best you can do is ensure they have a smattering of knowledge before moving them on. Some companies have just about abandoned the idea that cadets should do practical shipboard work and confine them to bridgework. I must question how such trained cadets can ever become seamen. To be a seaman, the officer and Captain must not only have experience of the work the crew is being asked to do, but have an understanding of the difficulty of the work and the conditions under which it is being carried out.

> *I will always remember a time on Captain's rounds while I was a junior cadet and entrusted with the note book. The Captain was told that staining in the lavatory bowl could not be removed. He removed his gold braided jacket, undid his cufflinks and rolled up his sleeves, called for the cleaning equipment and proceeded to clean the stain from the lavatory bowl. He said nothing, but he did not have to. He simply demonstrated his training and why he was the Captain.* Every man onboard respected him for that.

It is a question of respect. Seamen will respect someone who has done what they do and can tell them how to do it. When we came to sea from our training ships, we could often go on-deck and splice wires and stitch canvas better than the ABs. Similarly, engineer officers had served a five year apprenticeship of hard knocks in heavy engineering before coming to sea and there was very little you could tell them about the practical side. Our cadets today, unless they come from countries that still retain proper pre-sea training, know very little. It is therefore most important that their time is not wasted but is carefully thought out and supervised. Work on the basis that, although they will not be able to do work for enough time to become proficient at it, they at least will have the time to experience it and so maybe understand the difficulties, the time required and the tools needed. Most cadets will be on a training scheme that has to be completed during their time onboard and I suggest that you check their books frequently to ensure that the programme is followed. Similarly, you must encourage your senior officers to ensure that not just the cadets in their department but also the rating trainees are accorded the same regard for their training.

The cadets are also there to learn to be officers. Many of them will be away from home for the first time and can be quite inexperienced in looking after themselves. If necessary, this must be taught by frequent inspections of their quarters and their appearance. If you have passengers onboard, after explaining to them the training purpose, put the cadets on their tables for the occasional meal with the hope that a few social graces will rub off on those that need them. Quite a number of companies will have laid down procedures for cadet training and the responsibilities the officers have for it. If there is not, have a junior officer from each department take on the role of Cadet Training Officer so that he can be the officer any cadet can go to with problems.

In the end, it is important to remember that cadets are in an unfamiliar world that has different rules and sometimes a different language. Quite often they are working and living with people from different countries and cultures. It can be a lonely life, especially if there is only one cadet or trainee. Your attention can help their integration considerably.

4   Sailing

You will find getting familiar with the navigational situation for departure comforting (Courtesy Stena)

Depending on the time available, and still hoping that you are not sailing on a wing and a prayer, then the bridge should initially be your priority. Rather than nipping down the gangway for a little bonding with the natives, a quiet evening spent checking the initial port and coastal charts, firing up the radars and operating them and checking any pertinent publications, especially local 'Notices to Mariners' and weather reports, will do wonders for the soul.

You should talk with the Chief Engineer about how he likes the engines to be operated and if there have been any past problems, such as blackouts. At this stage, there is little point visiting the engine room unless the Chief is particularly proud and wants to show you round. Generally though, it is a hot and noisy place and no one really wants the Captain there.

I know Captains that have never been in the engine room. When I was a junior officer, one Captain on his rounds always used to make a point of asking where the engine room door led to. Worrying thing was, on that ship, the Chief Engineer used to ask the same question!

Have the Chief Officer give you a quick walk round the decks. At this stage, you are not making an inspection, it is purely for your own knowledge. When you get away to sea you will have time for a better look around. As a seaman, you will obviously see things that are wrong or that you may have done differently, but as yet you do not know the situation regarding the stores available or the quality of the deck crew. It is a continual surprise that the modern day seaman seems to have an ability to walk past equipment that is broken or missing, gear not stowed properly and leaking pipe work and neither fix it nor report it, especially in the case of safety equipment that is there for your protection.

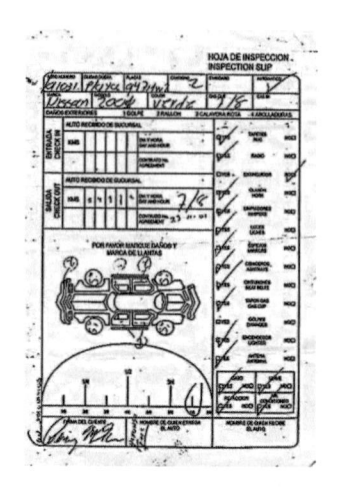

Check your new ship for damage, just like you would for a hire car

Have a walk along the berth and check the condition of the hull, especially in the area of the quarter and the shoulder. If there are any large dents, check with the Chief Officer if they are recorded on the hull plan and in the log book. If not, make a note of these for advising to the company. After all, why should you be blamed?

You have by now checked most of the basics and should know enough about the ship to get it safely out of the harbour and into blue water, with a course set for the next port.

Here are some of the items you should now be thinking about.

4.1   Gangway Notice Board with ETD

This is very important and should have been updated the afternoon before. When stating the ETD, always allow at least 3 hours in reserve. The reason for this suggestion is simple. Crew tend to go ashore the evening before sailing. If they don't come back and there was no ETD stated, they will (and do) claim that no one told them when the ship was sailing. The fact that everyone knew and it should be their responsibility to find out is neither here nor there. It now becomes your fault. The three hours allows for car breakdowns, taxis not coming and the fact that the love of his life has pinched his wallet and he has to leg it back to the ship!

4.2 Crew Lists Ready

Ensure your name is now on these and on the Stations Bill. Visits from Port State on sailing day are quite common. While on the subject of Port State visits, make sure you know where your lifejacket and survival suit is stowed. It is embarrassing having to look around for these with Port State looking on. Also make sure that you have completed and signed your initial familiarisation document.

4.3 Other Forms

These depend on the port and country that the ship is in. A departure form might be required and immigration and customs will possibly board with the agent to check on crew and bond seals.

4.4 Stowaway Search

It is most important that this is thoroughly organised, particularly if your ship is heading to the UK or Europe from African ports. Hopefully, all the deck storerooms will have been locked on arrival as, if not, the only thing left in them may well be stowaways. Don't forget the holds and the hatch entry spaces. On a large ship you will need all the crew for this search so allow the time. This can be entered into the log as the security search.

4.5 Draught Read

Sometimes this is a problem as a large bulk carrier has to read the draught on both sides, often through the use of a boat. If there is a large swell on the water or the sea is choppy the reading can be somewhat variable.

4.6 Pilot Boarding

Find out from the port control if the Pilot is coming by road or boat. If by boat, ensure that the pilot ladder or gangway is ready on the outboard side and that the manropes are rigged, regardless of whether they are used or not.

4.7 Weather Reports

If possible, obtain the latest local weather report. If you use a weather fax or email, these may not give as good a view of the local situation as the port can.

4.8 Tide States

Hopefully, your Navigating Officer will already have these in the passage plan. However, do remember that they will have been taken from the tide tables and so will differ slightly from the local conditions. Many times you will find that when the tide should be going out it is coming in, and vice versa, especially near high and low waters.

4.9 Testing Navigation Equipment, Steering and Engines

**Allow more time than the obligatory 1 hour before for testing the gear.
This gives more time to fix anything**

Although it is normal to test gear 1 hour before sailing, this does not really allow much time to fix anything that is wrong. Equipment tests should take place at least 3 or more hours before sailing. There will be an ISM check list. Ensure that clocks are synchronised, especially between the engine room and the bridge. If there is any defect and it cannot be repaired in time, you will have to make an assessment of how it will affect your departure and voyage to the next port. If it is an engineering problem the Chief Engineer will keep you advised. Clearly, if the fault is of a serious nature and the engine doesn't work, then you can't sail and the decision is made for you. In such a case, the agent will be advised and the Chief will already be on the phone to the company for shore assistance and/or parts.

It is astonishing how many insurance claims have been lost due to errors between the bridge and engine room clocks.

In the event of an engineering defect that could interfere with the safe progress of the ship, you must consult with the Chief Engineer before taking any decision to proceed. If he advises against it, then do not sail. Should he use the word 'might', then do not sail. You are not in the business of 'might' and you may not yet have the experience to quantify this. The same stance must be taken with the bridge equipment. There is equipment that you can proceed without and equipment that is, in your opinion, essential. This decision will depend on the repair facilities at the port you are in and those at the next port, together with the distance to that port.

As an example, you find the auto pilot is not working. If you do not have an Electronics Officer then there is probably not much you can do yourself except test the power source and give it the traditional smack. Many modern systems are really not designed for ship's staff to attempt to repair anyway. While this is not an emergency, is it a serious problem? The first evaluation is whether or not a technician is available in the port? If there is, have the agent organise him to attend as soon as possible. If time zones allow and your head office is open, get on the phone and advise them of the situation, especially as there might be a delay in sailing the ship.

If there is no technician readily available, or he attends and finds that spares are required that are not in stock, then you must now consider all of the factors. If your next voyage is for a few days to the next port, then obviously you can sail so long as you have enough sailors who can steer the ship. However, if you are heading off for a forty day haul across the oceans, the problem becomes more complex. While you may well have sailors that can steer, quartermasters they are not, so your passage will resemble the anti torpedo zigzags of World War II, with the additional fuel consumption and time. More serious is the fact that you will be stripping the deck department of most of its personnel for the entire passage. If you start with only five seamen, this will completely disrupt all the work of this department, including essential safety maintenance. However, the port will not allow you to stay alongside for very long either, especially if you are on a busy cargo berth, so the chances are that after a few hours wait, you will be required to leave for the anchorage if you elect to remain.

The real answer to your problem lies in the time element and in your operations department. If they can get parts and technicians quickly to your vessel, you may be allowed to wait, but the clock is ticking. If you go off hire, what is the cost per day? If you are not chartered the question of the cost still remains. However, if you sail, the cost is to the ship rather than the office accounts. I assure you that, after only a very short wait, you will be sailing!

There are more serious problems, such as gyro failure, that you will have to decide on. If the spares and/or technicians are not readily available to repair this equipment in the present port, there will be pressure for you to sail. If you are a senior Master of many years standing with the company, you can tell them what you are going to do and, despite their grumbling, get away with it. However, if you are a first trip Master, it is not so easy.

In the case of the gyro, we know perfectly well that the ship can sail safely using the magnetic compass and that any company would be reasonable in its expectation that you sail if there is no possibility of a realistically quick repair. The problem is that it also affects the automated radar plotting system, which is a SOLAS requirement. It becomes a matter of common sense in interpretation of the regulations. Personally, I believe that if there is no shore assistance possible in the port you are presently in, then you are justified in sailing. After all, if it broke down an hour after sailing you would continue. However, remembering SOLAS, the real answer to the situation is to apply to the authorities in the present port for a SOLAS exemption certificate, which will allow the ship to sail for a specified period to a specific port where the repairs can be affected. If they do not have a spare blank exemption certificate, copy one from the annex of the SOLAS regulations.

4.10   All Crew Onboard

If the gangway board gave an ETD with 3 hours to spare, then the fact that someone was missing should have been advised to you at that time. The sensible thing is to then question the missing crewman's mates to find out when he went ashore and if they know were he might be. If the gangway has been manned with a security watch, the time he left should be recorded. If it is a relatively small port there may be time for the agent to see if he can find the absent crewman. Meanwhile, get his belongings packed up ready for landing, together with his documents and passport.

Finally, before you sail, if you do not have one, buy a small pocket recorder of the voice activated dictaphone type (even iPods have a dictaphone accessory now!). This is a very handy little tool and one that could save you from a number of problems in the future. While on your shopping expedition, also buy a cook book. If you do not need it on this ship, you could well need it on the next.

4.11   One Hour Before Sailing

The following reports should be made to you during this last hour:

- Stowaway search completed
- all navigation equipment checked and in order
- charts ready for use
- steering and engines tested and in order
- the ship is secured ready for sea.

The last one can be problematic. In many ports, the agent and the Pilot could be onboard and the tugs standing by before cargo is completed. In the case of a bulk carrier, you could have still two holds open. Do not allow these factors to influence your decision to sail until you are satisfied the ship is secure. There are circumstances in good weather when half dogs and cleats can be put on the holds and secured fully as the ship proceeds out of port, but this situation can only be judged with experience. On your first voyage take no chances and put up with the grumbles. You didn't order the Pilot. If you are responsible for ordering him then wait until cargo work is completed. Never sail with your holds open. They are not designed for that condition or the forces that heeling can put on them during port manoeuvres.

4.12 Draught and Stability Information

If fully loaded, you should have already checked the anticipated draught against the port depth at the estimated ETD, not forgetting the heel, especially (when manoeuvring) with a very wide ship.

4.13 Squat

When a ship approaches shallow water, the water flowing past the hull has to increase speed as the available flow area decreases. This causes a reduction in the pressure acting on the hull in the vertical direction, which has to be compensated for by an increase in the buoyancy forces, so the ship has to increase its draught to maintain the state of equilibrium. Because of the shape of a ship and because of the adhesive effects of water, the changes in pressure are not the same forward and aft. This causes the ship to trim forward or astern, depending on the hull shape. Therefore, the magnitude of squat depends on the hull shape, the side and under-keel clearance and the speed through the water. A ship with a block co-efficient of more than 0.7 will generally trim by the bow.

4.14 From the Agent

Certificates
Ensure that you retrieve any of your certificates that were ashore and check them against the agent's receipt. You will be surprised at how many times ships sail leaving these behind.

Port Clearance
Normally this is given to you by the agent. Be careful with it as often it can look like a laundry receipt and so gets mislaid more than any other.

Last of all; don't forget to give him the mail.

**Don't forget to give the agent the mail.
It's a fast track way to unpopularity onboard**

4.15 Sailing

With all visitors clear of the ship, the Pilot on the bridge, 'H' flag and the gangway hoisted, you are set to sail.

4.16 The Pilot

The Pilot should have been presented with the pilot card and shown the passage plan for departure. The idea of the Pilot being presented with a plan for departure, drawn up by a junior officer with no idea of local conditions, is an interesting one. The theory is good as it gives that officer training in planning large scale navigation in confined waters and, if he has done his plan properly, it will draw your attention to any foreseeable problems. Whether the Pilot has any intention of following your plan, and what you do if he doesn't, has never been fully examined but look at it this way, the Pilot has far more experience of manoeuvring ships in confined waters than you. He certainly has far more local knowledge and can communicate with the other Pilots on ships under way as well as the tugs. There is a chance that he will have his own plan for you to check, though do not depend on this. If you show him your passage plan and then ask him how he intends to depart, if the verbal plan sounds reasonable go with it.

4.17 Tugs

How many tugs is enough?

You may be asked what tugs you require. However, tugs are often a racket worked between the port, pilots and agents and, without doubt, in many ports you are persuaded to take tugs you do not need. Your first voyage is not the time to make a stand on this, so go with what the Pilot wants unless it is ridiculous.

> *One time in India, with the ship facing out to sea in calm weather and on a 200,000 dwt vessel, the Pilot wanted 4 tugs, which I told him was nonsense. He went into a rage and stated that if I wouldn't have the tugs I must sail the ship myself, which I did. He left the ship in rather a temper.*

If the tug's lines are taken, ensure that they are put onto the right bollard in the correct manner. Again, on large vessels, be aware that some bollards are intended for barge moorings, rather than mooring or towing, and that these have a lower SWL. If your lines are sent to the tug try to ensure they are your best ones, although this is not easy as you are probably using your mooring lines as they are let go from the jetty.

Make sure that the crew stand clear of the tugs lines once they are made fast.

4.18 Berth Clearance

If possible, try to have the berth area alongside the ship clear of cranes, loaders and dischargers, especially those in way of the bridge wing and bow. Some ports co-operate, others do not. If you still have these obstructions in the area, ensure that the Pilot's attention is drawn to them.

4.19 Anchor

Check if there is an anchor down. You were not there when the ship berthed and probably neither was the Pilot. You certainly would not be the first ship to try to leave while forgetting the anchor on the bottom.

4.20 Bridge Orders

Ensure all orders are repeated clearly

Ensure that all helm and engine orders are repeated back loud enough for the Pilot to hear. When the order has been carried out it must again be stated. If you are way out on the bridge wing on a large vessel then you must advise the Pilot when his order has been carried out. There must be no doubt that the Pilot knows what is being done with the helm and engines. The bridge Duty Officer should be stationed in the wheelhouse, checking that the helmsman is correctly applying the wheel, checking the ship's progress on the chart and, if there are no bridge wing controls, operating the engine and/or thrusters controls.

4.21 Lights

If it is night time before sailing, reduce your lighting to just the work lights fore and aft. This will let your crew work safely while enabling your night vision to develop faster once you leave the berth. Check that your navigation lights are on.

4.22 Leaving the Harbour

Sailing is easier than arrival. You are increasing speed instead of reducing, the area of manoeuvring becomes larger the further you progress, at least until you get to the fairway and breakwater, and you are leaving port, which in modern times is always a relief. While we will look at pilotage later, it is enough to say at this stage "do not completely trust the Pilot". He is human and his attention can wander in the same manner as anyone else. It is critical that you watch all his manoeuvres as well as the traffic, drawing his attention to anything that you think might affect the safety of the vessel. A good way for you to do this is to put yourself in his place and think what you would do. In this way you learn and become more confident about driving your ship in confined waters.

Unless the trip is going to be a short coastal voyage and you are sure the weather is good, have your mooring lines stowed below. Apart from losing them over the side, getting them in the propeller is a sure way of stopping the ship, making yours the shortest command in history.

Don't forget the engine room. If the harbour or river passage is prolonged, keep the engine room advised of progress, especially the time you estimate Full Away will be. Apart from it being considerate, remember that the Chief Engineer, also has preparations to make. Watch out for smoke from the funnel. Tolerance for smokey ships, even in harbours, is fast disappearing.

4.23 Disembarking the Pilot

Find out the side from which the Pilot will be disembarking and have the ladder or combination ready for use. Where and when the Pilot will want to leave the ship will vary. Some want to leave almost as soon as the lines are let go and others as the ship enters the approach channel to the sea. Although there is a pilot area clearly marked on the chart, rarely will this be kept to. If there is bad weather outside that will be hazardous for the pilot boat he will obviously have to leave inside the breakwater. However, if there is not, and you are not too confident about carrying on through the remainder of the harbour passage without him, then say so. There is no shame in this and you are just doing what many of us did in our first commands. Once the Pilot appreciates that these are the early days of your command he will understand and co-operate, if he doesn't *he* is the idiot. It is his duty is to take the ship to the pilotage area whether he likes it or not. Of course, you could be lucky and have a helicopter. These are lovely things that do away with all the problems of boats and weather. Just have your Helo deck area clear, the fire party standing by and away he goes

Agree where the Pilot will be dropped

Off the harbour, make a lee, if required, for the pilot boat and have the Pilot escorted off the ship. As you know, an officer or cadet is required to see the Pilot away, but do not allow this to leave you alone on the bridge. Call another officer out or, if there isn't one, have a seaman take him down. It is more important that the bridge is manned properly at the entrance to a port than to follow the niceties. You can always tell the officer forward to go to the ladder and see the Pilot off, as per regulations.

4.24 Speed

Watch your speed going out. If the wind is blowing down the throat of the harbour a swell will develop inside the breakwater. This, coupled with any squat building up, will increase your draught. Of more concern are your men on the forecastle, who are probably still stowing the ropes below and waiting for your orders to secure the anchors. Driving too fast into a swell, especially on a loaded ship, could bury your nose into the sea and seamen have been killed in this way.

5 At Sea

MV "World Vale" approaching Cape Horn"

5.1 The Fairway

When heading out to sea it is wise to keep clear of the anchorage area, which will generally be to either one side or the other of the main fairway leading out to the fairway buoy. Short cuts to the next course across this area are not a good idea as you have no way of knowing when ships are about to move.

Strong winds or currents can be running across the fairway so care should be taken to allow for this set. Particularly with a light ship, this set can affect the ship very quickly so be alert for it and alter course earlier rather than later.

5.2 Securing the Anchors

You still have men on the forecastle waiting for your instructions. If you are heading straight out to deep water then you can have the anchors secured. If you are remaining in coastal waters, you will want to have your anchors available for immediate use if required, so have them clutched in and on the brakes. Once you leave coastal waters for deep sea, don't forget to have them secured. Wait until your crew are finished and clear before increasing your speed.

5.3 Securing Ship

Haul your flags down as they are expensive and can be torn to bits in one night by strong winds. If it is night time ensure that all your work lights are switched off once your crew are off the decks. Hopefully, the crew will have secured the pilot ladder/gangway when the Pilot disembarked and the Chief Officer has now secured all of the hatches and cargo equipment.

5.4 Full Away

Once clear of the fairway buoy, and if you are happy with the situation, ring full away. Again, do not feel pressured into doing this. Poor visibility or dense shipping in the approaches are both reasons to keep the engines on standby. If you are uneasy, then wait.

So, on the assumption that you are at last away from the port, you can breathe a sigh of relief and congratulate yourself on having survived so far without anything too drastic. Once satisfied with the bridge and the progress of the ship, you can get below and square your office or cabin away.

5.5 Standing Orders

Day 1 draws to a close...

There is this one important task to complete before you can relax. It is most important that your officers not only know what you require of them, but that they acknowledge they do by signing this document. Currently on the ship will be the last Captain's orders and, while you can incorporate the good points that you read from them into yours, you must make your own. Once they have read these, the bridge officers will sign them.

You will have read lots of these in the past and will have your own ideas about what you want. Therefore, the example below is only a guide to some of the items you may wish to include.

Responsibilities

- The Chief Officer is head of the deck department and is responsible to me for all matters of deck crew, watch keeping duties and bridge maintenance. He is responsible for correct completion of the bridge log book and it is essential that this is done properly. The basis is that, if you are in doubt, enter your remarks
- the 2nd Officer is the Navigating Officer and is responsible for all aspects of navigation. He will prepare the passage plan and charts for the forthcoming voyage in good time and advise me if there is any chart or publication required. He is required to draw my attention to any area on the chart that the ship will pass that might require my attention. In addition, he will bring to my attention any navigation warning that might affect the ship
    - he will advise the times of high and low water throughout the ships stay in port
    - he is responsible for the readiness and good order of the bridge equipment.
    - prior to arrival in port, he will advise the bridge of any special national or port requirements
- the 3rd Officer is responsible for all signaling equipment and flags. He will ensure that the required flags are ready for use prior to port entry. He will assist the Navigating Officer as required by that officer
    - he will prepare routine port and sea messages as required
    - he is responsible for the maintenance of all portable communication equipment
    - he will act as the ship's Met Officer and ensure that all weather reports are received in a timely fashion and that the ship's position is plotted on the weather charts
- for the purpose of these orders the following will apply:
  Good visibility : above 5 miles
  Restricted visibility : 2 – 5 miles
  Poor visibility : 1 – 2 miles
  Fog below : 1 mile
- these orders are not comprehensive. They are intended to compliment your own professional understanding and the company instructions and guidelines. I expect all officers to use their initiative in the following of them. They are to be read and acted upon in conjunction with the following:
    - International Conference on Revision of the International Regulations For Preventing Collisions at Sea, 1972 (1990 Edition)
    - Bridge Procedures Guide Fourth Edition 2007
    - Company Standing Orders

- - Company ISM Manual
  - The Ship Security Plan

- Should there be any perceived conflict between my orders and any of the above, please bring the order to my attention
- All bridge equipment and controls are there to be used if the circumstances require. All officers are expected to read the instrument manuals provided and have an understanding of the working and limitation of the instruments
- all navigational equipment and controls are to be tested at least 2 hours prior to departure and the test list completed. As part of this check, the gyro compass and all repeaters, including radar, are to be aligned. ER and bridge clocks to be synchronised. The steering gear is to be tested in main and secondary modes
- I am to be advised of the following:
  - any decrease in visibility
  - any malfunction of bridge equipment
  - any doubt whatsoever regarding the safe navigation of the vessel
  - at any time you require my presence or advice
  - any adverse weather reports
- I expect the OOW to act with common sense regarding the RPM of the vessel. Should the vessel start to pound severely, then reduce the RPM as required, advising me of the same
- when making large course alterations, I require the ship to be put into hand steering. The wheel is not to be handed over during any such alteration until the vessel is steady on the new course. When in traffic that requires a number of alterations of course, I require the Helmsman on the wheel
- when altering course for other vessels, early action is required and the alteration is to be substantial in order that there can be no confusion about your intentions on the other vessel. Under normal circumstances, alterations of course should take place not less than four miles away and ships should not be passed less than one mile away
- no other duties are to interfere with the keeping of a responsible lookout. If at any time essential work is required to be completed by the OOW, he will advise the Chief Officer who will ensure that adequate lookouts are provided for that work period. Under no circumstances is work to be done by the OOW in regular shipping waters
- my presence on the bridge does not relieve you of your charge of the watch. I will either verbally take over from you or give a navigational order. To prevent confusion, if you are in any way uncertain if I have command, you must ask me
- irrespective of me taking command, you must also check my action, continue with the plotting of the vessel's position and call my attention to the movement of other vessels or any unsafe navigational procedures I might be taking

- the OOW's prime responsibility is for the safety of the ship and he will take any action required to ensure this. If, at any time, he feels that the ship is standing into danger, or he is unsure of the situation, he will call me if time allows. Otherwise he will, without hesitation, take any action required to put the vessel into safety. These actions will include use of the helm and engines, change or reversal of course, or stopping the ship until the situation can be resolved

- in the event of an emergency stop at sea, if there is power to the rudder the ship is to be put onto a course away from any immediate danger. Generally this should be to steer the ship away from any land or ship in the area

- the OOW is not to take the watch until he is completely satisfied as to the ship's position and the safety of the present course. Should there be any dispute as to either the position or safety of the ship, I am to be immediately called and standing order 10 will apply

- in taking any immediate action, if there are other ships in the vicinity, and if time permits, use sound signals and/or VHF to advise them of your actions

- any defect or malfunction of equipment is to be entered into the bridge defect book with the date and time group and sent to the appropriate person or head of department concerned for his signature

- if, due to deteriorating weather conditions, the OOW feels that it is unsafe on deck, he will place the decks out of bounds by broadcast and by informing the heads of departments. If any personnel are on deck at the time, they are to be ordered into the accommodation

- the deck log book is an important legal document and I expect the OOW to ensure that all entries are properly made, particularly in respect of weather conditions. When the ship is rolling, I require the degree of roll to be entered. Remarks are to be made about any pitching and taking water on deck

- the OOW is responsible for displaying the correct flag and light signals in good time. The ensign is to be hoisted at the gaff when the ship is under way and at the stern when the ship is alongside or at anchor

- prior to arrival, the OOW will test communications, bridge and portable. He will also synchronise the clocks between the bridge and ER. He is responsible for ensuring that the pilot ladder is rigged in good time and that the crew are called to stations ready for arrival.

Under Pilotage

- When the Pilot is on the bridge, he is to be treated with all the courtesies as for the rank of Captain. The Pilot is responsible to me for the direction of the ship. His presence on the bridge does not relieve the OOW of any of his responsibilities for the safe navigation of the ship and he will continue with this, advising the Pilot of any navigation or shipping hazards he feels might endanger the ship

- should the Pilot at any time give an order that does not directly concern the navigation of the ship, or have any complaint regarding any aspect of the ship, I am to be immediately informed.

There are situations that will occur that I have not covered. I do not know the answers to everything and neither do you, but together hopefully, we will find a solution. Always call me if there is any problem.

5.6 The Night Order Book

Often repetitive, but remember that the night orders must be written up every night regardless of there being no changes. Always note the course the ship is presently on, any alterations of course that are to be made during the night and when you wish to be called. A simple 'as per standing orders' covers all your other orders. The night order book also exists to show that you have been up on the bridge before going to your bunk for the night.

5.7 The Watches

Inevitably these will be the standard watch system of three deck officers on a 4 on 8 off system, unless you only have two deck officers, in which case you will be expected to take a watch. The sea and those who work there are, in general, very conservative and any changes are a long and laborious task. The 4 on 8 off system was designed for the days of the open deck or bridges, based on the theory that 4 hours of standing in a howling gale being lashed by spray was enough. When you consider that the Watchkeeper in a nuclear power station can stand up to a 12 hour watch, as do the staff on the oil platforms, then surely we can accept that the system can be flexible and that flexibility can benefit the ship and officers alike. Obviously, in coastal and busy waters the four hour watch stands, but how about a six hour watch system when the ship goes deep sea? The advantage of this is that the officers have only one broken nights sleep in three and, with the changes in the times of the watches, all will have a chance to participate in the social life onboard. Strangely you might find that if you offer such a system, the older officers might refuse, being set in their ways. We are very conservative, but at least by offering this, it displays your flexibility in accepting change. Out of interest, the dog watches were designed purely to stop the repetitiveness of the same watches. For some reason these gradually disappeared and now we have the repetitive watch system again.

5.8 The Lookouts

The strangest anachronisms remain as a vestige of the very distant past shipping acts, completely ignoring the advances of electronic aids available today. A good example is where the degree of lookout continues to differentiate between day and night. Yet the speed of vessels in low visibility and the removal of many fixed navigational aids from the coasts *do* recognise that. In the question of lookouts, it is nonsense to differentiate between day and night. If a lookout is required at night then a lookout is required in the day. It is very rare for any Watchkeeper to detect a ship or danger to navigation visually before radar while, at night, the OOWs keep a better watch on the radar. By contrast, the bridge tends to be far busier with more tasks and distractions during the day than the night. Therefore, the case is stronger for lookouts to be appointed during the day than at night.

If the shipping regulations adamantly demand that a lookout, in addition to the OOW, is essential to the keeping of a proper lookout (and I have no disagreement with this), then again we must recognise that this must be maintained continuously. Therefore, the duty lookouts should not be allowed to leave the bridge for any reason, which creates the need for reliefs for these lookouts. No ships are so manned, or if they are the interference in maintenance duties would prohibit such a watchkeeping system.

Under present regulations on a well manned and managed ship, the watchkeeping system should be allowed to be flexible, allowing the Master to adjust it according to the weather, traffic or occupation of the ship (coastal, ocean, drifting or anchored) and, most importantly, the experience of the officers and ratings under his command

The pressure really comes on the Master who is appointed to a ship in poor condition, on a busy schedule, with a deck workload as long as your arm and chronically undermanned. In such circumstances, every man-hour on deck is vital and the Chief Officer, if he is any good, will want the lookouts on deck.

Under present regulations, and these are the ones we must work to, during the day the lookouts can work in the vicinity of the bridge where they can be on instant call. But on a ship that trades worldwide, carrying a worldwide folio of charts, the 2nd Officer has to correct all of these as well as constantly update all of the bridge publications. Therefore, he often needs a lookout during the day.

Having advanced all of the arguments, under present regulations you must comply with the lookout requirements regardless of the deck work requirements. If the company wants the work done, then let them man the ship properly. In the meantime, your first duty is to the safety of the ship and those onboard. (And do not forget your own career problems if there is an incident that could be put down to failure to keep a proper lookout).

6   Your Ship

Captain Lloyd's first deep-sea command, the MV Arya Gol, in 1973

Once at sea, and before tackling any other issues, you will have time to find out about your ship, its standards and pervading attitudes. Be careful about judging the abilities of the heads of departments during this tour as a lot of what you will see will be at the level tolerated by the last command. You might even be pleasantly surprised. This tour is not for criticism, but is more to judge the current situation and consider areas that you feel need to be improved or changed. While procedures can be improved, changes take longer and will only be effective with the willing participation of those concerned. On deck, you will initially be looking to see that the planned maintenance system is followed and working and that it is not just a series of items filled in on paper. Most importantly, check that the safety equipment is in good order and well maintained. Take this tour with the Chief Officer. It is courtesy to ask him and as it is his department only he will know the answers to your many questions. When you make this tour don't forget to wear a hard hat, even though the only thing that can fall on your head is from a seagull. It is now part of the safety procedures and if you don't wear a hat, why should the crew? It is important to establish a safety culture in the ship so, regardless of your own feelings about it, you must take the lead.

Finally, don't forget to take a note book! As a recent Chief Officer, you should know what to look for so regard the following as a suggestion.

6.1 Items for Attention

- Are the rollers free in the fairleads?
- check the grease nipples on the machinery to see if they are greased or painted over
- is the anchor ball in good condition?
- how many shackles are there on each anchor and are they clearly marked?

6.1.1 Windlasses

- Are the brakes in good order?
- when were the liners last changed?
- check the grease on the brakes and clutch. Debris can mix together with the grease and over time build up to a solid mass that can stop the brakes from being fully applied and the clutch from being properly engaged
- check the vent covers, rubbers and gauzes
- are the anchors well up into the hawse pipes and not moving?
- are the spurling pipes cemented or foamed and the covers on?
- are the forecastle weather doors watertight?
- are the chain lockers self draining or pumped? How often are they sounded?
- where is the emergency fire pump and how is it started? Have all the deck crew been instructed in the starting procedure?
- what fire prevention system does the paint locker have? Is the eye bath maintained and are the chemical data sheets present?
- is all the gear in the forecastle well stowed and securely lashed, especially any oil drums?
- is it current practice to remove the lifebuoys from the forward part of the ship at sea and stow them in the forecastle? While this prevents them being washed away, should there be a man overboard and there is no lifebuoy to throw over the side very serious repercussions could follow. Do not stow these away. You must accept the occasional disappearance and order more
- where are the forward life-rafts stowed, are they in date and are the hydrostatic releases in date?
- what is the condition of the hatch rubbers? Are these repaired by the crew and is there spare rubber, glue and tools onboard?
- are all the hatch dogs and cleats present and free?
- if you have a midships gangway, is this in good order? When was the gangway last tested?
- are the pilot ladders and manropes in good order? Make sure that they are not painted and that they are not used for any other purpose
- are the fire boxes complete with hoses and nozzles and do the nozzles turn?

- if you have a helideck or Helo landing or transfer area, is this properly and clearly marked?

Take time to find out about your ship when out at sea

- is there appropriate rescue equipment stowed close by?
- what is the condition of the hydraulic lines?
- is there any oil on deck?
- is the pollution equipment in good order and complete?
- if you have cranes, check the flexible couplings
- what are the conditions of the crane cabs?

6.1.2 Deck Lighting
- Whose responsibility is cleaning and replacing lights?
- are the insides free of water?

6.1.3 Lifeboats
- Are they secure in their chocks?
- are the boat ropes properly led forward to the lowest deck?
- if enclosed boats, check that the helmsman's perspex screen is clear and can be seen through. If not, these can be ordered and replaced. Also look to see if there is condensation inside the boats. This can be cured by having a schedule for opening the entrance hatches in good weather. How often is the inventory of equipment checked? This should be done frequently because of the pilfering that can take place
- when were they last lowered?
- is the policy to end the wires and, if so, how often and when was it last done?

6.1.4 Rescue Boat (if carried)

- If an inflatable hull, check where the rubbers rub against the retaining strops
- how often is this exercised?
- if a petrol boat, how much petrol is carried onboard?
- are the lights working in these boats?
- are the batteries charged?
- are the MOB lifebuoys on the bridge free running and the lines clear?
- are the batteries well maintained and checked regularly? Who is responsible for them?
- is the magnetic compass easy to see from the helmsman position? Is the light working?
- are the halyards properly fitted with cleats?
- are the flags in good condition?

There will be many more points that you wish to check on a tour around the decks and you should now have a far better understanding of the ship you now command.

6.2   Engine Room

Ask the Chief Engineer if he could show you around the engine room or, if he is busy, arrange for someone else to show you round. Never go down to the engine room on your own at this stage. While your visit to the engine room is purely a courtesy visit, if you see that it is dirty, the bilges are oily and unpumped and dirty rags are lying around, then you could well have a problem. However, it may be that they have just finished a major job and still have to clean up so do not be judgmental at this stage. If you are disturbed by what you see, wait a short while and then have another look. That will give you a more accurate view of the situation.

6.3   Weekly Inspection

There is a purpose to the weekly inspection, apart from it being the 'parade of the unemployed' as I have heard it so delightfully put. It is the opportunity for you, along with the heads of department, to inspect the accommodation and make on-the-spot decisions on any problem found. It displays to the crew your interest in their quarters, it allows you to visit the officers' accommodation and, if the stewards clean, to see they are doing their job. If the officers maintain their own accommodation, you can check that they are keeping it in good order.

Have the Chief Steward/Purser, or if you don't have these then the Cook, Chief Officer and Chief Engineer accompany you. If you only have a Cook onboard, it might be that the Chief Officer is responsible for the organisation of this department. Does he know this? If you find that he is not and things have been left to the Cook who, with the best will in the world, should not be allowed to do what he likes without some supervision, you might find that you will have to assume responsibility for this. What you are looking for here is evidence of how the department is organised, the cleaning the catering department is responsible for, and the standard of cleanliness maintained, especially in the galley and storerooms.

6.3.1 Accommodation

- Are the alleyways clean and polished?
- are the lights all working?
- is there any private wiring that has not been approved?
- is the bedding in good order?
- is there any broken furniture?
- are there boiler suits in the cabins rather than in the working lockers?

6.3.2 In the Galley

Does the galley resemble an efficient kitchen or is it more like a truck stop café?

- Are the scuppers clean and free of debris?
- is there any sign of insect infestation, especially cockroaches?
- are the seals on the fridges clean and secure?
- is the Cook equipped with clean aprons and headwear?
- is the hand basin in the galley equipped with soap and clean towels?
- are the stove uptakes free of grease and are filters cleaned regularly?
- when was the galley Cooker vent last steam cleaned?
- is the refrigerator temperature recorded daily?

6.3.3 In the Storerooms

- Is there any ice build up?
- are the scuppers free and clean?
- lift the hatch boards and see if the deck is clean underneath
- are the room temperatures recorded daily?

Check the dates on a sample of the provisions. A few days over is neither here nor there, but you can sometimes be surprised by what you find.

> *I remember checking a ship in Vancouver, that had just been provisioned, and found the meat stamped 'Not fit for human consumption'. Perfectly fit for sailors then!*

7 Ship Management

Organisation and administration is a major part of the Shipmaster's role today

> *Twice in my career, I have joined ships where there had been no previous administration, with a complete new ship's company of officers and men, none of whom had ever sailed together before. In a way it was refreshing as we had the opportunity to have the ship's administration the way we wanted it to be rather than following the ideas of a previous incumbent or the office.*

Because of the large number of crew onboard (around about 60) and the number of problems we were dealing with, I decided to hold management meetings every week and this worked well. What was important was that I was kept up-to-speed with what was happening around me rather than have senior officers keeping me out of the loop.

In a number of instances we were able to abandon the traditional concepts of who does what and when. It did not work all the time, and there were some traditional things we could not change owing to safety and officer reluctance to accept completely new ideas. But, without doubt, we were able however to tackle a number of problem areas that I have noted exist on many ships.

The following is not a complete management system for your ship, but it will provide you with an idea of a type of management that not only was applied to the ship we were on but was in the process of being adopted for the fleet (before the fleet disappeared!)

The following were itemised by number in separate sections in a ship management book that was issued to every officer and key ratings, with copies in the crew messroom.

7.1 Defects - Deck Safety

If shipboard repair is required:

- The Chief Officer to be notified
- a repair chit will be issued to the Head of Department required to make the repair
- the repair chit will be marked "priority" and treated as such
- on completion of the repair, the Chief Officer will be notified
- the repair will be logged in the safety log book

- the safety log book will be given to the Chief Officer every Sunday morning for his signature
- the Chief Officer will advise the management meeting of all repairs in that week.

If shore repair or assistance is required:
- Shore repairs will be decided by the Chief Officer
- the Chief Officer will make out the appropriate work order
- the Chief Officer will advise the Captain
- the Chief Officer will advise the company and request the repair
- if there is any attending shore technician, he will be attended to by the Department Safety Officer
- the Department Safety Officer will advise the Chief Officer that the repair has been carried out to his satisfaction
- the completion of the repair will be logged in the safety log
- the Chief Officer will advise the Captain and the company that the repair has been completed.

While that might seem long winded, do not forget we are dealing with a mix of nationalities, many of which do not have English as their first language. Safety and clarity was the aim of providing a step by step guide that, if followed, would cover all the bases.

7.2　Safety Training

Action Officer: Deck Department Safety Officer
- The Deck Department Safety Officer is responsible for producing the ship's training programme
- the formal safety training will take place each week after emergency drills, until 1700
- the Captain will stand the watch during this period
- all officers, as required by the Deck Safety Officer, will be involved in this training
- the programme should be constructed such that a mixture of practical, video and classroom instruction is given
- the Deck Safety Officer will keep a record of all instruction in a training record book

Remember that this was before ISM was introduced by the IMO. Also, we were dealing with a crew where many had never been to sea before, some had never seen the sea! The last of the crew were delivered by a bus with the army guarding it as they had been taken from the town jail to make up our numbers. The Radio Officers wife steered the ship down the river and there was the occasional splash as various intended seamen decided that whatever lurked in the river was far preferable to whatever was lurking at sea.

7.3 Bunkering

Ref Captain's standing orders: Port
Action Officers: Chief Engineer Officer, Chief Officer, OOW

- Prior to arrival in the bunkering port, the Chief Engineer Officer will complete the company check list and the oil spill contingency plan
- the Chief Engineer Officer will ensure that he has a copy of the emergency contact list
- the Chief Engineer Officer will check that all pollution precautions have been taken
- the Chief Engineer Officer will ensure that all shipboard communications are in working order and will be responsible for communications with the shore or barge
- the Chief Officer will ensure that the fire fighting equipment is in the vicinity of the bunkering position and that this is ready for use
- the deck department will be responsible for making any bunkering barge fast alongside, they will assist with hoisting the bunkering pipe onboard and will be responsible for the ladder to the barge
- the deck department will put up the 'no smoking' signs and rope off the bunkering position from shore workers
- the Chief Engineer Officer will take fuel samples as required and place them with the Administration Officer for posting
- the Chief Engineer Officer will agree and sign the receipt for fuel oil received, and advise the OOW when bunkering is completed.

Once again the intentions are to lay out the sequence of events so that there are no disagreements about who does what and who is responsible for each sequence.

One interesting change we made was the idea that the Radio Officer came out of his little cave and was integrated completely into the deck department as the ship's Administration Officer. As such he dealt with a considerable amount of the paperwork, assisting on the bridge for entry and departure and standing a watch in port as OOW provided there was a senior officer or myself onboard.

7.4 ISM

When it was introduced, the ISM Code was a way of ensuring that those ashore took responsibility for the impact of their actions on the management of the ships. Regrettably, as time has gone on, we have seen it become more and more of a paper chase.

Ships that were already well managed will have benefited little from ISM, while those ships that are poorly managed and operated often have either convenient ISM inspections or block falsify their entries. However, it does provide some level of lever to the authorities who are trying to upgrade the worst offenders.

> *In the not too distant past I was present when an ISM auditor passed a vessel with over one hundred defects and proudly awarded it the ISM certificate. He had been flown in by the owner of the ship, licensed by his marine administration as an auditor and had a new boilersuit with ISM inspector hastily printed on it. I think that was the only connection he had with the ISM code.*

The ISM should be helpful to us at sea in the safe management of our ships, so it must have our support, regardless of our personal feelings, as we have to encourage our officers and crew to follow the codes. However, it must be recognised that harassed officers trying do several jobs at once will fail to make an entry or write a signature. This really should not warrant some of the deficiencies that are subsequently handed out by auditors, which are then jumped on by companies as examples of bad management that demand explanation.

As Captain, it is your function to see that your ship and officers conform to your company's ISM system. If you find that there are elements that cannot be complied with because of the particular circumstances of your ship, you must advise your company and suggest a change that will allow your ship to conform. Those who wrote the ISM book on your vessel did it for the whole fleet, or may well have written parts of it when in another company, so only you can point out problem areas. Communications regarding ISM should be kept in a separate file for production at the time of audits.

While our conduct on the bridge and management of navigation of a vessel is fairly rigid, being bound by regulations, the internal management of a ship is not unless it is laid down in the company regulations. Even these should be seen as a guide as it is important that your approach to the ship management is flexible. Involving junior officers in the management not only brings their fresh ideas but gives them confidence while training them for their next step. An example would be to hand over full control of bridge maintenance from the Chief Officer to the 2nd Officer. The bridge work done by the watchkeepers would come under his direction, as would the ordering of all bridge stores and equipment. On some ships this might be done already but certainly not on many. Why should we not try to reverse our present thinking and learn to delegate again? Only in this way can our present day junior officers be prepared for the future and have more interest in the ship.

8   Discipline

I have the very bad feeling that with the way political correctness is going 'discipline' is another word that will be soon removed. But whatever they do ashore, it is one word that no ship can operate without. In the armed forces discipline is more easily maintained as they have crew trained in discipline, officers trained in exercising it and a list of offences and punishments that are rigorously enforced.

On the Merchant ships it is a bit of a quagmire. We all know it is required and governments provide a list of offences and allow certain punishments, mostly monetary, to be imposed. But disturbingly, in the Western registrations, even these are now mostly removed and many ISM books do not even mention discipline, although it is integral to the safety of the ship. Even the IMO, which generates booklets on various codes, does not have one for discipline. In the UK it is not unusual to find that a seaman recently signed on has just been released from prison, often for offences that mean you would not wish to have him confined with a group of people for a prolonged time at sea either.

Once again we need to look to the Flag States around the world as the discipline you can impose on your ship depends on the registry and the willingness of that registry to support their declarations.

Think about this one. Not so long ago, a few crew on a flag of convenience ship decided that they did not like the Chief Officer, so they hacked him to death and threw him over the side. When the ship arrived in the USA they were handed over to the authorities for holding until the registered flag authorities extradited them for trial. No such application was ever made and, after holding the crew for a few weeks, they were repatriated to their countries with no charges. Very shortly after, they were back at sea.

Is lack of discipline causing other problems?

This kind of situation continues to happen, which is why many Captains and officers lock their doors at night in today's strange world at sea. Many years ago, for anyone to lock their door at sea was unheard of and even frowned upon, which is why door curtains were provided. The reasoning was that if there was a collision it could cause distortion of the door frames, trapping the officer or crew member in their cabin.

Therefore, you must understand that, even though you may have a discipline code as required by your registration, too often it is purely paper and you will be completely unsupported when trying to impose it. Your owners or managers generally just want any problem to go away and would prefer that you do not make or create any fuss. Here is another example to consider. How many passengers on the cruise ships operating out of Florida have been apprehended by the ship's Captains for drug possession and handed over to the shore authorities for prosecution? I remember from my own days on the cruise ships how even quite serious cases of assault would be hushed up with compensation paid out instead of allowing the law to take its course.

On your ship you could have the situation where you have a crew untrained in discipline, officers unskilled in implementing it, you unsupported by the regulations of the Flag State and your operator not wishing to know about your problems. However seamen, in general, will want some level of discipline as it guarantees their personal security onboard. In making the rules for your ship remember that once you have declared them, you must stick to them with no deviations, otherwise they will become meaningless. Discipline must be constant but not oppressive, with as few regulations as possible. Its main aim is to produce a fair and reasonable society onboard where all are treated as adults and with equal respect.

If discipline is to be effective you must support those who are in authority and responsible for maintaining it in your name. Your officers must feel secure that, provided their authority was correctly applied, any adverse response will bring the dissident party or parties into conflict with you. Equally, any crew member who has a complaint about a superior must be listened to with respect and courtesy, even if you consider it a minor matter. What is a small matter to you can be a major one to him.

When dealing with an offence, it is essential that you remain impartial in your questioning and judgment. Before having any hearing, ensure that all is ready. The person's head of department should be there, as well as the Chief Officer (if he is not the head involved) because he is the nominal head of discipline of the ship. Any witnesses to the event must be ready to be called. Have your voice recorder on as you will find that after any hearing there will be different versions of what was said. Above all, you must provide the accused every facility to allow his side of the events to be told. Finally, ensure that your flag state rules on the administration of discipline are followed.

You must make those onboard aware of the levels of discipline you expect

I suggest that, having decided on the course you wish to follow and the authority you will give to your officers, you have at least the senior officers in for a chat about discipline onboard. You can then advise them on the system you want in place with, for example junior officers giving an unofficial reprimand for minor offences, heads of department issuing written reprimands and you dealing with the more serious offences.

I have always worked on the principle that there are three bad problems that can completely unsettle a ship until the source is removed. These are physical assault, theft and drugs.

8.1 Assault

There are always degrees to assault. A drunken thump between two friends in the night that has them apologising to each other in the morning can be dealt with by a warning and, if at sea, their tap stopped. But an attack by one crew on another that results in injury is a different matter. If the injury is serious then the only course of action that you can take is to send ahead to the port that you require the police to be present on arrival. Make an entry in the log book of the occurrence and make an incident report with the witnesses' statements. Warn the crew member who made the assault that he is to keep away from the victim and ensure that work details are arranged to separate the two. Only if a crew member continues with violence that will endanger either the crew or the ship can you restrain him. This can be difficult on the average ship as not only do you not have a cabin or locker for this purpose but ships rarely carry handcuffs.

> *In the distant past, when we used to make our rounds on the passenger vessels with the Masters at Arms, any misbehaving or abusive crew or passenger would be hauled off to the cells, which on one ship I remember was on the boat deck. There they would cool their heels off for the night before being brought before the Captain next morning. Passengers were given one warning and then off the ship. I bet that there are many modern cruise ship Captains and officers who wish they could still do that today!*

If the assault is upon an officer who is carrying out his duties, then this is an assault on you as well and must be treated with all the seriousness of such an act. In some ports you might have the opportunity of requesting the sentence and, if this is allowed, you should go for the maximum.

8.2 Theft

Theft is a nasty business that generally happens only in port, where it is difficult to tell if the culprit is crew or shore side personnel. The problem is that suspicions always grow and these, and the subsequent accusations, can easily disrupt the ship. It is only with repeated offences can you determine that it is a crew member involved and, unless he is caught red handed, it is a long and laborious process to determine who it is. Anyone who is caught must be landed and repatriated at the next port, as much for his safety as for the well-being of the ship.

8.3 Drugs

Strangely, I encountered very little of this problem while at sea. Except for a few cases, it was users bringing drugs onboard for themselves, but even this was rare, probably because many seamen are economic refugees and don't get paid much. But if you have, or suspect you have, drugs onboard you must take action. The action you take will depend on where you are.

> *When I was running between Brazil and Canada, I had a very good relationship with the Canadian Customs in the port we used and a message sent directly to them would ensure that, on arrival, the situation would be dealt with. There were more drugs in every bar ashore in Canada than on my ship, but that was not the point. If your ship is found to have drugs onboard, and it can be shown that you knew and did nothing, the consequences can be dire.*

The rule here is to bide your time. If you or your officers do find a stash of drugs and no one knows of their discovery, then leave them alone. The reason for this is that the Customs in the next port might wish to follow them to the receiver. Wait for a port that you know will deal with the problem intelligently and provide the information ahead of the ship's arrival. Obviously when you do send such information, you discuss this with no one else onboard, either before or afterwards. Always send the information directly if possible, rather than through the agent. The reason I say that is that agencies can be open places so you cannot always be sure where your information might end up.

There are a few good books around dealing with the problems of drugs at sea, the best I have found is put out by the International Chamber of Shipping and is called 'Drug Trafficking and Drug Abuse'. In the back of this book there is a list of customs contact numbers.

Having dealt with the major offences, there are still a number of others that you cannot disregard and must be treated seriously. However, these can usually be dealt with internally.

8.4 Disobedience to a Direct Command

While this sounds as if it should be fairly simple to deal with, it is not always the case. All too often young officers, especially those unschooled in leadership, will give what they might interpret as an order but in actuality is not. Owing to their lack of confidence in giving a direct order it can come across more as a request. This can particularly be a problem when dealing with a crew that is perceived as being 'robust' in their general attitude. Before dealing with apparent disobedience and issuing the appropriate warnings or fines, do try to find out how the order was made. However, once the point has been made, should this occur again by the same person to the same or another superior, then you cannot tolerate it.

8.5 Insolence and Verbal Abuse

This can often be caused by a superior's over familiarity with the defendant. If the two had been ashore drinking together the night before and are on first name terms, then who is the cause of the problem?

If you do have a problem crew member on your hands who, even after issuing the required warnings and fines, is determined to carry on challenging all authority, then that person must be removed.

This is not always as easy as it seems as the question of cost and travel budget will be used by the operation office through the personnel department. Regardless of the company, you still hear nonsensical responses such as 'wait until the ship comes back then we will deal with it' or 'can't you get them to shake hands', suggestions that demonstrate a failure to understand a ship and its management. Remember that it is not just you that wants the person off the ship, the unsettling influence will mean the rest of the crew will as well. If they are not removed, they will have shown that they can break the ship's regulations with impunity and their status will have grown amongst the more boisterous of the crew. Never mind their reputation, establish yours. Put them down the gangway and don't take any nonsense from the office on this. Call ahead to the agent and tell them to arrange the travel and advise the personnel department that under no circumstances will the ship continue with them onboard and, if required, you will sail shorthanded until replacements can be organised.

You might expect that, after receiving reports regarding a crew member that was dismissed from his ship, those ashore would take steps to ensure that the facts of the case were reported to the appropriate national marine administration. Unfortunately this is rarely the case and it is not unheard of for the same company to re-employ him.

To counter this, if you do have such a crew member who has been a constant source of trouble and who, after agreement from your senior officers, you believe should not be allowed on any ship, you have a duty to your fellow Captains to stamp the discharge book with the reasons for the dismissal and advise the issuing authorities. In the United Kingdom the discharge books no longer have a place for this and writing to the authorities will have very little effect. There are those more intolerant amongst us who write across the discharge book the fact of the dismissal, but this has no legal standing. However, at least they will have to obtain a new discharge book if they are to go to sea again.

The above descriptions are of the problem cases that can come your way and that should be dealt with by yourself. For many good reasons, other more minor matters should be left to the heads of departments. It is important that, when crew members are brought before you on a disciplinary charge, they realise the seriousness of the matter. Another good reason is that it allows your senior officers a certain freedom of action to discipline their own departments, hopefully making them more effective as superiors. Minor offences can often be dealt with unofficially. An example of this might be where a seaman is AWOL for an hour or so in the morning and the Chief Officer gives him the choice of making it an official offence or working off his offence with extra hours. This is a good solution for everyone, provided that it does not become a repeating offence, when you will have to take action.

A few last thoughts. You are not the ship's policeman, you are the magistrate. You may well see things on your movements around the ship, but if they are of a minor nature, bring them to the attention of the Chief Officer and do not try to deal with them yourself. Remember the blind eye that every good Captain acquires and try to acquire yours quickly.

As a final point, discipline exists not to make the ship oppressive, but to make it a peaceful, fair and safe society for those onboard. Jack Sadler, in 1983, wrote a superb book on discipline at sea and I sincerely recommend it for further reading.

9 Safety

Overdoing safety messages, or posters that become wallpaper-like, turns safety to graffiti that is ignored

If yours is an average ship, there will be books, posters, signs and even videos all about safety crammed onto the shelves on the bridge and mess rooms. In addition, you will have the volumes of ISM coupled with forms to fill in for every possible event. However, it would appear that few people onboard are interested and I often used to say that, as Captain, and after the Chief Officer and Chief Engineer had once again given me all the reasons why exercises could not be held or equipment could not be used, I was the only one who was interested. I think that one of the problems is that most of these publications appear to live in a world that is far away from the ships I have commanded. They talk of bridge teams and fire teams, BA parties with helpers, hose parties, lookouts, record keeping and communications when, in reality, you only have three officers, five seamen, a couple of oilers, a Cook and a Steward available to you. I am not saying that these books are wrong, you should read them and understand what should be done. But, having done that, you must then look at your ship and work out what **can** be done in emergency situations to give the best chance of a successful outcome. Without doubt the best way to deal with any emergency is to be prepared and this can only be done by repetitive exercises, with a debriefing and amendment of the procedures afterwards and then doing it again if necessary.

It important to determine what is possible with the resources you have.

9.1   The Paperwork

The list of paperwork to be completed is endless and is well documented in your ISM guide book. While you may feel that much of this is unnecessary, it must be completed and so you might as well do it properly. I don't need to tell you that, if there is any accident, the correct completion of this paperwork can appear more important than the accident. However, once items such as risk assessment are completed, they are pointless if stuffed away on the bridge and although you can tell the crew that they have access, few will actually bother to read them. Keep them in the crew mess room or lounge instead and have the Safety Officer spend an hour with them assembled, going through the various jobs for discussion.

9.2   The Safety Committee

This can be a very valuable tool in the pursuit of safety onboard your ship but, like all tools, it must be used correctly. All too often, everyone just sits and listens to whoever is chairing the meeting as they read the last minutes then list the latest safety bulletins from company and flag state. They are either just waiting to be dismissed or they will use the opportunity to ask for equipment that there is no chance of them being supplied with, using the meeting as a time to grumble about the Captain, the ship and the company and, of course, the Cook.

Whoever is to chair the meeting, and I recommend that it not be you, must operate to strict guidelines and not allow the meeting to move away from the subject of safety onboard using the existing equipment. To stimulate some debate, review the exercises already held and ask for comments and suggestions for future exercises or changes in the way the present ones are conducted. The reason that you should not chair the meetings or, better still, not even be present, is that your presence may interfere with the free flow of debate the meeting exists to encourage.

9.3   Your Equipment

The correct equipment is essential and herein lies the first problem. Most companies have a standard quantity and type of equipment that they supply to their ships. In the majority of cases those responsible for supplying the equipment have never used it and the only criteria used for selection is that it meets the SOLAS requirements and is the cheapest. Lada and Mercedes are both cars and approved for the road but there is quite a difference in the capabilities!

There can also be a problem with the compatibility of the equipment. A breathing apparatus might be SOLAS approved and of good design and so might the fire suit provided. But can the two be worn together? Quite often, only with extreme difficulty.

First then, examine your equipment to see what is available to you and check that it is in good order.

- Are all the fire extinguishers colour coded and date marked as to the last recharge?
- are all the hydrant covers valves greased and easy to turn?
- when were the hoses last pressure tested and are the connection rings free of rust?
- are the dual purpose nozzles greased and easy to turn?
- is the pressure of the BA bottles checked regularly?
- how many are there onboard and what is the condition of the compressor?
- check the fire suits and ensure they are complete with gloves and boots
- fire torches - are they charged up and holding the charges?
- what is the communication method between the officer in charge of the emergency party and the BA set teams?

9.4   The Fire Detection System

Many of these systems are defective because their extreme sensitivity means they give out false alarm signals. When this occurs frequently the crew response inevitably lessens. As each alarm sounded is shown to be false, eventually no one will turn out until it can be confirmed that it is definitely a fire, which of course can be too late. So many ships have this problem, with its inevitable human response, and yet there does not seem to be an industry attempt to solve it. Fire detectors are repeatedly changed in the problem areas but often with no improvement. All too often you are left with two stark choices. To continue to let the alarm be sounded throughout the day and night and try to enforce crew to respond on each occasion, or isolate the offending area and hope that if there is a fire it is not at that particular location. Naturally you must try to get the system attended to but, in the meantime, to allow the crew to sleep but retain responsiveness, you may well have to isolate the offending detector. If it is in the accommodation area, as a compromise, you can purchase a home battery detector unit and temporarily use this. Not the perfect answer by any means but possibly an idea. Of course, in the engine room such a unit would be ludicrous. Therefore, the Chief Engineer will have to institute a frequent physical check of the area by the duty Watchkeeper.

9.5   Emergencies

The emergencies that can occur at sea are generally covered within your ISM manuals. The problem with these manuals is that many of them are bought 'off the shelf', especially if the company is small. Therefore, what you are likely to get is a manual written, sometimes by a consultancy, for another company. If ISM manuals were read by all and were followed they would manage to bring situations to a satisfactory conclusion. So why do many incidents and accidents end in messy circumstances? The answer is simple. At sea, we rarely live in a perfect world.

What is an emergency? If you believe the output of many safety departments, almost everything at sea can be interpreted as an emergency and you are left with the distinct impression that all we do is lurch from potential disaster to potential disaster. The following are some examples that are listed as emergencies within an ISM manual.

9.5.1 Main Engine Failure

Is this really an emergency? Surely that depends on where it happens? It then goes on to say that the Chief Engineer 'should try to start the engines'. Possibly end of the "emergency"!

9.5.2 Enclosed Space Entry

Care has to be taken and procedures followed but is it really an emergency?

9.5.3 Severe Weather

Again, I would say not an emergency but situationally dependent.

9.5.4 Electrical Blackout

An emergency? Unfortunately, on some old ships, it's still a way of life.

These are a sample of contingency plans and lists that somehow have found their way onto our ships in the dramatic guise of "emergencies" rather than as incidents that are part of normal seafaring life. Incidents can be planned for and procedures provided for their occurrence. The unfortunate effect of so many lists is that no one reads any of them, let alone takes the time to understand and comply. Personally, I would classify an incident as something that can develop into an emergency if the correct procedures are not followed. Whether an emergency can be controlled by following procedures is doubtful as each one has its own characteristics that require initiative and ability.

Crossing the North Atlantic in a 500 ton ship

The last emergency I was involved in was at 2am when, on a ship we were delivering, heavy seas broke through the outer plating of the engine exhaust trunking on deck and water began pouring into the engine room. Not an emergency, but an incident that could be resolved by simply starting the bilge pumps and pumping the water out. However, it did become an emergency when all the bilge lines were found to be blocked and rotten. We now had a rapidly filling engine room in heavy weather 150 miles from land. Strangely enough, no one thought about reading the contingency plan for such an event or even took time to study the risk assessment. Instead we set about trying to plug up the hole and rigging the emergency fire pump. Our attempts failed twice owing to the force of water and the fire pump could not cope with the water ingress. Just before telling the Cook to make some sandwiches for a life-raft exercise, we had one more attempt at putting a crew member over the side on lifelines to secure the hole from that side. This worked and, after dragging a very wet and cold man back onboard, we managed to reduce the level of water in the engine room and limp back into port. So we broke every rule in the ISM regulations, we endangered the life of a crew member, but we managed to bring our ship back and did not have to go boating. We also failed to make out a work permit.

What I am trying to illustrate in the above is that, in any real emergency, the books tend to go out of the porthole and it's your training and initiative that take over. By all means, read the advice given and remember the useful bits as part of your training, but in the end there is only one rule, cope with the problem. If you succeed, good for you, if you don't then get off the ship.

In any emergency, we deal with two main factors, equipment and people. If both are good quality and used correctly then, with luck as well, the situation can be dealt with. Coping with the failures of those factors is the nightmare that the modern Captain must sometimes deal with.

You are unlikely to be able to change the equipment, at least not until you can prove through an incident that it should be changed or upgraded, usually through an incident. For years and years I tried to have at least one BA set that was worn on the chest, to make access into tanks and getting through lightning holes easier, but without success. 'If it is in SOLAS then you can have it, if it isn't forget it', has been the general stance of most companies. So you work with what you have.

You are not going to change your officers and crew easily either, especially when they haven't done anything wrong. Some of them will be incompetent but that is not unusual in any walk of life. It is your job to evaluate them, assign them according to their abilities and then try to bring those you are critical of up to, or close to, the standard that you require. If you have a competent Chief Officer, it is important that you work through this with him and that your decisions are made in accord. After all, he will be the emergency party leader, at least out of the engine room, and will be responsible for making things work. Similarly, consult with the Chief Engineer. If neither of these officers is the Safety Officer, bring him in on the discussion as well.

9.6   The Stations Bill/Muster List

Again you see the same printed card on ship after ship and in company after company. Fill all the slots in and win a prize (I am certain you know what I mean). Once again, in many Companies, stations bill cards are bought off the shelf or the same ones that were used when the ships had larger crews are still used. While writing this I am looking at a bill for a ship with a total of twelve officers and crew on it.

The sections are for:

- The bridge team
- the control team
- the emergency party
- the back-up emergency party.

Without a doubt it looks good and it is indeed impressive that so much can be done by so few, and so naturally the tendency is to fill the sections so that you have three persons in each section. However, such a stations bill is for decoration only as no Captain in his right mind is likely to deal with an emergency in such a way. Instead, why not place your personnel sensibly and train in the same way that you would deal with an emergency? With larger crews there is a tendency to give every person a job, such as Steward 'a' will release the forward gripe on the port lifeboat and seaman' b' will tend the safety line on No2 BA set. I suggest in your planning you move away from this as the more rigid your plan the less flexible it will become. Within the first five minutes of most situations, your plan will start to unravel, so the less rigid your plan is, the easier your team will adapt to the changing circumstances of the emergency. By all means have your core plan, which in an example such as a fire situation will centre on the BA team and the hose party. Other members of the team should then be trained in the various tasks required to support the core and appointed to these as required.

9.7 Exercises

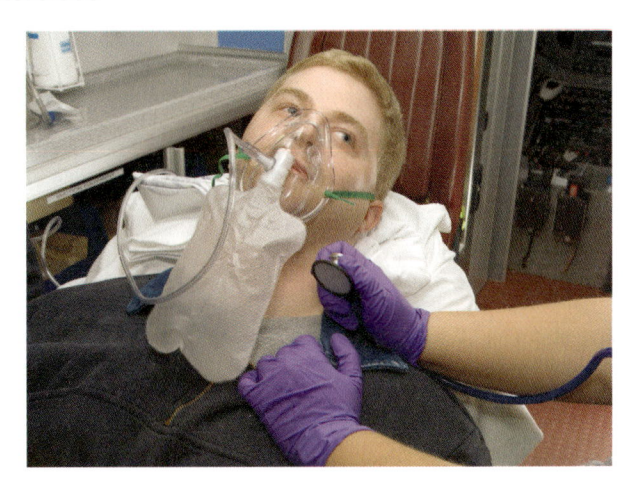

Realistic training helps

If you are to have any chance of coping with an emergency on your ship, good, well thought out and frequent exercises are essential. The area and type of emergency must be changed for each exercise so that the team or teams gain familiarity with all parts of the ship in which they may find themselves operating. Try to make situations as realistic as possible. Instead of a dummy being carried out of an enclosed space or the engine room, use a real crew member. Make sure that he is wearing a hard hat as, if they have been exercising with a dummy before, they are going to be initially quite careless in their handling of the stretcher.

Through the chandler you can obtain smoke canisters that are completely non toxic and non-staining. These are excellent for using in places like the forecastle, and to give your BA team a realistic setting to operate in. Failing this, pull the fuses in the accommodation with all the doors closed and have them go through a couple of decks with the hoses, or try the fall back option of blacking out their visors. Have people 'killed off', and see how the team copes with the problem. If you can, either yourself or the Chief Engineer should be a silent witness to the exercise, making notes where you think improvements can be made and then reviewing the exercise with all of the participants when it is completed.

Although many companies are trying to stop this, I personally advocate lowering the boats at sea to the embarkation deck and I have done this regularly through all my years at sea. After all, provided that no one is in the boats if they fall away, is it not better we find this out now rather than in a real emergency?

The point I am making is that you have a choice. Your exercises can either be boring affairs where the crew stand around being checked off and putting a hose over the side for a few minutes, which is completely pointless, or they can have real meaning and prepare your ship, as much as possible, for any emergency. Obviously some aspects will be repetitive, such as the hose party and the fetchers and carriers, but you want them to be. Repetition is a way of guaranteeing that, on the day, they will carry out what they are trained to do.

It is important that the crew realise the seriousness with which you regard these exercises, regardless of what they were used to before you came. If you are not satisfied with the way an exercise was performed, or feel that the crew did not give it the attention it warranted, then do it again and again until they realise that it is better to do it properly.

The debrief is equally important and this must be a self critical debate. This is where your notes from watching the exercise can be very useful. Where did the exercise go wrong, who failed to carry out their duties? How can it be improved on? Who did well and is deserving of praise? If you can give your crew a sense of achievement and participation, then regardless of the ship or the company, you will have done well and are starting to make your crew into the team that you want.

9.8   Fire

This is the emergency that will test your organisational abilities and the capabilities of all those onboard. Regardless of the type or size of ship, the threat is the same. Theoretically, everybody has undergone the basic fire course with some, mostly officers, also having undertaken Fire II and Fire III. However, I say theoretically because quite a number of crew will have had the certificates and stamps in their discharge books issued without undergoing any such course. This has been going on for so long that we now all accept it as normal and are not surprised when personnel often know little about firefighting. Also, as there are no refresher courses required, elements of a course attended many years ago tend to dim a little with time.

We fight fires to save life which, as always, is the priority. The fact that the ship is saved in the process is coincidental (and it is probably well insured). The criterion must be that, if at any time life is more endangered by fighting the fire than by abandoning the ship, it is time to leave. There are no bonuses from shipping or insurance companies for staying, and, unless you are a cruise ship, no one to declare your heroics either.

If you accept that statement, it follows that the aim must be to put the fire out as soon as possible. Ships have more fires than are generally disclosed because most fires are of a minor nature and are put out on the spot by the person/s that discover them.

While understandable, it is a pity that they are not reported as lessons can be learned from every fire, regardless of the size. In many companies it would also be a serious disciplinary offence not to do so. As examples, here are some of my own fire experiences.

Cabin fire caused by a cigarette burning bedding
Smoke detected by passing crew member who ignoring a nearby extinguisher, went into the officers' saloon and took a jug of water from a table and put the fire out with that. While causing far less damage than the extinguisher, when asked why he did not use it, said he didn't think he was allowed to use it as it was an accommodation one and always clean and polished. This went unreported as the ship was alongside a tanker berth and would have been thrown off, with all the subsequent recriminations.

Hold fire caused by shore worker's cigarette
A pile of rubbish in an otherwise empty hold was on fire, but with no danger to the ship. The fire party went down and cleared the area way around the burning section, creating a fire break. Our attempt to get two hoses down met with a problem as, by the time they reached the bottom, the weight of the hoses caused such a pressure where they went over the lip of the sharp coaming of the hatch that no water would come through. Eventually, one hose was able to be used when the Bosun cut a fending tire in half, put the two halves together across the coaming edge and put the hose in the middle.

Electrical fire in locker on passenger ship in main lounge
Smoke was observed by the night time duty watch patrol. Fuses were pulled and a foam extinguisher used. The fire party was not called and it was logged as an 'electrical fault'.

Fire in rubbish and ropes on poop deck
This started while in the harbour sailing from Rotterdam and was caused by burning soot from the funnel. Full emergency stations were called, and the fire party first tackled the fire aft and then moved to the funnel casing. The port was quite concerned as the funnel was giving a nice glow to the night sky, but we advised them that all was under control, which it was very quickly. An interesting aside is that the Pilot disappeared from the bridge during the emergency. I later discovered that he had called the pilot boat alongside and abandoned us in the middle of the harbour!

From these incidents, you will note that I have never experienced a fire in either of the two danger spots, the engine room and the galley. What it does show is that fire can breakout anywhere at any time and you must have a crew who understands both this and the need to tackle it as quickly as possible by any means at hand. From the Captain's viewpoint you must have an organisation in place that, once an alarm is raised, will give you a fighting chance of putting the fire out. Never mind filling in the boxes in the emergency party stations bill, see what you need and who you have to fill the positions.

9.9   The Emergency Party

The aim of the emergency party is to have been trained so as to be able to cope with the worst of conditions. Some fires will not require a fire suit to be worn and sometimes two hoses may not be required. None of this matters, only that the party is ready for any condition.

The Chief Officer will be in charge at the scene, maintaining communications with the bridge and the hose parties. There must be two hoses available at the scene of the fire and each hose must be manned by one man wearing fire protective clothing. If the party is going to be multi departmental, with the ability to fight fire anywhere on the ship, then one man should be from the deck and the other from the engine department. Examine the fire suits and accessories. Do they fit? It is pointless putting a crew member who is tall or rotund in a small suit. Next, does the suit when worn with the accessories completely cover all the exposed parts of the body? If they do not, then they are a major problem in fighting any fire. What about the boots? Are they proper fire boots or does the company, like many others, supply ordinary rubber boots that will melt?

It is reassuring if you have faith in the ability of your fire party

The condition of the fire protective wear will determine how close to the fire the hose party can get. It is not just the flames that you are to be wary of, but also the air and metal in its vicinity, which can burn skin if it gets hot enough. While the hose party is getting ready, another two crew need to get the hoses and correct nozzles and then help serve the hoses as the hose party advances.

Who must wear the fire suits? If you have a seaman from the deck in one then the other should be worn by a person from the engine department. If this is an officer it is a bonus.

So far we have used up four crew. In the fire party, apart from the hose party, we also need the Electrical Officer if there is one, or if not an Engineer Officer for dealing with electrics and isolating areas. If the fire is not in the engine room, the Chief Engineer will be at that station and the Captain will be on the bridge.

In Command — Safety

So far we have used eight, leaving one man, probably the Cook, for boundary inspection. I say inspection rather than cooling as one man cannot do much more than find and alert. That has taken up nine of the ship's company and there are thousands of ships sailing around with that number or less.

There are other essential tasks necessary, such as lowering the boats ready for embarkation in the case of a need to abandon the ship. A first aider must be ready to deal with any casualties. The Captain also needs another officer on the bridge and preferably a helmsman as well. Boundary cooling needs to be properly done. Ventilation, especially engine room vents, must be closed off if you are considering CO_2 injection. All of these tasks can be planned as crew numbers become available. There is really no debate about the use of CO_2. If the fire is in the engine room and it has not been put out immediately then, provided everyone is clear, this is your best option. The only reason to risk fire suited crew stumbling around in smoke and heat is to get someone out if they are missing.

If you have another officer on the bridge, with possibly a helmsman as well, at least you will have assistance with communications and be able to leave the bridge for an on-the-spot evaluation. This is most important if the situation is approaching critical levels.

> *The last real emergency I had at sea was with a nine man crew. It was not a fire but I was alone on the bridge. Dealing with communications on my own was such a problem that I told everyone "don't call me, I will call you"!*

The description above is not a tutorial on how to fight a fire. There are many courses and books for that. The aim is to show that, regardless of the excellent advice you will find in all of these books, whatever they say has to be adapted to suit your crew and circumstances. You cannot have an officer who cannot speak English properly dealing with communications. You cannot send a hose party into the engine room if they do not know their way around and you cannot have someone dealing with a casualty if they have no first aid experience.

Few of the books and training aids deal with the realities of small crews, language problems and crew capabilities, which is not a criticism because what they set out to teach is the correct way.

> *I remember seeing one training video showing the emergency party control setting themselves up with a desk, with persons to keep a log of events, another to check the pressures of the BA sets and another just for communications. Surprisingly, there was no steward for making tea.*

In the end you make do with what you have so make sure your emergency team is based on practicality and realism.

9.10 Radio Medical Assistance

The assistance available to you decreases in proportion to how far you are away from land and the part of the world you find yourself in. No matter where you are, there is always radio medical assistance available and, having used this on a number of occasions, I would say that excellent advice is given. The closer you are to the shores of an industrial country then the better it becomes, often with helicopter-borne fire fighting or evacuation services and tug support. Often the decision to call for this assistance will be taken out of your hands the moment you initiate your first mayday calls. Many industrialised countries, reacting to indecision by Masters in the past, will send a tug if you are drifting near their coasts, regardless of the owner's wishes. To the question about when to call for assistance, the answer must always be sooner rather than later and if the helicopter comes with the firemen and by the time they get there the fire is out it doesn't really matter. It could have gone the other way and they could have found you drifting in a lifeboat. The primary task is to keep everyone who might be able to assist up-to-date with what is going on.

In port, in most cases, you will have far more support to call on and in the event of fire you assist the fire services rather than them assisting you. However, I can think of a few places up various rivers where, even if you are alongside, you are on your own. At least you will be able to get your people off and watch the bonfire from ashore if required!

10 Difficult Circumstances

10.1 Port of Refuge

Any port in a storm

IMO resolution A949(23) states:

"Place of Refuge means a place where a ship in need of assistance can take action to enable it to stabilize its condition and reduce the hazards to navigation and to protect human life and the environment.

When permission to access a place of refuge is requested, there is no obligation for the coastal state to grant it, but the coastal state should weigh all the factors and risks in a balanced manner and give shelter whenever reasonably possible

Under International law, a coastal state may require the ship's captain to take appropriate action within a prescribed time to stabilize the situation with a view to halting a threat of danger. In the case of failure or urgency, the state may exercise its authority in taking responsive action appropriate to the threat."

In earlier times, ports recognized that they owed their existence to ships and the seamen on them, so 'port of refuge' was established as an international obligation to take in and provide assistance to ships in distress. Today you are quite likely to find a 'closed' sign on the door, especially if there is any danger of pollution. If you are really in distress, and it is your opinion that you are endangering the lives of your ship's company if you proceed further, what are your alternatives when you are advised that the port is closed to you?

Your main aim is to protect the lives of those onboard. If time allows you might be calling for assistance from salvage tugs/helicopter and rescue services. But, in the meantime, the prudent Captain will be closing with the nearest safe place, which will be land or a nearby port.

While I personally accept that there is no obligation for a coastal state to give permission to use the place of refuge, the IMO states that it must weigh up all of the factors and risks, which must mean to human life first and pollution second.

The port will often seem to have only one interest, regardless of the lives onboard, and that is the pollution dangers that your ship could cause. The IMO guidelines in resolution A949(23) discuss the Master assessing the situation together with the salvor and any others involved. However, I find I cannot agree with this as all other parties are likely to have their own agendas while the Captain has only one, regardless of how many tons of oil might spoil the beaches, the safety of those on board.

This is not a callous disregard for the distress such pollution might cause, but it does put human life first and ahead of the environment. If you feel that the options offered will not guarantee the safety of life you have to take the action required to preserve it.

If you approach a place of safety and you are forbidden to use it, I can only recommend that you press on until you have reached a place where you can either safely disembark your crew or until your ship is sufficiently stabilised that repairs can be made. You will then have done all you can.

Then you can call the media, because you can hardly be blown out of the water on television. You may well find yourself in hot water over such an action, but you will provably have followed the rule that puts the safety of your crew first!

I did use such extreme measure in the Pacific. I had a critical medical emergency with a crew member who was getting steadily worse. The only island near was to the north and was an American naval base. When I contacted them to explain that I had no charts for the approach and asked for assistance and guidance, they told me that they could not assist and to go elsewhere. So, having checked the draught in the pilot book, I turned up in the middle of their channel which as it wasn't very wide. My ship was a 50,000 dwt container vessel so it completely blocked it. With very bad grace they removed the sick crew member but refused to treat him there, instead putting him on a flight to Honolulu. I was warned of America's displeasure with my actions and never to darken their base again. I unblocked their base and carried on my way.

There are two things to note about this story. First, those pilot books, some of which were written a long time ago, are truly excellent in their approach advice and I have made a number of approaches without charts based on their recommendations. Second is that the seaman made a full recovery after an emergency operation.

10.2 Abandon Ship

As I have never had to deal with this particular emergency, I am not really in any position to advise you how to go about it. With a well trained crew who are exercised regularly in abandon ship procedures, the normal seamanship aspects will govern your actions. In an emergency that is the prelude to taking such an action, it would have been prudent to have the boats readied. But, as discussed earlier, this depends on the number of crew you have available. If they are not ready you must allow time to separate yourself from the emergency to prepare and lower the boats without any panic.

If the ship still has power and is an automated system, you can abandon the engine room and still be able to give the boats a lee as they are lowered. I need not have to remind you that, as Captain, you are last off the ship. However, even if it is your fault, staying onboard while saluting is only for the movies.

10.3 Grounding

When is a ship aground not aground?

Be careful how you use the word 'grounding' as it rings lots of alarm bells. 'Touched' or 'caressed the bottom' sounds so much better. 'Moved through the mud and stopped' was another interesting expression I once saw. You could also try 'when proceeding down the river, the current was stronger than anticipated and the sandbank hit us on the port side', but do not expect too much success with that one.

The ark - Allegedly the first "Blameless" grounding.

'What do you mean, no cure no pay?!'

There are groundings and groundings. The real ones are when you come to an abrupt stop with a crunching noise and the ship takes on a different angle of repose. If your engines have not already stopped, then emergency stop them. If after sounding around and checking the tanks it is obvious that you have a piece of rock sticking through your hull, take a moment to calm yourself and your officers down before taking action. It is not as if you are going anywhere. The main task, after sending the appropriate emergency messages, is to ensure your hull integrity while establishing your exact position. It could be that you have found an uncharted shoal area or single rock outcrop. More exist than is recognised, especially when you are navigating in seldom used waters with a deep draught vessel. If this is so, then you now will have your ship's name on the charts of the future. Check for pollution. Those ashore are likely to consider this far more serious than your ship or even your sailors' lives. If there is any sign of pollution immediately try to alleviate it by transferring the oil to other tanks. In the meantime, provided that it is only your double bottom that is breached and you are satisfied that the ship will float in a stable state when you are afloat, you can attempt to get the ship off.

If it is hard rock you have found the chances are that you will not have gone very far into it, so it will just be the forward part of the vessel that is affected. Sound around, especially aft, and check the state of the tide. If it is a rising tide then wait until it is at its highest point. Meanwhile, empty the tanks you can forward and fill them aft. If you are in ballast you can also consider ballasting your after holds, provided that your stability can take this. In a small ship in good weather, consider using your boats to run your anchors astern. This does not have to be very far, just enough to give you extra assistance. When the tide is at the highest, provided your propellers are in deep water, come astern using your helm from hard port to hard starboard repetitively. There is a school of thought that says that if this does not work then try coming ahead and then astern. If there is nothing else to try it might be worth it, but ensure that all else has been tried first. If there is a tug available this should be engaged, even if only to standby and escort you to wherever your managers or owners wish the ship to go for repairs.

I remember as Salvage Tug Master being called to pull a ship off the rocks and being surprised at the ease with which it came off. We later discovered that the crew had done nothing to try to get off, just waited a day for a tug to arrive.

My one experience of grounding on hard ground was actually on concrete. I was making an approach to a port in Canada, when we grounded on a disused war-time seaplane slipway that was not marked on the chart. As the port was close and had shallow water that I could get to if I was taking in water, because of the rapidly falling tide I took my chances and immediately ran the ship full astern using port and starboard wheel. It was a bit like coming unstuck from glue, at first reluctant and then suddenly free and traveling astern at a rate of knots. Watch this if you are in confined waters! Luckily there was no water ingress and, after calling for divers, they presented me with photographs of a chunk of concrete embedded in the now very twisted port bilge keel. We had a rippled bottom that required 70 tons of steel in the next drydock. The last time I saw a chart for the area it was still not marked!

If you are to use a tug, it generally be its hawser that is used. This is very heavy and, as an example, a 9 inch wire towline would mean the messenger line will have to be heaved onboard using the windlass. In good weather the tug might send someone over to ensure that the line is made fast as they require, if not, follow the tug's directions and ensure that all crew are clear of the line when tension comes on. There is a possibility that the towline will be shackled onto your anchor cable, which gives a certain spring to the line. Care must be taken to avoid any nips where the lines come onboard the line should have as fair a lead as possible. Where nips exist, ease them into a new position at least every 24 hours. In addition, if the line is in a position where it chafes against any part of the ship, it might also be necessary to parcel the wire with canvas and grease to ease the wear and tear. Most towing Masters have their own preferred ways and you should be guided by them.

There are certain rivers in Africa and South America where towing off with ground tackle and low powered tugs is the method still used. The tug will help lay the tackle, which consists of heavy wires run from your ship to anchors, and you then heave your vessel off. If you are a small vessel they might well use your own anchors and cables, but this entirely depends on the weight. If the tug's wire is to be attached to your anchor cable there is a rough rule of thumb of 3 shackles of cable to 150 fathoms of wire and the size of wire about 2 ½ times the size of cable.

Aground on sand or mud is a very different situation. With both of these conditions, if you are at full ahead and the shoaling area is gradual, the ship can go a good distance onto the bank before stopping and quite often without anyone noticing. Generally, in such a gentle shoaling situation the hull will be intact although the sand is likely to have taken all your bottom coatings off. If the ship is secure your immediate problem, especially with mud, will be your engine cooling water intakes becoming fouled. Once again, wait for the tide unless you are in the unfortunate position of going aground at high water. If that is the case, then you will probably need to have tugs to get you off.

River or estuary groundings are the "bottom caressing" ones and are far more common.

An interesting one I had was in South America in the Berbice River in Guyana, which is not a good place to take a large vessel. We loaded to our maximum, allowing for the high tide in the channel out, and always sailed just before the high tide. The problem was that, going out, the thick weed that grows very tall on the bottom hampered the speed of the ship and we were not able to clear the channel in time before the ship got so close to the seabed that the weed blocked the engine intakes. We had to stop the ship, which meant that very quickly we settled on the bottom, and we sat there for the night with no power, waiting for the next tide to refloat the ship. As it was going to be a while between floating and restoring power, I let go the anchor to hold us in position during this delay. Then, with power back on, up came the anchor and away we went. That was caressing the bottom. We went aground regularly in that river, which you can also do quite easily in the further reaches of the Mississippi and the Amazon, especially in the tributaries.

In any of these situations try to get the ship off as soon as you can as, unless you are unlucky enough to find a hard lump of rock sticking up in the mud, there is no danger of a breach in the hull. There are times when the ship might be on the edge of a bank and this is generally indicated by the ship lurching to one side or another when going on. In such a case, if going astern doesn't do much, try going ahead with the wheel hard over to the side opposite the lurch. In most cases you can get the ship off with engine and wheel movement unless you are on a rapid falling tide, in which case you will have to wait until the next high tide. In this case sound around and see where the deep water is because, if you are on the edge of a bank on one side, by pumping out your ballast or changing around your fuel oil you may be able to list the ship and slide off.

10.4   Piracy

**Piracy is a growing industry and becoming
more competent with strong leadership**

At least one sector of the shipping industry is growing! There was a time when the warships of the first world nations roamed around the world with little regard for the waters they were in or the nationality the pirates were when they blew them out of the water. No one bothered about any inquiry afterwards either. In those days pirates confined their activities to the more local shipping in their area. With the withdrawal of the international responsibilities of the established Navies, control of these sea areas was placed into the hands of governments that had neither the naval resources nor the inclination to police. More recently the pirates have found, I believe much to their initial surprise, just how easy it is to extend their activities to the deep sea sector. They were probably even more surprised to find that the majority of ships have their arms removed, in keeping with the policy of peace and goodwill to all men. The only problem is that, in the areas of the world where law and order do not exist, there is not always an understanding or agreement with this peaceful policy.

Since then, as Captain, I have voyaged regularly through the known pirate areas of the east, notably the Sunda, Lombok and Malacca straits and the Cebu Sea areas, mostly on very large vessels. The advice has not changed - keep a good lookout, try to isolate the accommodation, secure all entry points, rig hoses and have the decks well lit. This is from government authorities who ensure that, when their government ships travel in such waters, there are armed guards onboard! A case of do as we say, not as we do. I did try to get rolls of razor wire supplied to put around the rails but, as this is not a SOLAS requirement, it was not supplied.

Here is a point to ponder on. If you are attacked by pirates in territorial waters and there is a naval vessel nearby that is not of the nationality of the country whose waters you are in, the warship is not allowed to interfere with the pirates without first obtaining authority from that country, by which time the pirates could be back on the beach counting your money. The good news is that the warship is allowed to help you afterwards. Everything is alright then!

All the advice is against arming ourselves. This is for reasons such as we are not trained in the use of weapons and that the weapons might be stolen. Much of the advice is open to debate, with strong views on the merits of each position from both sides. What I will say is that it is a debate that should be raised and discussed. For me, it all seems very strange. In the years leading up to the Second World War and into the 60's, ships trading around the world regularly carried weapons. As a Cadet and as a junior officer, on a Saturday morning I was allowed to practice with the Webley 38 revolvers that the ship carried. Ships trading on the China coast were quite heavily armed.

It is obvious to all of us at sea that, without adequate law and order, piracy will continue to grow. There is no sign yet that all of the governments in the piracy areas are able or willing to take the appropriate action. We often sail our ships in waters where the rule of law is not as it should be, and in some parts the governments and armed forces themselves are known to participate in acts of piracy. Shipping agencies in these areas must be treated with caution as considerable information is able to be passed to the pirates through them.

The choices you have are to either offer no resistance in the hope that they will appreciate this co-operation and treat you civilly or, when walking in the jungle, carrying a big stick. I believe a sensible route might be to institute a proper Master at Arms course in handling and dealing with weapons. This way we could have one or more crew onboard trained properly in their use and maintenance, with the weapons under their control. However, for now we must continue to navigate through these areas of danger without any self protection.

Both my experiences of piracy were when I was a Chief Officer on the West African coast in 1971. The first was when anchored in Lagos harbour where we were boarded, in daylight, by pirates looking for cargo from the containers. We had an armed watchman onboard who was provided with a bow and some arrows! When we urged him to shoot his arrows he was rather unwilling as this might upset the pirates, who were busy looting the cargo. Further, he knew the pirates as they were from the Nigerian army. So we stood on the bridge and watched the cargo being removed into a lighter and transported to the shore, where it was placed into Nigerian army trucks. They didn't bother us and we didn't bother them.

The second time was in Cameroon, again in port but this time alongside. We were boarded at night by five armed pirates looking for cargo, but our decks were clear. The ship astern of us was a German ship so we called them on the VHF and warned them what was happening. Shortly afterwards we heard several bursts of gunfire and then silence. The pirates were rather unlucky as the Captain of the German ship was not heavily into peace and goodwill, so his ship was well armed with automatic weapons. The three pirates who boarded were shot dead and the two remaining in the boat drove off. The authorities were not concerned, declaring that the pirates could not have been from Cameroon as piracy was not allowed!

My advice is to take all of the recommended precautions and, if you perceive you are in danger of being boarded, try to steer away. However, with the regard to the advice to use the hoses, be very careful as you could well be putting those manning the hose in considerable danger. From my own experience, it is amazing just how much more confident you feel with a couple of automatic weapons on the bridge, but the moral and safety debate will continue to be a strong one.

10.5 Medical Emergencies

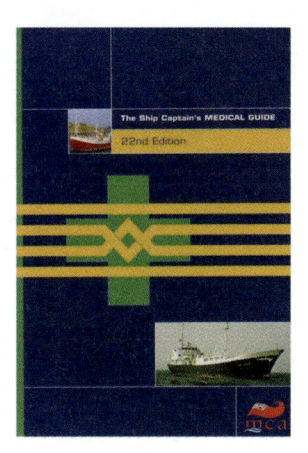

Ship Captain's Medical Guide, one of the most practical books onboard a merchant ship today

'The art of medicine consists in amusing the patient while nature cures the disease'
Voltaire.

I often feel that this type of emergency is one of the most difficult to deal with, mostly because of the feeling of total inadequacy that passes over you as you attempt to cope with the problem. With all other types of emergency you have at least a professional base to fall back on, enabling you to get your teeth into the predicament. A medical emergency can appear at any time in many ways, leaving you scrambling for the Ship Master's Medical Guide. This is the best guide book you will have onboard and it has been honed and polished since it was first published in 1868.

If the patient is conscious you must maintain an air of complete confidence, even if you haven't a clue what to do. Even if it looks serious, tell the patient that it is not as bad as they think and that you will have it fixed shortly. This will help to stop the patient becoming agitated and maintain their morale. If they are in pain, try to relieve it. If you are successful at this the patient will calm a little, and you will feel a lot better too!

With anything that is at all serious, get medical advice. When you do this, ensure that the patient is never left alone. Try and leave them with someone who will be sympathetic to their condition, the last thing you want is someone asking if they can have his TV!

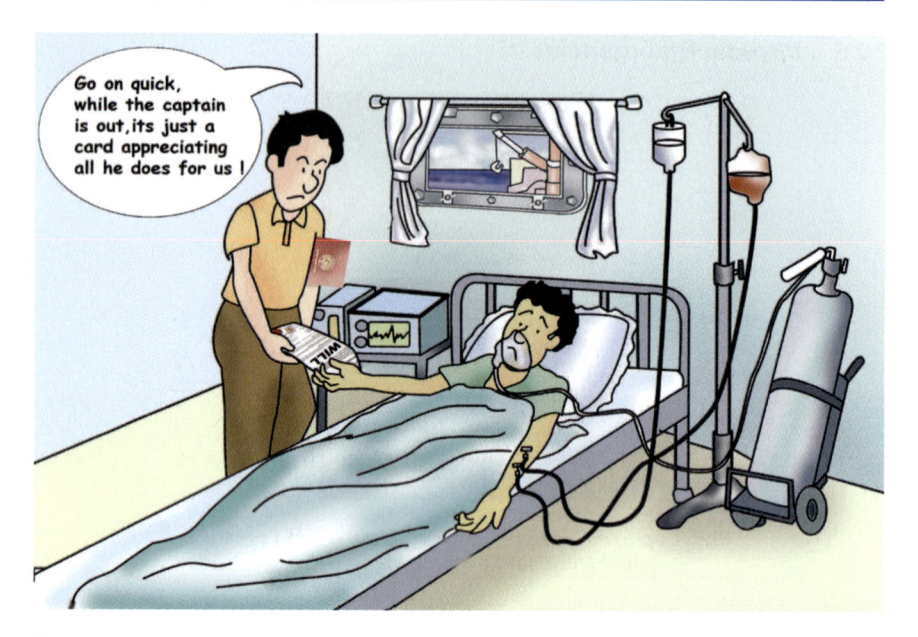

First use the Sat-phone and call the best medical centre near your position. The numbers are found in the Admiralty List of Radio Signals, Volume 1. However, if you are crossing the oceans regularly, or are trading on a regular route, it is an idea to write these numbers down near the Sat-phone so you won't have to waste time looking through the book.

When you call make sure you have to hand all of the information suggested in Chapter 13 of the Medical Guide. This is another good time to have your tape recorder handy, as I doubt if you will have a Sat phone extension in either the treatment room or the ship's hospital. If you have to be talked through procedures, you will have to rely on an officer who can speak good English on the Sat-phone using a portable transmitter to relay to another officer standing near you.

Do not forget other ships in the area. These days there are a lot of cruise ships sailing around and, although few cross the oceans, you never know who is around or the facilities or experience they may have. Who knows, even amongst your crew you could find ex-service personnel with practical medical experience. If there are naval vessels or cruise vessels they will have medical staff onboard and usually a dedicated rescue craft for transfer. If you are within range of land or naval ships, helicopter assistance can be provided to either transfer the patient or to bring medical staff and equipment to you.

11 Collisions

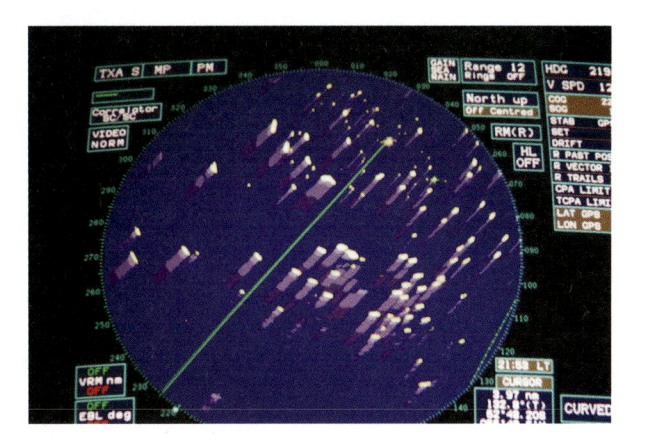

A collision at sea could will ruin your day, trip, career...?

My only experience of this was the day my 2nd Officer was making noon calculations on the bridge on a perfectly clear day in the China Sea. He did not notice a fishing boat which, from a perfectly safe position with the ship passing clear, inexplicably decided to try to cross the bow from the port side. The 2nd Officer did not ensure that his lookout was on the bridge while he did his noon calculations. At the last minute he looked up saw what was happening and yes, you guessed it, went to port just as the fishing boat decided not to continue across the bow and went to starboard. He was very lucky, as our ship at the time was around 200,000dwt and the fishing boat was only thirty feet long. We grazed him as we went by but it was enough to take his foremast down, along with a portion of his deck rail. We stopped the ship and sent over the lifeboat to see if he was safe to carry on. Once he confirmed that he had only superficial damage we resumed our course.

The best way to discuss collisions is to consider the reasons for them and try to deal with the problem at source. The trouble is, most of the real reasons are going to be beyond your control.

11.1 Why Collisions Really Happen

Every casualty produces a flurry of documents, rules, advice on how not to collide and the inevitable "we fail to understand" pronouncements. Blame, is apportioned without going too far into the reasons and we settle down to await the next "inevitable" incident. If we accept that the majority of collisions are caused by human failure we must examine the cause of these failures and determine the actions that can be taken to alleviate them while, at the same time recognising the limitations of this approach. We can list the failures under three broad headings: political, financial and human.

11.2 The Ideal Situation

The ship is properly manned so that at all times a Watchkeeping Officer and a properly trained lookout are on the bridge. Today, few ships can claim this ideal.

The six men such manning implies should be the dedicated navigation team of the ship, required to perform no other duties at sea unless they are directly connected to the navigation of the vessel.

No ship today can claim this.

They should be highly motivated, of good morale, properly trained and with certification from recognised and respected government departments. Prior to joining any vessel with navigation and control equipment that an officer is not familiar with, a course in such equipment should be undertaken. A watchkeeping course should be undertaken for the ratings who will be employed as lookouts and who are, by default, part of the navigation team.

Whatever they are being trained in these days, it does not seem to include acting as a lookout.

All of the above is perfectly normal in the air industry and no one yet has been able to present me with a logical reason why the shipping industry should not follow the same standard. If it were instituted on a worldwide scale, the incidents of near miss and collision would dramatically decline.

11.3 The Prevailing Situation

The 2nd or 3rd Officer is recruited through a manning agency from a third world country with certificates that no one can check as, if they are sighted at all by the employing company, they will be in Photostat form. In the past we had economic refugees as seamen, but now they also come as officers. The officer does not want to be on the ship or work for that particular company, in fact he may not want to be at sea at all. But the pay, although poor by international standards, is better than anything that can be achieved at home.

Our reluctant officer will be flown out to the ship, which will often be sailing the same day that he joins. The Chief officer will have been working for 16 hours without break and, with cargo loading coming to an end, has no time to show him round. The ship sails and that evening he is on watch in traffic with navigation and control equipment he does not know how to operate properly, with a lookout who cannot speak the same language and little idea of how to perform his duties.

Under these circumstances, the real wonder to me is that there are not more incidents.

Of course, this does not happen on every ship and many Captains and Chief Officers try to ensure that their officers have a degree of understanding of the bridge equipment. But with unwillingness from many companies to train or recruit and pay properly qualified officers, the complete workload often now falls on the senior officers. At the same time, ISM has added considerably to the workload of these same officers, causing further deterioration of the navigational vigilance. All too often it is "never mind the watch, fill in the paper".

So why does all of this happen and why is it allowed to carry on irrespective of the STCW and ISM initiatives? Let us look more closely at that.

11.4   STCW (Politics)

With the signing of the STCW convention in 1995, the standardisation of training and certification was to herald a new dawn and it was a brave attempt to at least try to get some control on certification and training. However, while examination requirements may be the same, the examination protocols certainly are not. STCW led to adverse effects on standards as it reduced the examination standard to the lowest common denominator, reducing the value of the certificates of traditional maritime nations from a professional to a technical standard. They also allowed holders of certificates from nations with low standards and corrupt administrations to sail legally on all vessels and worse, to be able to trade low value certificates for high value ones, once again debasing their value. The result has been an overall lowering of standards. Traditionally qualified officers began to leave the sea as their professional qualifications and value were debased and their salaries reduced.

11.5   The Financial Dimension

Financial considerations lie at the heart of many of the problems, with profit maximization causing low pay, poor conditions and inadequate manning. Consider the illogicality of the present manning regulations. A deep sea foreign going ship of 500 tons voyaging across the Atlantic in winter can be manned with just the Master and one officer. The number of ratings carried is decided by the flag state whose decision is based on the details of the ship that have been submitted by the owner or manager! Yet that ship might have a speed of 15 knots, a speed at which it could punch into a far larger ship, sinking it in minutes.

If you have not had the unpleasant experience of watchkeeping six hours on and six off for over a month, I can assure you that it does not improve the standards.

My own experience of this was while making a deep sea tow in the Atlantic, with two deck ratings from the Spanish fishing fleet who could not steer or speak English! We had an oven timer on the bridge to wake us up because we kept dropping off to sleep towards the end of the watch!

Unconventional deadman alarm

I believe that the majority of the ships steaming around today are undermanned. Many have language problems on the bridge and crews of mixed nationalities. These often exist in a system of voluntary apartheid with poor pay and conditions and whose only 'friend' is a shore-side personnel department that is purely a hiring and firing agency. All of this contributes to a general attitude of indifference and poor morale.

It is unfair to blame the Captains as most of those in the office ashore, including those ex-seafarers and the safety departments, know that these problems exist and do little to alleviate them.

Here is a question. If the Master of a ship feels that the manning of his ship is such that it causes him concern regarding the safety of the vessel, or if he feels that the lack of a common language onboard interferes with safe watchkeeping, what are his alternatives?

We all know the "professional" answer, but if the Master refuses to sail, will he be supported? In the international shipping world there is no union to come to his rescue. In other words, he is on his own against all the guns a shipping company can bring against him. So, the Master generally sails regardless of the state of his officers and crew, unless he is in one of the few Companies that would support his position.

I am including fatigue in this section as, although it is a human condition, the causes are financial. Chronic under manning on most ships today means it is not uncommon for bridge officers to work over 16 hours a day in port, with the Chief Officer sometimes sailing without having slept for 24 hours. I know that there are forms stating the required hours of work, and forms to fill saying how many hours have been worked, but they are often falsified. Of course, they shouldn't be, but where is the support for those who fill them in correctly or refuse to sail? Let us go back to our "better world" and imagine a ship that truthfully completes the forms and then finds that it cannot sail, or even more startlingly, advises the port of this. I wonder if there is any oil or bulk terminal in any port that will accept the ship remaining alongside after completion so that the crew can rest before sailing. Or any port that has set aside berths that ships can be moved to for this purpose? The argument that is sometimes made, that the ship could go and anchor, is ludicrous as not only would the fatigued officers have to go about their duties unberthing the ship, but they would still have to do anchor watches, utterly defeating the purpose. Under-manning, coupled with incompetent crew putting a greater workload on the competent, causes fatigue. Rather than producing meaningless paper trails we should be tackling this. It is important that you recognise fatigue in your officers and, when possible, assist them by doing the occasional watch for them. I know that this is giving in to the system and arguments for additional reduction of the Deck Officers, but if you have sailed from port with a Chief Officer who has not slept for over twenty hours it is in the interests of everyone onboard to assist.

11.6   The Human Element

Something we all know is that as long as we have humans on the bridge there will be accidents. Of course we must do all we can to alleviate the problem, but the constant flow of 'how to keep a watch advice' will not help until the basic underlying causes are solved.

The bridge library continues to grow. One can only assume that companies expect these books to be read on the bridge while keeping watch, which I think rather defeats the object!

At one time, ships sailed through areas such as the Singapore Straits or the Dover Straits without the Master on the bridge and without routeing. It is a very foolhardy Master who leaves the present day junior officer alone on the bridge in such places, even with routeing and VTR. The colleges and examination bodies continue to claim that their standards are the same as in the past yet all of us who are out there on the seas have significant doubts about this.

The continually increasing workload caused by planned maintenance, updating publications, completion of ISM requirements, Safety Officer duties and the latest Security Officer duties, have been added to the ship with no increase in manning. These duties always fall on the bridge officers, as if there were no other officers onboard. As the extra workload increases, officers are understandably reluctant to complete their watch and then go to work for hours in their cabins.

- The majority of ships are undermanned for the tasks they are required to perform
- manning assessments by flag state that are based on tonnage of the ship and the operators' statements of crew requirements are unreliable and unacceptable
- the qualifications and training of many officers are often deficient for their designated responsibilities
- falsification of hours of rest documents is accepted as fact by many companies and ignored by the agencies whose job it is to ensure their enforcement, so many ships are sailing from ports with officers suffering from fatigue
- there is little support for Masters that try to ensure their ships are properly manned, with all required safety procedures followed

- the ports feel that they are divorced from the issues of ship safety and fatigue and have little interest in the safety issues of the ships, except where they interfere with the port and the speed of turn around
- the regulations regarding lookout are out-of-date and should accept that day and night require the same levels of vigilance
- the training of bridge seamen as lookouts is poor and requires a specialised course
- we need to accept that the bridge team should be dedicated and unhindered by other duties.

When trying to deal with many of these problems, often you will come against an age old excuse, flag state. If the flag state allows the ship to sail with a Master, a monkey and an organ grinder, it must be safe. If the flag state agrees that 12 nationalities can all converse perfectly well because the operator says so, then it is so. These illogical rebuttals to any reasoned case continue as the excuse for not dealing with the increasing problems. Over the years, many of my colleagues who work within these official bodies have expressed their concern on these matters, but are often powerless to act.

I have wondered why the insurance companies are so disinterested in the root causes of our problems. The only explanation I have ever been given is that the costs of the accidents are factored in, although personally, I have no idea how you factor in the cost of lives. If the governments are satisfied that the flag state solves all problems, charterers and insurance companies are disinterested and unions, associations and professional bodies have no power to act, then owners and operators will continue to ignore all reasoning, and collisions will continue.

12 Man Overboard

Will a man falling overboard even be seen on today's minimum manned ships?

I remember the very first man overboard situation I experienced. It was while I was a cadet on a ship in the Mediterranean. It was a pleasant day with a slight sea running, little wind. A seaman, working in a lifeboat that was stowed in the falls, fell back over the side. The call went up which, as the boats were located on the boat deck not far back from the bridge, was heard. Not surprising, as the bridge was manned by the OOW, the Cadet of the Watch, the Quartermaster on the wheel and a seaman as lookout. The Radio Officer was also on watch in his office on the bridge. I was immediately detailed to sound three long blasts on the whistle. This, apart from being the recognised signal to other ships for MOB, was also the ship's MOB action stations signal. The OOW ordered the wheel hard over which, as the wheel was manned, was instantly carried out. The lookout let go of the MOB lifebuoy and smoke marker. Responding to the signal on the whistle, the Captain had arrived on the bridge together with the 4th Officer and two other cadets, the two seamen designated as lookouts arrived and picked up their binoculars and each went to a wing of the bridge and took over the lookout from the bridge seaman. The Chief Officer, a cadet and the boat lowering party were already assembled on deck. The boat was lowered to the boat deck and manned by the 3rd Officer Junior Engineer and five crew. The ship turned round and slowed down, the boat was lowered and went away while the ship was making around 5 knots, using the boat rope to clear the ship's side. The man was found clinging to the MOB buoy, hauled inboard and returned to the ship.

The whole incident took around 15 minutes and no one seemed particularly excited by it. The man was put into dry clothes, given a large tot of rum and in the afternoon was back working in the boat. Entries were made in the log book and that was that, and so it should have been. Every voyage we practiced MOB, with the boat being sent away at sea. In addition we used the boats regularly. Liberty boat, barbeques, beach parties and ship visits were all occasions to use the boats so there was a seamanlike familiarisation with boatwork among all onboard. The six cadets carried were all from training ships where they had been immersed in boatwork for two years, and the ship's ratings were all intimate with boats. In addition, the lifeboats were, although quite cumbersome, open boats and capable of being used for boatwork. Similarly, as a young Captain, we rescued several men from a boat that had sunk, finding them easily in comparatively good weather, with an open lifeboat.

Well, the sea has not changed (a phrase I find myself repeating more and more the older I become), but everything else has. On the positive side is the fact that the safety culture now has managed to influence even the most recalcitrant, and safety belts, non slip decks and a general acceptance that maybe it is not a good idea to have sailors dangling over the side in a force 9 has certainly reduced the incidents. However, there are now many at sea who are not as familiar with the ship and seamanship as they should be. In addition, there still exist conditions when seamen have to go out on deck in bad weather. Individuals still do foolish things regardless of the technology surrounding them and despite precautions, lectures, posters and safety departments. People still have a habit of falling off of the ship and into the sea and it is our job to bring them back, preferably alive.

12.1   The Present Predicament

Today, unless the ship is leaving or entering harbour, the steering is likely to be in auto-pilot.

If it is day-time and in open waters the OOW will be the only person on the bridge. This is often the case at night too. There is a requirement that during the day, if he is not on the bridge the duty seaman should be within instant call by the bridge. However, this often means that he is within a call, a situation exacerbated by the chronic manning situation on many ships.

Ships are now generally larger, the bridges wider and the wing doors often closed, so not only will shouts of 'man overboard' not be heard, the dash out to the wings to release the MOB lifebuoys will be longer in a situation where every second counts.

The boats, unless you are lucky enough to have a purpose built rescue boat, are two enclosed lifeboats, one of which will be named the rescue boat because the davit motor is faster. They will, in many cases, be stowed high up on the ship. Add this height to the possible height of a large ship in ballast and the drop can be extreme.

In addition, the modern ship has the lifeboat davits aft, as part of the accommodation housing. This means that the boats when lowered, rather than being against the side of the ship they are in considerable danger of being swept under the stern counter.

With such difficulties in using the boat you would expect that the expertise of the seamen and the officers to be better than in the past. Regrettably the seamanship training of present day ratings and officers is very basic, with little boatwork knowledge or practical training.

Enclosed lifeboat (approved by Class as a rescue boat – but not by Captain Lloyd)

You can now see a number of problems are likely to arise in any attempted rescue venture, particularly if you are paying attention to the sensible caveat of not endangering the lives of your men, but it is still your duty to do all you can to rescue the person from the water and get them to a place of safety. Further, you must be able to demonstrate that you did all you could to affect such rescue. Putting it bluntly, if the rescue is successful all the rules broken will be forgiven. If it is not successful you can be sure that every decision and action you made will be pulled apart by every governmental deskbound mariner in the flag state concerned, even to the requirement that you must have pulled the risk assessment and issued a work permit for lowering the boat!

12.2 Preparation

The remark about the risk assessment is not as facetious as you may think. Regardless of your feelings about risk assessment, it is well established and is not going to go away, and for the more junior officers it has always been part of their normal seafaring culture. Many of us older Masters tend to leave bits of paper to the officers but it is worthwhile pulling the risk assessments and running through them. They will often have been written by junior officers and unless you amend them, you and your ship will be governed by what they say. Having assumed command of the ship you are responsible for ensuring their observance, so it is not much use leaving your disagreement with them until they are read to you at the Court of Inquiry.

Not only should you read the risk assessment but you should also ensure that all those who may be concerned with a MOB situation read them as well. If there are any changes to be made you will all know both the changes and the reasons why and so the assessment will be up-to-date. At the same time this provides the Master with the opportunity for a discussion with all of the officers, especially the deck officers, the problems of MOB on that particular ship. Not only will this provide an opportunity for all opinions to be evaluated, but it presents you with an occasion to evaluate your officers by listening to their responses to the difficulties. After all, if the 2nd Officer states that he has never been in a boat before and is frightened of the sea, he is probably not the man to cox the rescue boat, even if the stations bill says it is his duty to do so!

Fast rescue craft

This discussion also allows you to leave the officers in no doubt about what you expect of them in such a situation. Once all the opinions are listened to, accepted or dismissed, the framework of a plan can be established, taking into account factors such as the regulatory requirements and the limitations imposed by the ship and its equipment. It would also be interesting to gauge your officers' reactions to taking your boat away in differing sea states. From this you will have to scale your ideas on what to do.

Another most important preparation is to gain knowledge of your own ship's handling capabilities. All too often we join a ship, sail around on it and leave, without really knowing how the ship handles in an emergency situation. This is not good enough if we are to call ourselves seamen. How fast will the ship turn at full speed with maximum helm? What speed will the ship slow down to during such a turn? How will this turn affect the sea state alongside the launching area? Will two full turns calm the seas enough to launch? Can you bring the ship alongside an oil drum floating in the water and what is the best angle of approach? These are questions that you, as Master, should be able to answer. No one can seriously question your decision to take a few hours to try these manoeuvres out after joining a ship, and think of the difference they could make between saving or losing a life.

Out of interest, while playing with your ship, try a 'Williamson Turn', which is so beloved by certificate examiners. Rarely will it bring you back completely on track because it was designed for very different types of vessels. The Williamson Turn was named for John Williamson, USNR, who used it in 1943. However, according to 'Uncommon Carriers' by John McPhee, the manoeuvre was originally called the "Butakov pipe" and was used in the Russo-Japanese War as a way of keeping guns at the same distance from an enemy. It could not have worked very well then either as the Russians lost that engagement! The Williamson Turn is deemed the most appropriate at night or in reduced visibility, when the position of the MOB is still close to the ship. For other situations, an Anderson Turn (quickest method) or a Scharnow Turn could be used. The choice of method to use has often depended on the prevailing wind and weather conditions.

However, while all three turns are interesting, ever since GPS positioning gave us the ability to fix our position instantly they are largely redundant. I am quite surprised that, as we no longer have to know the points of a sail or how to trim an oil lamp, the use of these turns is still required by certificate examiners and taught extensively in the Nautical colleges. It creates the problem that the belief continues that these turns should be trotted out, like some religious mantra, with all the subsequent delay in any rescue operation. Even if the GPS is not working, the wake of a modern ship lingers sufficiently for a ship to be conned back into the path.

The final preparation is MOB avoidance. It is essential that the Master provides detailed instructions about what he will allow in differing weather conditions. Equally, any prudent Master should ensure that, before the onset of bad weather, all deck fittings and cargo lashings are checked and secured. Better this than sending men out in the middle of a storm. These are precautions that any good Chief Officer would make, but now the Master has to check it is being done.

A last though on preparation is that it would be useful to know which of the crew can swim and which cannot. I am willing to bet that no Captain reading this knows this fact about his crew. I certainly didn't. If crew members can swim, they might be more confident in the rescue boat. In some circumstances there could even be a need for a strong swimmer to enter the water from the boat to assist the survivor.

The MOB plan has one aim, to retrieve the man from the water in the shortest possible time without endangering other crew members. So how long do you have? If the person cannot swim and has no life-jacket, then it could be said you have as long as you like. However, if we are a little more positive than that, the chart that follows provides some indication of the time scales you should be concerned with. I do not intend to deal with hypothermia in detail, but you should realise that it is a very real problem and requires knowledgeable treatment as even when someone is recovered alive from the water they can still die. It is surprising that while working at sea, we seem to know so little about hypothermia and its treatment.

WATER TEMP	WATER TEMP	EXHAUSTION/ UNCONSCIOUSNESS	EXPECTED TIME OF SURVIVAL
	32.5°F	Less than 15 mins	15 to 45 mins
0.28°C to 4.4°C	32.5°F to 40°F	15 to 30 mins	30 to 90 mins
4.4°C to 10.0°C	40°F to 50°F	30 to 60 mins	1 to 3 hours
10.0°C to 15.6°C	50°F to 60°F	1 to 2 hours	1 to 6 hours
15.6°C to 21.1°C	60°F to 70°F	2 to 7 hours	2 to 40 hours
21.1°C to 26.6°C	70°F to 80°F	3 to 12 hours	3 hours to indefinite
>26.6°C	Over 80°F	indefinite	

Of course the time scales are improved if the person was correctly wearing a survival suit, so when they were last tested?

I once did an exercise on an ice class ship in the ship's swimming pool. Of the twenty seven suits tested, eight had leaks through deterioration of their sealed seams and six crew suits had leaks through poor or incorrect fitting. Over 50% failure, which was our fault for not testing them correctly and for not ensuring the crew could wear them properly.

At least the testing of these suits is now mandatory!

The only way to properly check these suits is in water, so do it if you have the opportunity. Also make sure that all crew know how to wear the suits, especially remembering to remove their shoes!

12.3   MOB - The Plan

Letting go the lifebuoy (preferably with smoke float) will boost the man-overboard's morale. He's been seen!

The following are the actions that are required from the OOW (not necessarily in order):

- Sound the Alarm
- fix the position
  once the bridge is alerted, the first action should be to establish the position. The fastest way to do this is hit the MOB or Way Point marker button on the GPS. At least we now know where to turn back to
- let go the MOB Buoy and markers
  not only will this provide confirmation of the area in which to find the person and give that person something to hold onto to keep him afloat, but it will also show to them that his accident has been seen and that the ship is taking action. His morale will be greatly enhanced by this. Now the ship's alarm for MOB can be sounded and hopefully there is a separate alarm for this. If not, then you end up sounding the general emergency stations alarm which rather pointlessly sends all the crew to fire stations. If you are not on a ship where the alarms are triggered so frequently that no one bothers any more, this will at least alert all onboard to the fact that there is an emergency. It also should draw the Master and others to the bridge without further calls
- alert the engine room
- post lookouts
- maintain continuous watch on person in the water if still visible
- call the Master
- sound MOB on the ships whistle
- log the events
- contact nearby vessels on VHF and alert them to the situation
- send out the MOB alert on the emergency channels
- hoist 'O' signal flag
- commence turning the ship and conning back to MOB position
  at this stage do not worry about reducing speed, although while the ship is turning the engines can be put on standby, alerting the engine staff to prepare for manoeuvring. As the ship turns with hard wheel the speed will reduce dramatically so that by the time the ship course is reversed, the speed could, as a rough guide, be a third of the initial speed.

With the above actions all carried out within a couple of minutes, the OOW will have done all possible and further assistance will be arriving. Of course, if there are others present on the bridge at the onset of the event, actions can be carried out more quickly.

If there is someone else on the bridge and the MOB has just occurred, it is essential that visual contact is maintained. I would opt to keep visual contact rather than put the spare man on the wheel as, if the suggested sequence is followed by the OOW, the ship will be coming round soon enough.

It will not have escaped your attention that I have omitted the phrase, 'Put the wheel over the same side the man has fallen from'. I don't include this because the initial intention of this manoeuvre is to increase the distance of the ship's propeller from the person in the water. When this rule was written, ships were far smaller and slower, mostly with manual steering. Even if the bridge sees the man going into the water, the speed of the average ship and the initial slow response to the wheel means that by the time your action makes any impact, the MOB will already be astern. A quick calculation for your ship can easily be made but as an example, if you take a ship of 183 metres at a speed of 15 knots and if the person falls over the side from the very forward part of ship, it will take 23 seconds for the man to be astern of the ship. If an MOB report is made to the bridge, it will almost certainly be too late to attempt any clearance of the propeller. If the OOW witnesses the event, could he get to the auto pilot, change to manual and turn the wheel in that time? On some ships there maybe a chance, but I believe that for the majority there is not.

However, here is a reason to consider which way to put the wheel. If the person is actually seen to go over the side, it does no harm to put the wheel over on that same side, not necessarily because you will help clear the person from the propeller but keep from swinging the stern across the line of sight. The final judgement of where in the priority list to put the turn of the ship must rest with the characteristics of each individual ship. If the man is seen to enter the water by the bridge, and there is a chance of clearance, then the wheel hard over manoeuvre should be made as the first priority.

With the new arrivals on the bridge, and you taking command, the plan can be further developed.

Lookouts should be posted, with binoculars if you have enough and searchlights manned if you have them. This is, at the moment, the only way you are going to locate the person if he is not already being observed. Depending on the assistance that exists at this stage on the bridge, alerting other ships in the vicinity and logging the events must follow. I accept that keeping an accurate record and time of events is important, but it is not as important to the person in the water. Which or who has the priority?

If you really want to hoist the 'O' flag and have spare hands for this, then do, although no ship is really going to notice and many will not know what it means!

12.4 The Execution

If the MOB has been located and the ship has returned to his position, recovery can take place. By this time the bridge will have more information on the incident, most importantly the exact time interval between the person entering the water and the alarm being given. This is critical, especially if there is no visual sighting of the casualty. You should also know by now if the person can swim and if there was any other recovery aid used by the person raising the alarm.

The choice of recovery options will be dictated by the weather conditions and the condition of the person in the water. If the rescue boat cannot be used, are there other ships close enough to immediately launch theirs? Is it possible to bring the ship alongside the casualty? Can a net be put over the side on a crane? These are some alternatives that may be available.

In all decisions made to use the rescue boat, if you consider the weather makes a successful launch possible, the final decision should rest with the Cox'n. If the person in the water is seen to be alive the pressure to recover is intense. If the body is located and no sign of life is observed then, while not yet accepting death, the allowable risk factor must lower.

Thinking about risk factors, all rescue efforts are subject to the safety of the crew. While this is sensible and correct, would we actually follow this course? Where does risk begin? When using boats at sea there is always a risk element, so at which point does it become unacceptable? I think that if the persons in the water were a couple of children, and the only way to recover them was using the ship's boats, even in gale force seas we would launch, or at least I hope we would. If we can agree to that, it follows that there must be an acceptable risk level in any launch decision that is particular to the circumstances and, as Masters, we must accept the consequences of any decision we make.

Before picking the best crew for the boat, consider the number that will be required. If a dedicated rescue craft is being used the number will be limited to a Cox'n and two or three and, by regulation, these crew will have rescue craft training. But if you are using an enclosed ship's lifeboat, additional equipment can be added, such as a lifebuoy to assist in recovery, blankets, even a life-raft if it can be got through the doors or lashed onto the deck. This is not a comprehensive list, but is a number of items that may be included. Any lifeboat, if being used for rescue, will be light in the water. This means that it will be harder to control, especially when the Cox'n is trying to peer through a scratched perspex screen. When considering numbers, the difficulties of heaving a man up out of the water into the boat must be anticipated, particularly if you have to try to get the person through a small hatch in the side. It could well be that a crewman might have to enter the water to put a harness on the person to lift him, or that men may have to go out onto the deck of the boat. Therefore, safety harnesses should also be included.

Prior to launching the boat, if the sea state is anything but low it might be prudent to take a turn out of the ship, producing a 'dampened area' in which to lower the boat. Smaller ships might even find two turns more effective. Whether to give the boat a lee on launching again depends on the roll of the ship and the height from which the boat is being launched. With the ship beam on and with a heavy swell, as the boat lowers the swinging will increase with the dangers of it either contacting the side or getting swung under the stern counter. If you have lower deck access to the falls this swinging can be lessened by running a line around the falls, moving the fulcrum of the swing to that lower level.

On smaller ships it may be better to make two full turns to dampen the sea before lowering the lifeboat/rescue boat

However, if the sea is not sufficiently dampened it might be better to try the ship with the sea a few points off the bow, sacrificing some lee for less roll. The boat rope should be led well forward from the lowest deck point. As the boat lets go, the rope must be immediately taken in to avoid fouling the boat's propellers. At this stage this would be catastrophic.

The greater problem is the recovery of the boat. The positioning of the ship has already been discussed so it really is now in the hands of the Cox'n. An enclosed plastic lifeboat is totally unsuitable to use as a rescue craft, but without a dedicated FRC it may be all you have. One item that may help is nylon pennants. If you have these already made up for such an eventuality, after the launch haul up the hooks and put them on. They will make an immense difference to the ease of recovery and in the past many ships had them supplied for just this purpose.

The boat rope must be ready to lower down to the boat. This will be the only chance of lining the boat up while trying to engage the hooks. There is a possibility that you will not be able to recover the boat or that the boat is so damaged in the recovery attempt that further attempts cannot be made, at least until the weather has abated.

This situation is not one that any Master would wish to find himself in. Alternatives such as going to another ship that may be easier to board, waiting for a helicopter if one is available or even escorting the boat to land if it is near enough would have to be contemplated. In the end, the only alternatives may be waiting for weather to improve or trying to take off the personnel and abandoning the boat, which could be a dangerous action. At least a lifeboat is designed for survival, which would be about the only plus in the whole affair!

Going to a SAR condition if the MOB is not located is a specialised subject that I will not deal with here. It is certainly worth reading about the various search patterns and to understand the aspects of command and control when searching for survivors. I would like to add that if the person is not located and it is felt that the ship is in the correct position, if the weather permits and manning allows, consider lowering both the lifeboats. Set them off each side of the ship at about 2/3 cables then shut off their engines. Sound carries very well over water so if the MOB is blowing a whistle or shouting there is a good chance that those in the lifeboats would hear. Also, with the boats in the position you are ready to make a parallel search pattern.

I recently held an exercise involving both my FRC's (fast rescue craft), a number of dummies in the water, significant wave heights of 3.5 metres, night time and heavy snow. No previous briefings or warning given. Indeed, conditions were such that the crew felt themselves safe from any exercise. We made mistakes and learnt many lessons, and this was on an Emergency Response and Rescue Vessel where the crews are fully trained in rescue and are exercised constantly.

12.4.1 Conclusion

The Captain of the average merchant vessel, that has only enclosed lifeboats carried, on a ship alone on the high seas in poor weather and trying to cope with a MOB, is in a desperate predicament that is not of his own making.

I have not covered every aspect of rescue in this chapter, nor every piece of equipment or actions that could be taken. I have also dwelt on the worse case scenario, which is the ship alone on the seas and with no dedicated rescue craft. The aim is to provoke thought about an event that might never happen to a Master, or could happen at any time. If it does happen, a life is at stake and it could well be that the instant actions and decisions of the Master, coupled with the general preparedness of the ship, will decide whether someone lives or dies.

As a final item, I know of one occurrence of a MOB at ~ 04:30 where the ship searched all day without success. As the sun set and twilight set in one of the many lookouts saw the twinkle from the MOB's lifejacket light.

Just when you think you won't find the MOB, there's a light to show you the way

13 Welfare

Drastically shorter port stays, reduced manpower and increased paperwork all take their toll on welfare and morale

This is not a subject that is often discussed during any of our training or college lectures, probably because there are no examinations in the subject. It is a very much neglected issue, both ashore and afloat, but it is terribly important if you are to have an efficient ship with a contented crew.

There was a time when you did not have to consider this problem too much because ships stayed in ports for considerably longer than they do now. Ports themselves were 'crew friendly', with the berths quite close to the town and its facilities for relaxation. This has all changed and on some types of ships it can be rare for the crew to be able to go ashore. When they do, it is often some distance to any population centre, requiring taxi fares they can ill afford.

If this is the situation on your ship, it is important to consider the various alternatives that can be provided to try to ensure that the crew have the opportunity of some form of social life onboard.

Crews tend to be a mix of cultures, each with their own attitudes to mixing and the type of leisure activities they enjoy. You should not force integration of the various nationalities on each other and it is my own my experience that when you have just two or three nationalities, each group tends to exist in a type of voluntary apartheid, only joining together for the odd social function. When you have several nationalities without any one group dominant there is likely to be more mixing but, either way, there are some basic welfare items that you should not ignore.

There was a ship that the owner visited and that had a meeting in the bar to discuss welfare. During the course of it the owner enquired as to what they did for religion onboard? The stunned silence was interrupted by the Electrician who piped up "I don't know about the rest of them, but I'm in here religiously every Sunday!"

13.1   You and the Ship's Company

As the Captain of the ship you wear two hats, one as Captain with authority over all onboard and the second as the company representative. It might well be considered that there can be a conflict between the two, for example where does your first loyalty lie, to the crew or to the company? The crew generally have little or no loyalty to the company unless it is an old established concern with long time employees, yet you expect them to be loyal to you. If this is the case, then should not your loyalty be to them? There really should be no conflict, as if the loyalty between the Captain and the crew is fixed, the company benefits. Unfortunately not all companies appreciate this.

When there is an issue between the crew and the company, it is you who must act as the broker between the two parties, and it is you who must be responsible for advancing the crew case if they are justified in seeking redress. It also falls to you to explain the company's position to those onboard. If there is no obvious resolution then you must try to effect a compromise between the two parties. If you feel that the crew has a good case you should say so, going as far as the seriousness of the matter requires. This will not win you many friends ashore, but you may not have many there anyway! You are the only person who can represent the crew if they have no union to put their grievances to.

13.2   Social Relationships

The hard lines of demarcation that used to exist in the past have blurred and this has resulted in a better understanding of everybody's contribution to the working of the ship. However, mixing in general between officers and crew is to be discouraged as it often leads to problems with discipline, where if assault or direct disobedience is involved can lead to serious consequences.

Today's officers have to follow a more difficult path than when the divide was clearly defined. If an officer is on a ship where all mix and he doesn't, he is criticised. If none mix and he does he will also find himself in trouble. You must tell your officers what you require or expect in this matter. The smaller the ship the closer relationships can become and while it is perfectly common and reasonable for this to happen on occasion it may well cause problems.

It is good to have the odd occasion when the officers and the crew can come together for a social occasion, such as darts matches and barbeques. This kind of event can break the monotony of long voyages and add to the friendly atmosphere on your ship.

13.3　Newly Joined Personnel

The ship may not be luxurious, but crew should expect clean and prepared quarters

Newly joining personnel have a right to expect that their quarters are clean and prepared with bedding, soap and towels. If they have been travelling all night to join the ship then they should, if possible, be allowed a rest period before any other activity.

Once ready, the head of department can bring new personnel to meet you, sign on the articles of agreement and handover documentation. When reviewing these you will be checking seagoing records, last ship, looking for long intervals ashore and the reasons. If the company or crewing agency has not sent a list of certificates and their dates then you will have to check them. In particular, I advise looking for medical certificates and dates.

Next there should be a basic induction of the ship and, if anyone has not recently been on the ship, this must be completed before they engage in any duties.

A small introduction pack prepared for the cabin can be very useful for explaining the ship, mealtimes, who is the Safety Officer and for the Security Officer, bond times and all the other small items of the ship organisation a new joiner would want to know. This pack should be permanently left in the cabins. Some Companies, although not many, already organise this but if yours does not subscribe to such niceties there is no reason that the ship cannot make them up itself.

With all new entrants to the sea care is required during their first few weeks, making sure they understand the type of job they are scheduled to do and that they know how to wear protective equipment and use the various tools. What appears commonplace to experienced seamen is a new world to someone completely new to the sea and the majority of the pre-sea courses are often too brief to prepare them. Under no circumstances during their first few weeks should they be appointed to any task aloft or on deck at sea without another experienced seaman with them.

As experienced seamen, we tend to have a rather blasé attitude to seasickness, ranging from mild sympathy to blaming it on the unfortunate individual who is suffering. The fact that when we were cadets no one cared and made us work is really no excuse for ignoring it today. I do agree that keeping the person busy is better than having them lying in their bunks, but have consideration for the safety of the work they are required to do. I wouldn't let them work in the galley either!

13.4 Dependants

I think it is true to say that women generally have a civilising influence on us. As dependants onboard they can, like passengers, have a pleasant effect on the ship and promote more social activity. However, there are some points that must be carefully consider with regard to this matter

13.4.1 Dependants Onboard

Some ladies who come to sea wish to wear their husband's rank. Often the husband does not notice, or at least chooses not to, but those junior to him certainly will. If it is the Captain's wife we are talking of, then everyone suffers as no one will tell him. If it is anyone else's wife you will have to step in. There is only one way to do this, very very carefully! I found that on the infrequent occasions I have had to broach the subject of a wife's behaviour with the husband has agreed and asked me to speak to her!

Once, after a particularly rotten voyage, and we all get those, I thought that it might be pleasant to come ashore. At the interview, a lady on the panel asked me if I could accept coming from being a Captain to this perceived lower position and I said easily, I was married! Captain at sea, AB at home. Not that I am complaining, it worked well with me in command of the ship and my wife in command of the home. It was always nice to be off the ship and have someone else making decisions for a change! At sea it is different and if your wife is onboard, especially if it is the first time away with you on a ship, there might have to be a fast learning curve if you are to have peace and happiness.

I once sailed with a very competent and pleasant Chief Engineer who, on occasion, used to appear at the door to my office with his blanket and pillows. His loved one used to throw him out so he had to bunk down in my office!

The relationship between a husband and wife is not all sweetness and light. If you are married, you need no lessons on that. It is important that any relationship problems are not taken out of the cabin by you or anyone else.

We had a very prim lady onboard at one time and, prior to her planned departure, I noticed that our menus were becoming more exotic. Instead of chicken and chips, 'Soft breast of Chicken smeared with raspberry sauce', and 'Shaven thighs of duck spread with succulent honey' began to appear. It was when the Stuffed Banana incident occurred that she walked out, telling me that I ran a ship of degenerates. As the cook's age and general state of deterioration prevented him from any form of degeneracy and his English and cooking had not suddenly blossomed, the culprits were found in the cadet's berth.

Although you can limit your own dependants accompanying you, generally control is restricted by what your company allows onboard, especially if you join a ship and they are already there. Sensible companies have a policy that limits the numbers and age of children. Regardless of what the company allowed I used to refuse point blank to have babies in arms onboard.

I was always amazed at those who actually wanted to bring children of this age, especially when on a long contract. My reasons for keeping them off the ship were purely medical and in their own interests. It is bad enough dealing with the ordinary medical problems that can occur at sea but the medical needs of babies are special. To protect the child, the parents, the company and yourself, you should think very hard before you are willing to sail with children of such a young age. Short stays on the coast are acceptable as there are ports within reach or, even better, helicopters to get them off if required. Ensure that all dependants onboard have their own insurance if the company does not insist on this. Diversions can be quite expensive.

Junior officers' wives are generally happy and excited to be away from life ashore, but 40 days steaming on a bulk carrier can get pretty tedious. With wives, as much as their husbands, cultural differences will exist and while their husbands have been exposed to other cultures for some time, this may be their first experience. Do be understanding about this. Regardless of the flag, the ship today is often an international community and while the dependant might be under your command, she is not part or trained to be part of the disciplined structure of the ship. I remember it taking over a week to persuade one lady to emerge from their cabin after joining.

So we must consider cultural differences and understand the probable lack of experience of a ship and its ways.

> *I remember one officer locking his wife in her cabin whenever he was not present. Apart from being insulting to everyone else onboard, it was obvious that this was against the poor lady's wishes, so he was given the option of ceasing this behaviour or having the door removed. Common sense prevailed.*

Another area to watch, are the relationships between those who have their wives onboard and those who do not. It is not that there is resentment but there can be a sense of others having something that you don't have. It is important that those with wives do not form a clique onboard and, by the wives presence, exclude the others from their group. This applies especially to the smokeroom/bar/lounge that can be taken over by wives and children if allowed. This place belongs to the officers and it is there primarily for their use. It is not a playroom or the wives club. By all means, if the officers are agreeable, times can be put aside during the day for children and wives, but when the officers wish to use it, or when the bar is open, I suggest that it is not the place for children or their toys.

With regard to children, safety is of the utmost importance and, depending on their age, you will have to have strict limits about where they can go and who must accompany them. Ships are fascinating, at least to those unfamiliar with them, and children are adventurous.

I once walked out onto the bridge wing one morning on a coastal voyage and saw that two children, unbeknown to their parents, had climbed up into one of the lifeboats!

With older children, consider putting them through the safety induction course both for their interest and their safety onboard. The problem with modern ships is that, while little thought tends to go on the interior accommodation, absolutely none goes into any thought of recreation space outside, so care must always be taken with all dependants.

Another problem to watch for is flirtation. This is a harmless word often describing a harmless event and more frequently done in fun and humour. While it stays at this level there is no problem. The difficulty is that it is not always taken that way or can go beyond the harmless. Be very careful if you have a state of affairs like this on board as it could be a potentially dangerous situation. Should this be occurring and you feel that it has gone beyond harmless, consider getting one of them off the ship, sooner than later.

Do consider the ratings as well. If you are with a company where only the officers are allowed to have their dependants on board then care has to be taken that they do not interfere with the crew activities or that by their presence extra workload is put on them. If there are ratings wives on board it is most important that they receive the same courtesies as those of the officers and that there is no perceived social division between them, particularly if there is only one ratings wife. In such circumstances I suggest that, if officer's dependants are onboard, the use of the officers lounge is extended to the rating and his wife for her time onboard or it could be quite a lonely existence for her. Ensure that the ratings wives are included in any shore activities that you have arranged or at least extend the invitation for this. Sometimes, if the ship is calling close to where crew members have their home, it is possible for their families to visit the ship. Should the ship be in such a position ensure that the agent does all he can to assist with this and see if they can be accommodated onboard for the ship's stay, especially if cash is short. On the other hand, you might consider granting a few days leave where it is possible.

If the ship is going to an interesting port where there is opportunity to get ashore it does no harm to advise the agent that there are dependants on board and ask for some tourist brochures to be brought down to the ship. You will be surprised at what can be arranged if there is a little thought given. Even if the husband cannot get off owing to his duties, at least a shopping trip might be able to be organised by the agent. The occasional transport bill can be lost if your relationship with the agent is amenable.

The aim should be for all dependants travelling on the ship to enjoy their time onboard and leave with pleasant memories that they can look back on. With humour, understanding, and your desire for their wellbeing this will occur most of the time.

13.4.2 Dependants at Home

The dependants at home should also be remembered. I have said that most of us are at sea for the money and these are who the money is for. Once again different cultures have different emphasis on how they perceive their responsibilities. In many countries, particularly those without the benefit of a free and organised health service, any illness can give rise to financial problems, especially if the crew member concerned is taking responsibility for an extended family. It is useful to know about your crewmember's families. Who is married, how many children, who they are caring for.

> *I was often surprised and humbled by the awesome responsibilities some of my crew accepted. One Chinese Chief Steward, who became a firm friend and with whom I still correspond, put three children through university in Hong Kong and Canada and they are now well established in various professions while he continues to live in his small flat. He worked on the ship for long contracts and then worked while on leave to achieve this.*

Often the company will have no knowledge of a case of severe illness at home, especially if the crewing is done through an agency. As well as contacting the company in these circumstances, contact the crewing agency direct and ensure that you receive regular updates on the situation. If there are financial problems, while you may not be able to provide an advance, the Company or crewing agency can. Advise them of this problem as well. If the illness is of critical severity and of an immediate dependant, you will have to get the crewmember home and do this with utmost urgency. In many cases the reaction of your company will depend on their contract obligation. However, all companies should recognise their responsibilities in the case of wives and children. If they do not then you must remind them, immediately and forcefully if necessary. The chairman or owner's private number can be useful in such a situation.

13.4.3 Death

The very worst situation is notification of the death of a dependant. When you receive the notification, take a little time to think about who you will be giving the news to and how you are going to do this. There is no easy way and every person will react differently. Will you send for the person or will you go to his cabin and tell him there? Get his head of department and the Chief Officer and tell them of the situation. Check that you can take some time away from all other responsibilities and that the Chief officer can deputise for you. If the person is in their cabin, I always found it best to tell him there, as if he was elsewhere I had to send for him to come to my cabin.

Do not do this in your office as it is too formal a place. Ask him into your cabin where there will be privacy for both of you. From you, at this time, must come compassion and understanding. Details of 'what next' can wait. It never got easier each time I had to do this, it was always different and always hard to know what to say or do. What you can do is provide a shoulder to lean on and cry if that is what they want. Sometimes you end up holding a man and on occasion crying with them, especially if it was one of their children or their wife. Word gets around very quickly on board and a quiet descends on the ship as it affects everyone. Apart from their natural sympathy, there is always the feeling that it could be them next. Another task for the Captain that people ashore rarely think about.

If you have good office support then this is where they can demonstrate their abilities by getting the person off and home as soon as possible. Remember that even if you are not calling in at a port, for critical illness and death there is often a helicopter service available on the coasts although quite often the companies will quibble about this. It would be nice to think that the company would help with any arrangements and that flowers could be sent but not many see their responsibilities extending to this. We don't have compassionate leave in international shipping and the chances are that pay will be stopped as soon as the employee leaves the ship. Never mind that. What you can do is ensure that flowers are sent from the ship on behalf of the ship's company.

I was handed my message as we passed within sixty miles of where my Father had died, on the South coast of Spain. There was nothing I could do, although my mother never understood as she was used to the Royal Navy and excellent family support services.

You should keep a watchful eye on the person and his reactions, especially if you cannot get him off quickly. I must admit I often question the wisdom of telling someone about this when you are in the middle of the ocean with a few weeks to go before reaching land. Obviously, if you are advised of a death then you have to tell the crew member but this puts the person through torture, wanting to be with his family but unable to do anything, then having to go through their deceased wife or child being interned without them being there. It might be an idea for the company or agency, knowing the position of the ship and the ETA, to go back to the relatives ashore and tell them of the situation and ask if they still wish the person to be notified immediately or to wait until nearer a place where he can be disembarked.

Often, if the person cannot get off to be at the funeral they will elect to remain. After all, all they can do is go home to mourn and stand at a graveside and then look for another ship as they need the money. They can mourn onboard and at least there they are with shipmates and friends. Different people, different ways, you will have to judge.

13.5 Provisions

Food is the fuel that the ship really runs on and the better the Cook and quality of food, the more contented your crew will be. For this reason, provisions must initially have your attention, ensuring that they are of good quality and quantity and served in a clean environment. There is nothing wrong in asking the senior members of the crew for their suggestions when ordering provisions for the ship unless they already have a separate system of ordering their own food, often using the cash they save to add to their wages. However, you must ensure that they are getting enough food to eat properly and that their food is not coming out of the officer's provisions, which can happen when such a system is in operation and there is one Cook for both officers and crew.

The galley should be locked at night, primarily for safety reasons although it does help if the steak for tomorrow is not eaten the night before. The galley is, together with engine room, the prime area of fire danger and Cooking in there at night cannot be accepted unless it is by the Cook.

Good food is the fuel that the ship really runs on

If the refrigerators in the mess rooms are kept stocked and there is a microwave available, there should be no problems for the duty Watchkeepers or those seeking supper.

13.6   Bedding

On most ships, crew are responsible for washing their own bedding while, on ships with a Steward, he will be responsible for the officers' bedding. It is essential when on rounds to ensure that the crew are properly washing their bedding and not just drawing a counterpane over the dirty sheets when you come round. The obvious hygiene benefits are in everyone's interests. Out of interest, check the condition of the mattresses. There is no SOLAS requirement to change the mattresses for the crew, and some companies are known to keep the same ones for over twenty years if they can get away with it. Very few companies have a periodic replacement policy based on date.

13.7   Work Clothing

The company has a duty to supply work clothing and this must be issued to newly joining crew and to those whose equipment has deteriorated. Many companies have a standard issue that is inadequate for the hard wear this equipment takes on a ship and unless the equipment is ordered on an individual basis, all too often the work

In Command	Welfare

gear issued does not fit. The standard work equipment any deck and engine crew have a right to expect is as follows:

- Boiler suits or work trousers and shirts
- safety shoes
- safety gloves
- safety goggles
- safety hat - ensure that the hat is "in-date" by review of the stamp inside it
- foul weather suits.

When operating in winter conditions:

- Insulated boiler suits
- parkas
- gloves.

For the Galley staff:

- Aprons
- Cooks hats
- galley trousers and tunics
- safety shoes.

If these items are not provided on your ship I suggest that you request permission to make a local purchase. Quite often, it is not that the company refuses to supply these items, but that they are unaware that they are not onboard.

13.8 Alcohol

In many companies there is a strong move to ban alcohol from being carried on ships in the belief that seamen cannot be trusted to have alcohol and be sensible in its intake. Safety is often quoted as a reason for this. However, the British Royal Navy, even in a war zone, has alcohol on all of its ships, including nuclear submarines.

When I first went to sea alcohol was very much part of the culture and much of the social life onboard revolved around its consumption. Many ships had their resident alcoholics, inevitably dayworkers, who could be found dozing in the afternoon sun while waiting for the bar to reopen in the evening. At that time ships' crews were large and we had enough competence onboard to be able to carry the odd one or two. On one ship I was on, it was the duty cadet's job to call the Bosun in the morning, and this had to be done with a large glass of whisky. Quite often you would go down and find him fighting off the various multi coloured animals that only the whisky could defeat. I grew up at sea thinking that this was quite normal and, in talking to other cadets from other companies, it was. But maybe in those days it was not much different to the offices ashore!

The only country that bans alcohol on ships, apart from countries with bans for religious reasons, is the USA. This means that "illegal" alcohol is often carried in cabins on their merchant ships and warships and, whenever the crew have the opportunity to hit the beach, the consumption of alcohol tends to make up for what wasn't drunk at sea, with all the resulting problems.

Officer's bar, Northern Venture

Today there is far less alcohol consumed on ships than in the past and there are far less daywork officers who are free in the evenings to do so. Without doubt, the young officer today is far more sensible in their consumption than we were and many of the crew and officers are from cultures where alcohol does not play the large part in social life that it does in European societies.

It is therefore rather ironic that at a time when drinking is in decline at sea, there is a move in shipping circles, most notably the oil companies, to ban it altogether. Bans never work. All you do is move the alcohol from the bond and the open to the cabins and behind closed doors. Once this happens, you have no control. Banning also encourages a binge drinking syndrome whenever the ship gets into port.

I am not arguing to support drinking to excess, but rather to advocate a sensible approach to allowing alcohol onboard. The issue of drink to those who want it can be controlled and watched from the bond account of each person.

The best way to control alcohol is through the bar system, another traditional shipborne social activity many ashore are keen to remove. Control is easy here as officers and crew, if there is a crew bar, have to record in a book their drinks as they purchase them and this is easily examined any time you wish. Further, if there is a bar, then there is no bond issue to the cabins.

| In Command | Welfare |

What! it says here only 5 units a day!!!

The officers bar, lounge, wardroom, call it what you like, is the centre of social activity amongst the officers. It gets them out of their cabins and a solitary existence and puts them into a convivial environment where the different nationalities, cultures and departments meet on common ground. The real value of this is not just the contentment of the officers but the fact that more aspects of the ship's work is discussed and resolved here than anywhere else. These days many of those who attend drink soft drinks, something I never saw when I was young, and this further demonstrates my opinion about the responsibility of today's young officer. Darts matches and the occasional Sunday luncheon buffet all add to a cordial atmosphere that considerably assists in promoting the general wellbeing of your ship and your command.

It's surprising how many items of ship's business can be resolved in the bar before dinner

The crew must not be forgotten either and, if there is a crew bar, the same systems apply. With a committee elected to be responsible for each bar, you have far more control over alcohol onboard than by issue through the bond or trying to ban alcohol onboard. Any problem in the bar and it can be closed for a determined period. Such measures, just by their existence, very rarely have to be exercised.

If bond is carried it should be prohibited to bring alcohol onboard the vessel. This should be strictly enforced. If there is a company regulation banning alcohol onboard you will have to try to enforce this but, regardless of what you do, there is no doubt there will be alcohol in the cabins unless the ship is on a short sea trade run and there is frequent opportunity to go ashore.

As a final word on alcohol, there may be an occasion or two when you look for your own solutions in a bottle. Of course, you know that they are not there, but it makes you feel better for a while. Many of us have done the same but my counsel is this - wait for port. The Captain who appears on the bridge on News Year'ss Night with a sprig of plastic mistletoe full of the joys of spring can be tolerated. The Captain who appears regularly 'under the weather' is a drunk and has no place on a ship.

At least in port you might find a friendly barmaid to tell your troubles to without them being repeated all over the ship, and you might even get some sympathy. Just make sure that you creep home in the dark and quietly. You will be amazed at how quickly a stumble on the gangway will be repeated in the head office a week later, with additional details about how they had to call out the crew to carry you onboard. If necessary and time allows stay ashore, but don't do what one Captain famously did in Northern Canada. He decided to sleep it off in a railway truck and next morning woke up a few hundred miles away from his ship. He was very lucky to have a good Chief Officer who kept his mouth shut and sailed the ship to the next port, which was not too far away, enabling him to return very chastened and very cold!

13.9   Bond

The carriage of bond is a privilege not a right, as customs officers never cease from telling you. As in many ports it is the first stop for these officials, ensure that your check of the contents is accurate and is as reflected in your bond declaration. Any discrepancy found can result in the imposition of a fine and the Scandinavian countries, particularly Norway, are the worst for this. There are horror stories of thousands of dollar fines for incorrectly listing the bond.

The bond is either company or Captains. If it is the company bond they decide the prices and take responsibility for the contents and insurance. This does not stop you adding cheaper items to the bond when the opportunity presents itself but you will be responsible for these items, passing on what has not been sold to the relieving Captain, providing that he is willing to accept these and pay for them. If the bond is yours, check that there is insurance arranged. With regard to pricing, 5% is usually enough to cover breakages and losses. What is carried in the bond is variable and depends on the trade the ship is on. Long distance voyagers tend to carry general shop items and confectionary as well as drink and cigarettes. Don't carry too much chocolate as it tends to go off when stored for some time.

Ensure the contents of the bond are correct as certain authority's fines are extremely punitive (particularly in the developed countries)

If food is the fuel of the ship, then bond is the oil that gets the ship through the ports. It is essential that, wherever you go, you ensure that you have sufficient whisky and cigarettes to ease the ship through the port formalities. I found that the only places in the world where this "oil" was not required were Japan, Germany and the USA. The quantities are variable but, if you go through the Suez or Africa, officials sometimes board with shopping bags and porters to carry the tribute! You have been warned. Sometimes, the plundering does not stop there, with many officials wanting provisions and medicines as well. You can put your foot down on this, especially if they have already visited the bond. I used to give them the choice, explaining that the provisions belonged to crew not to the company. It occasionally worked.

13.10 Wages

This is why everyone is here and when they are late in payment, especially if someone is living near the breadline, it can cause considerable distress to the family back home, which they are quite quick to pass on to the crew member onboard. This must be acted on very quickly. If it is an isolated case, it is generally a problem with the bank or the account numbers being used. A quick message to the company can usually clarify this and, with a switched on accounting department, can usually be speedily fixed as well.

If it is not isolated and is happening to others as well, then it may be an administrative problem within the company. An e-mail or telephone call to your operating department explaining what is going on and requesting confirmation that it has been dealt with should be the next path to follow.

When the wages are not received by anyone, alarm bells must ring. Give the company until the next port to pay or you will put a claim on the ship. Do not be persuaded to carry on any further until the payments are made and, at the same time, ensure that the leave pay to date is paid as well. If they are not paying wages, it could be they are also not paying other bills and the ship could be arrested at any time or the company could go out of business, leaving you and your crew high and dry on the beach.

We are all here to earn a living and it is important that we are paid on time

13.11 Medical

The ship's dispensary will be under the control of the officer delegated in the company ISM Officer's responsibilities section or, if not, the officer delegated by yourself. You should make sure you have an inventory of the stock carried. Any discrepancies between this inventory and the required items must be ordered as soon as possible.

The officer delegated as the ship's Medical Officer will also be responsible for the treatment of all minor problems and ailments, with the assistance of the Ship Captain's Medical Guide. He should consult with you if he has to deal with anything out of the ordinary beyond dispensing the usual pills and potions. It is essential that you establish a set time for this outside of normal working hours. In the smoko times or after 1700 in the evening is the best, otherwise the officer or yourself will be pestered by someone wanting aspirin or a contraceptive at 0200 in the morning.

Hygiene is very important and there should always be clean towels and soap in the treatment room. When dealing with any blood, gloves should be worn and any medical waste carefully disposed of. All treatment should be recorded in the medical

In Command │ Welfare

log. With regard to contraceptives, ensure that they are available but not in such quantities to allow the crew to go on leave with boxes full.

Visiting the doctor ashore is another problem area. The sheer expense of it is enough to make you think twice, especially in the United States where I recently received a bill of several thousand dollars for a crew member's one night stay in hospital. Often the visit will entail a long journey to a doctor or hospital that loses an entire day. On a ship with low manning and a short work time in port, this can disrupt planned work considerably. Obviously, if the crew member has a legitimate need to see the doctor there is no argument, but always consider if the visit is really necessary. Only you can determine this, taking into account not only the condition of the person but also his character. The crew member cannot demand to see a doctor, it is you that will decide to send him. If he is not the type of man to complain and never needed such a visit before then there is no reason not to send him. On the other hand, if he is always complaining about some ache or other, you may want to wait until a more convenient time and place. This is a difficult one to call as pains in the stomach or back cannot be diagnosed by you but a quick visit to a doctor ashore for a one off diagnosis, without being able to engage in long term treatment, is going to do very little except pay for the doctor's new golf clubs!

There are cases of crew members joining ships with a list of all of the family and relatives' complaints and, over a period of time, visiting doctors claiming their symptoms, getting the prescriptions and returning home with the cures! In the end it is your call and, if you are in any doubt, you will have to allow the visit. I accept that P&I cover the cost, after the deductibles for the year have been reached, but as these costs affect the next years P&I premium, it is again your duty to watch them on your company's behalf.

Mental problems fall into a completely different category and, as they are rarely if ever examined for in any seaman's medical, are more prevalent at sea than is generally realised. The problems have always have been with us but, through lack of interest, are no better today. When I came to sea there were a number of men who sadly were still suffering from the war and the change of personalities this caused was not surprising when you knew their stories. We also always had those we called 'eccentrics', who howled at the full moon or slept in their wardrobes!

The 'eccentrics' have mostly left us and whether we are poorer or richer for their departure is open to debate, but mental health problems still exist. Changes in behaviour are an indication of a potential problem, such as depression can affect anyone. You cannot diagnose this, only suspect it. If the underlying cause is on the ship you can act but often the depression is brought on by family news or an underlying condition.

If you do suspect a mental health problem onboard it will not be diagnosed with a quick visit to the local doctor. You could be lucky and have a local hospital near that can give assistance, but for that you have to convince the person to go. If he thinks that there is nothing wrong, what do you do? In these circumstances, you must immediately report your suspicions and their basis to the company. In doing this you are acting on behalf of both the person and the company and arrangement of a removal should be made.

13.12 Shore Leave

It is an unfortunate truth that most ports do not really want seamen to leave their ships. It is difficult for many who work in the port to think of the ship as our home, and the place where we live our private lives. Trying to get them to wipe their feet when they enter our accommodation decks is difficult enough, but the thought that we might have visitors to entertain onboard is often beyond their comprehension. Worldwide, the list of ports that try restrict access to the ships and the seamen access to the shore is endless. To these ports, security is used as a weapon to confine the crews.

Time to relax away from the ship is beneficial to general wellbeing onboard

It is most important that your crew have the opportunity of shore leave whenever it is possible. Just getting off of the ship and away from the closed environment for a while is enough. Should you find that, for some excuse or another, your crew is confined to the ship by a private authority or terminal, request a meeting with the terminal management to discuss it. If this is ignored and your ship is affiliated to the

| In Command | Welfare |

ITF, put the matter to them. It will not get you ashore on that visit but it might help for the future.

In the cases of national policy, as is the case in some Arab states, all you can do is accept the position. Your government will not be interested in pursuing the issue for a few merchant seamen!

13.13 Crew Mail

Communications have become easier with mobile phones and the abundant stations along the coast for using them. But there are many at sea who cannot afford to constantly use them so ship's mail is still very important and must be high on the list of your crew welfare commitments. If the crew have access to computers and the ship has an e-mail service they can use this can also help, although it must again be recognised that many will come from parts of the world where such access is not easy or cheap.

At smaller ports there is often no mail. To help with the delivery, a properly organised company should advise the ship when and where mail has been sent and provide the delivery service and number prior to arrival so it can be quoted to the agent. If this is not happening, try to get it organised. Some Companies wait for the mail to accumulate and then send it to a convenient port. Not only is this illegal in some countries but it also displays a total ignorance of the lives of the seamen they employ. Mail should always be sent out of the receiving office to the next port.

13.14 Cash Advances

Arrange your cash advances in good time through the agent and have the exchange rate that you receive posted on the crew notice-board. This way they can see that the onboard management is playing fair and square with them. The best companies arrange for the rate of exchange to be at the bank rate that day. There are other companies who prefer to use their own exchange rates, usually to their own advantage.

Regardless of the hard luck stories you receive, never advance cash to crew beyond what they have in the vessel and don't advance leave money. You don't know if they are coming back, especially in attractive places like Europe, Australasia and the United States. Also be very wary of handing out casual advances after the prescribed time. This is when you lose money as the chances are that you will be caught by someone in a hurry, you are in a hurry and you might just jot down the amount on a bit of paper or think that you will remember it. You won't and the bit of paper will get lost. Join the many others who have done this. At the end of the month, when your cash doesn't balance and you remember vaguely handing out cash but cannot remember who to, do not be surprised if the person you gave the money to also has a failure of memory!

Balance your cash after each advance, do not leave it till the end of the month.

Try not to carry large amounts of cash in your safe. If you get robbed in port, internally or by pirates, you will not lose very much but more importantly you will not become a target. Cash for a ship is delivered by outside agencies that, in some countries, have connections with criminals.

13.15 Visitors

I always remember a Captain's wife, long ago in London Docks, hurrying back up the gangway after a last minute shopping expedition to be met by a 'lady guest' coming down the gangway saying "you're too late luv, they're sailing soon".

Remember that the ship is home to you and your crew. If the port agrees, and there is no reason why they shouldn't, and provided that guests sign an indemnity, it should be acceptable for them to be on the ship on the ship.

In the case of female guests, if you put the question directly to your company, they would no doubt feel some moral obligation to surround their response to the request with various caveats about respectability, etc, and even the port joins in this moral crusade to protect us! But the point still stands – the crew and officers are effectively 'adults within their own home' while they are onboard. Within certain logical boundaries that maintain security and safety, they should be treated as such.

What a seaman does in his off duty time in his cabin is surely his own business, provided that there is no disruption to the ship. If the Captain does not complain to the port, what business is it of the port, provided that the visitor is escorted to and from the gate?

This is not an easy subject and little is written about it. You are not there to set the moral standard for any one person or sit in moral judgement, yet you are required to set the behavioural standards for the ship and ensure that your ship upholds those of your company. I would suggest that this might be the occasion for the blind eye, provided that all the heads of departments know that the port regulations must be complied with, indemnities must be signed and the persons are escorted properly. You should not be interested in the gender or race of visitors, just that their behaviour is within the bounds set by the company and yourself.

13.16 Uniform

If your company requires uniform to be worn then there is no discussion other than it must be worn properly. There is nothing worse than a part uniform, such as shirt and epaulets worn with a pair of jeans or with yellow socks. Merchant marine fleets traditionally form part of a nation's military resources and are legally obliged to serve their flag in war, and this is often supported by subsidies and other government inducements for strategic reasons.

Before 1918, the officers and men of the British and Commonwealth merchant fleets wore a mix of company livery and civilian clothes, which had a number of disadvantages. When captured, the enemy had no knowledge of the ranks or rating of those it had captured, including whether or not they should have military or civilian status. When on leave they were at a disadvantage compared to those serving in the military forces and often suffered harassment as it was thought that they were not serving their country.

An officer is entitled to wear the uniform of the highest rank that he has been employed in, provided he is not currently employed in a lower rank. There is no provision for a sword, which will spoil a few stories!

Uniforms are worn by merchant navies all over the world and are required by many companies who wish their officers to appear smart, especially in ports or when passengers are carried. It is advantageous to be in uniform when dealing with port officials, especially government employees who themselves often board in their uniforms. It also displays the authoritarian division between the officers and crew, an important factor in maintaining discipline onboard.

Wearing uniform also gets the officers to change out of working gear and into clean clothing in the evenings. Personally, I have worn it with pride my entire career at sea. There are those who oppose it but surely they knew that there was a uniform when they joined? In the enforcement of uniform there are always occasions for laxity, and at sea it is pleasant if after dinner the officers can relax in the bar or lounge in civilian clothes. Equally, at weekends when you may have a buffet lunch or something similar, then relaxation should be the rule. In other words, if uniform is worn on your ship, it should be discretionary. In this way, when you do want it worn everyone will be far more willing to make the effort.

13.17 Unions

For some odd reason, many Captains and senior officers are wary of unions, especially the ITF, which many ships are affiliated to. This wariness is probably instilled by the managers of the companies that employ them. However, in all my years of commanding ITF affiliated vessels, I have never encountered any problem with this union or any other. The unions are there for our benefit, a fact that seems to escape a number of Captains. In many cases, where Captains are trying to impress their owners by turning them way, the owner is quite content to have them onboard as he is already running his ships in accordance with their requirements.

Regardless of your opinion, if there was ever a need for a group of people to be represented by a union, a most worthy group would be seamen. They are all sailing in individual ships and rarely have an opportunity to get together to discuss their employment and terms so it is perfectly sensible that they have a union ashore to represent them.

In the days where Captains are being put in prison around the world for the strangest charges, I think that it is essential that you have representation and that everyone should very seriously consider joining a union that will provide such support wherever and whenever it is needed.

13.18 Animals

Sailors, especially when inebriated, have a strange habit of bringing various species of animals back to the ship. Ordinary dogs and cats tend to give way to exotic animals and it can happen that you only find the python during inspection when you open the wardrobe.

I sailed with one gentle lunatic of a Captain who insisted on fresh eggs, so purchased hens in Suez. Each morning the OOW had to collect the eggs from the monkey island, which had become the chicken coop. This lasted until a violent storm when the chickens, encouraged by a 70 knot wind, decided they could fly. I just hope that their swimming abilities were as good.

Animals can be a pain onboard as port officials are very keen on making sure that you sail with the same number as when you arrived. I know and understand the affection we have for the ship's dog or cat but they can be a headache if they go missing in port. More and more companies are trying to have them banned, but you can only ban what you know about. As long as sailors are around, there will still be the odd animal or bird onboard. You may well have to live with it.

13.19 Bullying

This is a newly used word in the workplace, especially at sea. There is a chance that it might exist and, if so, it cannot be tolerated. It is usually quite easy to stop it once you know about it and I am pleased to say that personally I have rarely had any cases of this at sea. However, the officers will not know everything that takes place on the lower deck, especially if the bullying is carried out by the senior ratings that we rely on to keep us advised.

I have always found the Steward to be the best source of information on such matters. It might also be wise to ask your senior officers to keep an eye out for any signs and maybe have a small discussion with the Bosun regarding your attitude towards this problem.

13.20 The Chaplain

In any port this is the one man who should always be welcome, regardless of flag. This man will be a friend to you, your officers and your crew and it makes no difference whether you hold a different religious belief or none at all. Anyone can raise problems with the Chaplain and he will always help if he can. He can also arrange for access to the religious services of various faiths and will be there for private counselling. Often, the Chaplains try to cover the services that many would feel the shipping companies really ought to be providing.

The Chaplain may be attached to the Mission for Seamen or some other welfare society. They often have access to exchangeable books or DVDs and will certainly have useful knowledge of the local port and area.

In my years at sea the concern and care demonstrated by the Chaplains I came across has always been impressive. Many crews I have commanded have benefited in some way or other from their presence.

In one incident toward the end of my career, my ship was diverted to a port just before Christmas. However, the Chaplain still managed to send the Christmas presents for each crew member from the original port before the ship sailed.

| In Command | Communications, Letters and Reports |

14 Communications, Letters and Reports

14.1 Communication

More often than not, the ship's company is multi-national in its make up. This is not unusual, ever since I came to sea in the 50's I have been sailing with foreign crew and even on my training ship we had cadets from various parts of the world. The language of the sea is English, for which I consider myself very lucky as it is my first language. It has always surprised me how well other nationalities can speak it, often better than ourselves. But there are many at sea who struggle to fully understand what is being said or written, especially when the conversation is between two non-English speaking nationalities.

The problem is often compounded by the unwillingness some have to say that they do not understand and so would like you repeat or further explain. Instead they say nothing and you walk away thinking that you have been understood and all is well, but the crew member now puts his own interpretation on your wishes.

Here is an example of how a multi-national crew can interpret a fairly simple statement.

The Captain's note to the Chief Officer
At 0900 hrs tomorrow morning, there will be a total solar eclipse. This is something that cannot be seen very day, so let the crew line up in their best clothes on deck in order that they may see it. To mark the rare phenomenon, I will myself explain it to them. If it is raining, we will not be able to see it clearly. In that case the crew should gather in the messroom.

The Chief Officer's note to the 2nd Officer
On the Captain's orders, there will be a total solar eclipse early tomorrow morning at 0900 hrs. If it is raining we will not be able to see it clearly from deck in our best clothes. In that case the sun's disappearance will be fully observed in the messroom. This is something that does not happen every day.

The 2nd Officer's note to the 3rd Officer
On the Captain's orders, we shall fully observe in our best clothes, that the sun disappears in the messroom at 0900 hrs. The Captain will tell us if it is going to rain. This is something that does not happen every day.

The 3rd Officer's note to the Bosun
If it is raining in the messroom tomorrow, which is something that does not happen every day, the Captain in his best clothes will disappear at 0900 hrs.

The Bosun's note to the crew
Early tomorrow at 0900 hrs the Captain will disappear. It is a pity that this does not happen every day.

What we learn from this is that if you really have a message or order that you wish to be understood by all onboard, then write it out in an order book and have the book taken around and everyone sign the order. Even if some do not understand, it will not become distorted in the rewriting.

The key to speaking to others of different nationalities is simplicity and clarity. Strangely, speaking louder and waving your arms around does not make any difference, you just become more frustrated. Think of what you wish to say, then say it slowly and distinctly, pausing between sentences. Use small words instead of big ones and then check that what you have said is understood. Your attitude will affect how officers are willing to tell you that they fail to understand what you want. If you are abrupt, authoritarian or impatient, they will be far less willing to ask you to clarify your requirements. There have been tragic situations caused by simple misunderstandings.

14.2 Letters

You would have hoped, with the introduction of computers at sea and the knowledge that we don't have secretaries or clerks, that the volume of letters and forms would decrease. This has not happened except for in Companies that have fully embraced the computer age and actively examined and tried to reduce the paper flow. In reality, everything could be sent by e-mail but we are still waiting for that to happen, especially with port documentation. Regardless of whether you are sending a letter by e-mail or by post, it has to be written and, if it is a formal letter, then it has to be written properly.

The standard rule for all letter writers is as old as the hills, but still has the same relevance today. Don't send what you write at night, re-read it in the cold light of day.

By all means blaze away on the keys and tell everyone how useless they are and why you are resigning, but don't send it. A problem with the computer is that it is too easy to press the send key then, in the morning when you see what you sent, you can't get it back. We can be quite blunt in our words and in our opinions sometimes, and your words can look very different away from the emotion of a situation.

Criticism is easy. We are all inclined criticise others, but yet are vulnerable to the same. If criticism is warranted, try not to make it personal. The Chinese have a saying about breaking people's rice bowls, that if you do this, they are in a far better position to do the same or worse back. Rather than criticise, suggest a change. Do not give your opinions until asked.

Remember that whatever you write to a company could become a legal document. If you write a letter criticising the fire equipment onboard and the ship then has a fire that damages cargo, all correspondence between the ship and the office will be displayed if asked for. The charterer's lawyers would have a field day with such a letter, even if it had no relevance in that particular fire.

Before you send a letter, read it and see if you could understand it if you received it without knowing the circumstances behind it. All too often letters are written to mind readers! Also check your spelling and grammar. Good points in your letter could easily be lost if your letter displays a lack of education in the language it is written in. If the letter is in English and this is not your first language have someone whose English is good or better than yours read it before sending.

Always keep a copy of your official correspondence, whether letter or e-mail, and have this to refer to as long as you are with that company. It is surprising how a year or two down the line, something will happen that is relevant to a communication you wrote.

14.3 Reports

Reports are more formal than letters and are likely to be seen by a series of people. The more serious the report, the more it will be viewed and commented upon.

Try this report:
It is with regret and haste that I write this letter to you, regret that such a small misunderstanding could lead to the following circumstances, and haste in order that you will get this report before you form your own pre-conceived opinions from reports in the world press, for I am sure that they will tend to over-dramatise the affair.

We had just picked up the Pilot, and the apprentice had returned from changing the G flag for the H. It being his first trip, he was having difficulty in rolling up the G flag, and so I proceeded to show him how. Coming to the last part, I told him to "let go". The lad, although willing, is not too bright, so I had to repeat the order in a sharper tone.

At this moment the Chief Officer appeared from the chart room, having been plotting the vessel's progress and, thinking that it was the anchors being ordered, repeated the "let go" to the 3rd officer of the forecastle. The port anchor having been cleared away, but not walked out, was promptly let go. The effect of letting the anchor drop from the "pipe" while the vessel was proceeding at full harbour speed proved too much for the anchor windlass brake, and the entire length of the port cable was pulled out "by the roots". I fear that the damage to the chain locker may be extensive. The braking effect of the port anchor naturally caused the vessel to sheer to port, just toward the swing bridge that spans a tributary to the river that we were proceeding up.

The swing bridge operator showed great presence of mind by opening the bridge for my vessel. Unfortunately he did not think to stop the vehicular traffic, with the result that the bridge partly opened and deposited a Volkswagen, two cyclists and a cattle truck on the foredeck. My ship's company is at present rounding up the contents of the latter which, from the noise, I would judge to be pigs. In his efforts to stop the progress of the vessel, the 3rd officer dropped the starboard anchor, too late for it to be of practical use, for it fell on the swing bridge operator's control cabin.

After the port anchor was let go and the vessel started to sheer I gave a double ring Full Astern on the Engine Order Telegraph and personally rang the engine room to order maximum astern revolutions. I was informed that the sea temperature was 23 degrees and asked if there was a film tonight. My reply would not add constructively to this report.

Up to now I have confined my report to the activities at the forward end of the vessel. Back aft they were having their own problems. At the moment the port anchor was let go, the 2nd officer was supervising making fast the after tug and was lowering the ship's towing spring down onto the tug. The sudden braking effect of the port anchor caused the tug to run in under the stern of my vessel just at the moment when the propeller was answering my double ring Full Astern. The prompt action of the 2nd Officer in securing the inboard end of the towing spring delayed the sinking of the tug by some minutes, thereby allowing the safe abandonment of that vessel.
It is strange but at the very moment of letting go the port anchor, there was a power loss ashore. The fact that we were passing over a "cable area" at that time might suggest that we may have touched something on the river bed. It is perhaps lucky that the high tension cables brought down by the foremast were not live, possibly being replaced by the underwater cable, but owing to the shore blackout, it is impossible to say where the pylon fell.

It never fails to amaze me, the actions and behaviour of foreigners during moments of minor crisis. The Pilot for instance is, at this moment, huddled in the corner of my day cabin alternately crooning to himself and crying after having consumed a bottle of gin in a time that is worthy of inclusion in the Guinness Book of Records. The tug Captain on the other hand, reacted violently and had to be restrained forcibly by the Steward, who has him handcuffed in the ship's hospital where he is telling me to do impossible things with my ship and my crew.

I enclose the names and addresses of the drivers and insurance companies of the vehicles on my foredeck, which the 3rd Officer collected after his somewhat hurried evacuation of the forecastle. These particulars will enable you to claim for the damage that they did to the railings of the No. 1 hold.

I am closing this preliminary report, because I am finding it difficult to concentrate through the police sirens and flashing lights. It is sad to think that, had the apprentice realised that there was no need to fly the pilot flags after dark, none of this would have happened.
Yours truly

You might well have seen this before!

Now let us try to rewrite it as a readable report. What we must try to achieve is clarity, explanation of the causes, resultant damages and, if you wish, the lessons learnt. As you become more experienced, you will learn how to spread the net to ensure that all of the blame does not come onto your shoulders. If you can spread the net to include shore management then all the better there is more chance of it being brushed under the carpet!

Sir,
Incident of the ……….. In the port of………..
During the river approach, the anchor was accidentally released. This was caused by language problems owing to the multi-racial crew onboard. (please see my letter regarding the probability of accidents owing to this very problem addressed to yourself and dated……..)

The letting go of the port anchor at full harbour speed resulted in damage to the windlass. The anchor caused the ship to veer to port and, although the ship's engines were immediately put full astern, as it approached a swing bridge the operator panicked and opened it causing several vehicles, persons and farm animals to be deposited on the deck. The 3rd Officer very quickly arrested any further forward movement of the vessel by letting go the starboard anchor, which held on a shore structure.

During this emergency the after tug, which could have assisted considerably in holding the vessel, ran under the counter and fouled the propeller, damaging itself to the extent that it started to capsize. Fortunately the 2nd Officer managed to hold the tug above the water with the ship's ropes, until it was abandoned

During the acciden, a high tension cable was brought down onto the main deck but I am pleased to report that no one was injured as the cable was not live, power to the scene by the underwater cable probably having been cut by the actions of the swing bridge operator.

In closing I would advise you that I am making an official complaint regarding the actions of the Pilot, who ceased to be of assistance after the anchor was let go, and those of the swing bridge operator for causing the damage on deck. In addition, I enclose a copy of my claim on the tug company for their failure to assist the ship and for probable damage to the ship's propeller.

A list of damage to the ship is enclosed together with the names and statements of the relevant witnesses. The company accident form is also enclosed.

Yours faithfully

So a little different, but hopefully you will see what the second report is intended to do, apart from trying to cool the incident and spread the fault. It cuts out the fluff and rambling, it gives a brief picture of what has happened and how. Obviously amplification will be required, but let the office ask for this. The advice they give you when being questioned by police is if you are a suspect is to never volunteer information. In any incident involving your ship, you are a suspect and, as far as the office is concerned, supported publicly but considered guilty privately until you prove your innocence.

The rules for initial reports are clarity, brevity and caution as this could well become a legal document if it is a report of third party damage or injury to persons. With regard to damage, spread your net wide and hold anyone of any consequence who was party to the incident to blame. It is always difficult to blame someone sometime after the event.

Some time ago I entered a Dutch port in winter and, during the berthing, the after tug displayed a considerable degree of disinterest in the proceedings to the extent that, when ordered to pull, failed to do so. This resulted in a hole on the starboard quarter of the ship from contact with the jetty. Tugs are similar to pilots, with the same protections of non liability in port operations. However, instead of contacting the port, I called the police and claimed that the tug was endangering shipping through bad handling. This was the first time the police had ever been called to such an incident. The police told the tug to wait for their boarding and the tug Master abandoned his tug and ran away, not just from the tug but from the town. Evidence was found that the Master was under the influence of a number of products, with the result that the tug company accepted the cost of all the repairs to my ship.

14.4 Meetings

These can be very unproductive and time consuming if you are unprepared and have no control of the gathering.

The first question to ask is if the meeting is really necessary? Some meetings are required, such as pre-planning for port entry or drydocking or monthly safety meetings, but they should be limited to a minimum on a ship. Apart from not wasting people's time, too many meetings can tend to give people the impression that there is democracy onboard, which you certainly don't want. Friendly dictatorship is fine!

Below is a list of reasons for shipboard meetings:
- Giving information
- discussion, but with an objective
- generating ideas
- planning
- finding solutions/solving problems
- crisis management
- setting tasks and delegating
- making decisions.

If you have decided that a meeting is essential, you should consider these guide lines:

- Have as few people at the meeting as possible. If there are people that may be required then have them standing by in order that they may be called if necessary
- prepare an agenda
- the first heading on your agenda must be the objective. What is the point of the meeting? What results do you want? Is the meeting just to advise those gathered of events to come or do you want a decision or recommendation to be the outcome? Put the items on the agenda in order of their priority. Start with the least important as these can be disposed of quickly before you get to the larger issues. The other way round will end up with smaller issues not being considered, or considered in haste through time restraint
- once the agenda is prepared, ensure that the other attendees have a copy in advance. They will know what the meeting is about and can prepare their positions
- choose a time that will cause the least disruption to the work patterns of the attendees.

When running the meeting you should sit at the head of the table and establish yourself as the Chairman. It is essential that you control the meeting by beginning with an outline about why the meeting has been called. Organise the timing of the agenda. You know how long you want the meeting to last and you know how many items are for discussion so you can write down the time you have decided to allot to each item. Do not be bothered about closing the discussion on a particular subject and making a decision before moving on to the next item. If members start to move onto other subjects not directly related to that under discussion, interrupt and bring things back on course.

Be wary of 'any other business' which all too often descends into the 'I remember when' phase. If you have timed it right, any other business should mean adjournment to the bar. Finally, at all times bear in mind that, on a ship and as Captain, those attending do not make decisions, you do. The meeting is to hear opinion and advice before you do so.

15 Surveys and Inspections

More added pressure

Without doubt, these can be the most disruptive pressure on a ship in port, especially if they are unannounced and with no appointment made. It also seems that there is now an endless stream of people coming up the gangway wanting to inspect the ship and, in many cases, anxious to find an item that justifies their attendance, especially if they are a private consultancy in the employ of others. The problem with these inspections is that they take place in port, quite often when the ship has less than a day to load or discharge the cargo, and they require essential manpower and time when both are in short supply.

15.1 Port State Control

I support Port State Control as they provide the most effective way to ensure adequate standards are maintained on the ships calling at the ports of the world. What I do not support are repetitive inspections. There is supposed to be some co-ordination between Port State authorities on the frequency of their inspections and they should accept other state's findings.

Recently my ship was inspected three times in two months in the United States, each with nil deficiencies. However, to a certain extent you can understand the problem from the Port State's point of view, especially when they board a ship with glaring deficiencies that has recently received a clean bill of health from another state.

> *In one incident in San Francisco the "inspector" boarding gave my ship a deficiency and told us we could not sail until the magnetic compass agreed with the gyro, and then could not be convinced that he was completely wrong. Instead we thought that this was so funny that we gave the story to the daily newspaper who also agreed with the stupidity. The ship was allowed to sail by an embarrassed coastguard.*

Port State inspections began in the United States with the coastguard inspections, and in the beginning there were some traumatic moments. The main problem was that those making the inspections had very little shipping or seamanship knowledge. Those boarding could, at times, be extraordinarily arrogant and insolent and a number of times I had cause to complain to their superiors (with little result).

> *On another occasion in the same port, our ship was boarded by a Coastguard Officer as we were singling up and, despite our protests and those of the Pilot, demanded to make a full inspection. Tugs and Pilots were cancelled as were the gangs standing by for the container ship in Los Angeles. I did not have to make any fuss about this as the charterers did it for me. The Coastguard Officer was removed from the port.*

All Captains visiting the United States during those early years have stories to tell about the Coastguard, but it is pleasing to note that in recent times a far more professional and courteous approach has developed.

If your ship has not had a Port State inspection recently, or it has been nearly a year since the last, then your visit could be fairly soon. Somewhere onboard you might find a checklist for Port State and it is worthwhile going through this at sea to ensure that all the items are covered. On a well run ship, which is what the Port State want to see, there is probably little for you to do and the inspector will form his opinion about how the ship is run within a few minutes of boarding. This will influence his inspection.

In some countries there is a problem where inspection is used as blackmail and so they find something regardless. If you don't pay up, you don't sail. There is only one answer in this circumstance, accept where you are, look after your company's interests and pay up.

15.2 ISM Audits

Sometimes those ashore wonder why we criticise the ISM system. The audit is often a good reason why. The internal audit completed by your company is not so bad unless it is done by a consultancy, when you are likely to have to deal with a lot of nitpicking.

The external audit can take two days if the ship is in port long enough, or will go into the night if sailing within a day. It involves most of your officers and crew. One of the anomalies of this audit is that they are insistent that the hours of work schedules are posted and that the hours of work and fatigue regulations are complied with, yet in all the audits I have done not one of them mentioned the fact that, after keeping the officers and crew on the go throughout the day and evening, while the ship had to cope with all the normal business of loading or discharging cargo, storing the ship and dealing with the myriad of other details of a port call, on sailing everyone was completely fatigued, going against the purpose of the ISM.

Are Captains judged by the number of deficiencies on their ships?

Audits in large companies, which pride themselves on their efficiency and safety, are often now looked at in a competitive way with the Captain judged by how few deficiencies the ship receives. The whole meaning of the ISM was to assist those onboard, a point that seems to be lost on many inspectors.

Again, there is a check list to make sure that you can prepare the ship for this audit and you generally have plenty of lead time to get all the paperwork filled in and the notices up. No matter how many times you drum into the crew who the company Designated Person ashore is, there are always the gallant few who will not have a clue when asked, though why the Chinese Cook should have to know this is beyond both me and him. Make sure that, on the day, your gangway is properly manned with the safety net secured properly, ie not wrapped around the gangway. There are often no anchoring points on the jetty for the ends of the safety net so fill two drums with cement, putting a couple of metal loops in the top and then when you lower the gangway where there are no anchor positions, put these on the jetty to create two securing points

Go through the previous deficiencies and findings and make sure that they have been closed out. There is no excuse for not doing so.

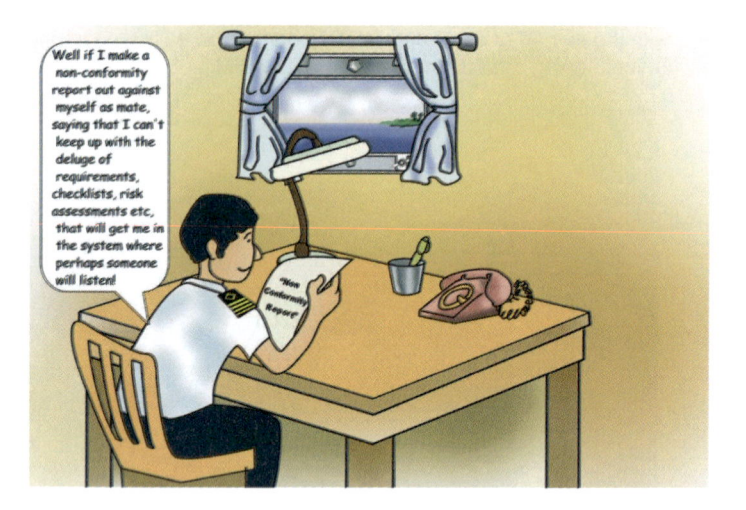

15.3 Security Audit

This is the latest inspection to join the list. Once again you should have a lead time on when this will occur and will be able to ensure that the gangway is manned by your 'security guard' making a list of all the allowed visitors. Standard questions and answers such as "can I see the security manual", "no you can't", pleases them. I don't really know why this manual is kept locked away as its security grading is only restricted, which does not officially require a locked safe and such security.
Make sure that the inspector is challenged on the gangway and that your security exercises are listed in the security book as well as the log book.

> *We had a security audit in a northern Scottish port and, when the auditor asked one of the crew what he would do if he found a bomb onboard, was told "f*** off". A very upset Maritime Coastguard Agency auditor had to be mollified and explained to that the crew member was simply explaining that is exactly what he would do. Good answer too!*

We must not be too flippant about this. There are undoubtedly ports in the world where security is now essential and risk does exist but, if that is the case, what on earth are we doing putting a crew member on the gangway when there are private security companies around who will do a far better job. If the company wishes to keep a watch on the gangway, why not equip the ships with CCTV ?

If there are suspected explosives on the ship in port, I firmly believe that it is far better to get the crew off and let the professionals get on with it.

In Command   **Surveys and Inspections**

Like the Keystone cops, ship security is a mild deterrent like a burglar alarm on the side of a house, where the aim is to push the would be perpetrators to another ship or make them rethink for another day

15.4 Charterer's Inspections

These are now usually carried out by private consultancies acting for the charterer's in response to increased pressure on them to show interest in the condition of the ships that they are chartering. For some companies this must clash with their desire to charter the cheapest ships. It has been my own experience that many are not really interested in the ship or the crew, they just want the job done for the least money.

As an example, a few years ago in Canada, a very reputable Canadian company chartered a ship that was subsequently arrested in a Canadian Port. The crew had not been paid, the bedding was found to be infested, the food was of a standard that it was condemned, and so the list went on. The company involved is powerful and can usually keep most of the bad press out of the papers, but on this occasion they could not. The ship eventually was allowed to sail when the deficiencies had been corrected and a few months later, at the end of the charter, it was re-chartered.

Sometimes ships are refused charter for the conditions onboard, the standard of the officers and crew or the manning, but it seems that they primarily exist to see if the ship can carry the cargo, if the engine can keep going and if the ship can complete the charter without sinking of its own accord.

However, if the ship is already chartered it is almost impossible for a charterer to take the ship off charter. There have been a number of cases where charterers have been appalled by the condition of what they have chartered, with engine breakdowns, fires onboard, flooded cargo holds, hundreds of safety deficiencies, etc. But they have been found against in the courts when they have tried to take action and so current legal precedents and rulings prevent them from assisting with the problem of sub standard ships. When the law changes, I believe that many of them will change their attitude and harden on these matters.

15.5 Flag State Inspections

Standard inspections are to ensure that you have your certificates stamped up-to-date. If you disagree with them you can challenge their findings and appeal back to the flag state.

You should first consider the ILO resolution 178, which is partly based on ILO 147, the Merchant Shipping minimum standards convention, all of which your flag state should have ratified. It requires member states to implement a formal inspection system of the following on their flag ships:

- Maintenance and cleanliness of working and living areas
- minimum age of crew onboard
- the Articles of Agreement
- food and catering
- crew accommodation
- recruitment
- manning
- qualification
- hours of work
- medical certificates
- prevention of occupational accidents
- medical care
- sickness and injury benefits
- social welfare
- repatriation
- terms and conditions of employment
- the right to organise.

You can see that many of the above cross over into the scope of other inspections that occur on our ships. While I am sure that many countries use other inspections to cover many of them, it does show that there is legislation that flag states have agreed to, ensuring that their flag ships comply to certain standards. But it would appear that many ships escape the net?

> *I had one occasion with a British MCA Surveyor when he insisted that Canadian medical certificates on the ship were illegal, even though we placed the MCA notice stating that they were acceptable in front of him. A call to his superiors prevented the ship being delayed.*

15.6 P&I Inspections

These do not occur too often and are usually the most practical inspections of all. Generally, they are carried out by hired-in consultants. Think of the P&I club as your local insurance agent. You will, over the course of the years in command, see quite a lot of them and they are usually most helpful in their deliberations. Over the years, I have learnt a considerable amount from them. Quite rightly, they stress the need for a properly detailed report of the events leading to and during any accident.

Here is some of their basic advice to Captains in the event of any accident:

In the event of an incident or allegation that gives, or may give, rise to a third party claim there are certain actions that you should always take and certain actions that you should never take.

Always:

- Call your owner or operator
- investigate every allegation of injury or damage
- collect evidence or documentation relating to the incident, including any defective equipment. Store them in a safe place and label them. Throw nothing away
- take photographs of any damage or circumstances relating to the incident
- instruct witnesses to write a review of what they saw and heard and, if possible, to draw a diagram. This should be done as soon as possible after the incident. Write your own personal notes about the incident.

Never:

- Allow a surveyor or lawyer onboard the ship or to interview crew members until he has identified himself and produced appropriate authorisation to satisfy you that he is acting for either your owner or your P&I club
- allow surveyors or lawyers acting for the opposing parties onboard unless you and they have written authorisation to do so
- give written material or physical evidence to opposing lawyers or surveyors. If in doubt, do not give anything to anyone or let anyone examine anything
- give a personal opinion on who or what was responsible. Keep to the facts. Again, if in doubt, say nothing
- allow crew members to express opinions
- admit liability, either verbally or in writing

| In Command | Surveys and Inspections |

- sign a document that you know contains incorrect information. This includes making false entries in log books
- think that the problem will go away if you do nothing.

I suggest that you engrave all of this advice on your heart.

15.7   Class Inspections

You can and should call class, in addition to the P&I club, any time that you suffer damage to the ship. This is particularly the case if there is damage to the hull and machinery as any repairs will be subject to their recommendations. If repairs cannot be made at your present port they can issue a temporary certificate of class, with a time limit that allows the ship to proceed to a port where the repair can be made. You will find that, just because a surveyor in a particular Port States that a certain repair must be done in a certain way, this will not necessarily be completed as he requires. Many of us have seen a surveyor require a repair to be done before sailing the ship but, after a phone call from his head office, issue a temporary certificate. A lot depends on the class society involved and how much clout your company has with them. Remember that class is also a business and there is intense competition amongst them. It is a growing sector of shipping with many new class societies are setting up and taking business away from the traditional majors.

Class

The standard class inspections, which are mostly carried out by engineering professionals, are for the renewal of your certificates, such as construction, loadline, etc. I have always found the large class societies in regular ports excellent in their approach and experience and their advice can be invaluable to the young Captain. Unfortunately, class inspection quality depends on where it takes place.

The way to approach all inspections is to be ready. If you have your records, checklists and log books all ready in one place, where they can be easily examined, it will save those making the inspection considerable time and effort. Once you know what has to be done, do it. If your ship is correct, all your documentation is up-to-date and your safety equipment is properly maintained, you have done what you can. If the officials are received properly and shown courtesy, then apart from the odd problem that some have to find just to prove their superiority, you have done all you can. Be careful to keep your frustrations with these inspections to yourself. If your officers feel that you consider them to be a waste of time, their attitude will reflect that.

16 Breakdowns

Where do all the ships come from when you blackout???

Just like cars, ships always seem to have breakdowns in awkward places. If you break down in deep water far from land your only concern is the weather, unless you have a blackout in which case you may end up Cooking on the barbeque.

If you are advised by the Chief Engineer that repairs cannot be made, your operators will have to arrange for tug assistance and decide which port to have the ship towed to for repairs. If you are in shallow waters you should have been able to use your anchors to good effect, taking the heat out of the problem. Even if you are drifting from deep to shallow waters, consider walking back on your anchors. Then, as the ship approaches a shelving bottom, the anchors will make contact and eventually hold the ship.

It is important to clarify your position in the event of a breakdown, particularly if the ship and those onboard are in danger or if the ship is drifting in such a way that the incident could develop into an emergency. If you break down in proximity to land and, either through wind or current, are drifting towards it, a safety or urgency message will alert the authorities of that country to your situation. If there is time the situation will be discussed with your operators. However, always remember that all decisions are in your hands so, regardless of their opinions or wishes, it remains your duty to safeguard the lives of those onboard. If this means that you need to call on assistance, this should always be done sooner rather than later. Bear in mind that Lloyd's open agreements can be made over the phone or VHF if required. Also, should you be faced with a tug making outrageous demands, there is usually legal provision for setting such agreements aside if they were made under duress.

17   Helicopter Operations

There are two types of helicopter operations that affect us. The first is for pilotage and the second is for evacuation. The only differences are that the pilotage movements are generally by commercial craft and evacuations are by specialist military or government rescue services. Regardless of the operation type, all the precautions to be taken by the ship remain the same. There is a good booklet regarding helicopter operations that is published by the International Chamber of Shipping, called Guide to Helicopter/Ship Operations, and this gives all the precautions required. You are required to have specialist equipment standing by with a team who can use it and who are trained to prepare for helicopter operations and how to react in any emergency, such as a crash on deck.

Transfers will take place with the helicopter landing on the ship if there is a proper designated and strengthened area. If there is no such area the transfer is completed by the helicopter in the hover position and a winched cable is lowered to the deck.

For all of these operations it is essential that the area is clear of equipment and personnel, especially loose gear in the vicinity. This is because the downdraft can be intense and, if there is loose gear in the area, it can be blown up and either injure personnel standing by or damage the helicopter.

Although you must always have the crash party nearby and ready, with normal transfers of stores and with pilots and personnel in normal conditions, the helicopter operation is a standard part of shipboard activity. It is only when you have an emergency case that more care has to be taken as, regardless of the prevailing weather conditions, you and the helicopter pilot will be endeavouring to complete the operation. At all times, follow the pilot's instructions. Helicopters can operate in surprisingly bad weather, up to 50 knots winds in normal conditions and in an emergency up to 70 knots winds. It is normal procedure when carrying out a medical evacuation to send a winchman down from the helicopter with their own stretcher for the patient to be strapped in, so check with the helicopter pilot if this is to be done rather than you strapping him up in yours. If the weather is extremely bad you must try to reduce the roll and pitch to avoid heavy spray in the winch area and in the helicopter engines.

For accurate communications with your officer on deck, it is essential that he is provided with an earphone and microphone system to plug into his portable radio.

My last medical evacuation was on a small search and rescue vessel in the North Sea, at night and in gale force winds. It went surprisingly well as we had a well trained crew, but we were told that even the deck lights, which were not directly shining at the helicopter had to be put out. This was on the instructions of the pilot as he preferred to use his own down lights to illuminate the winching area.

18 Stowaways

A Stowaway 'is a person who is secreted on a ship, or in the cargo that is subsequently loaded on a ship, without the consent of the Ship-owner or the Master or any other responsible person and who is detected onboard after the ship has sailed from a port and reported as a stowaway, by the Master, to the appropriate authorities.'

Stowaways are an increasing maritime problem that is no longer confined to the traditional stowaway ports of the African continent. In present times, they can and do board anywhere. The costs of dealing with them are staggering, ranging from an average of $20,000 to $40,000 US and sometimes up to $100,000, not including any incidental costs arising from charter party problems.

Despite your precautions and searches, stowaways have got onboard and now are found or, as is more usually the case, they have handed themselves in.

There is an IMO resolution, A871 of 1997, on the allocation of responsibilities regarding stowaways and it is important that you understand it. It is suggests that the following are your responsibilities:

- To make every effort to determine immediately the port of embarkation of the stowaway
- to make every effort to establish the identity, including the nationality, of the stowaway
- to prepare a statement containing all the information relevant to the stowaway ready for presentation to the appropriate authorities
- to notify the existence of the stowaway to the operators of the ship, the port of embarkation and the next port
- not to depart from your planned route to seek the disembarkation of the stowaway unless it has been prearranged with the authorities at the intended disembarkation point (so you cannot just drop him off on some deserted island!)
- to ensure that the stowaway is presented to the authorities at the next port of call (presumably to ensure that you haven't dropped him off at some deserted island!)
- (probably the most important) to take appropriate measures to ensure the security, general health, welfare and safety of the stowaway until he is disembarked. This means that you treat him humanely and provide him with bedding, soap and food etc. I find nothing wrong in having a stowaway do light cleaning duties in the accommodation to help pay for passage, provided that you accept that they cannot be forced to do this. You must also bear in mind the safety aspects, as they will not have had an induction course, nor be familiar with ship board procedures.

Having said all the above and assuming that you have complied with the provisions of the resolution, the onus to act is on the next port. It is often here that there is a problem as the resolution states that, after allowing the stowaway to be presented for examination and allowing your operator's representative, probably the agent, to have access to the stowaway, they should give directions for the removal of the stowaway to the port of embarkation, country of nationality, or to some other country to which lawful directions may be made.

This sounds fairly straightforward and, if complied with, not too much strain. However, the problem is that many ports have not read the part regarding their responsibilities.

The last time I had a stowaway on the West Coast of Africa, the next African port charged me 5000 cigarettes for telling them I had a stowaway and advised me to lose him at sea. The good news was we kept him onboard. The bad news was that we were going the wrong way and we landed him in South West Africa when he was hoping for the bright lights of Liverpool.

Many countries, such as Japan, refuse to allow stowaways to be repatriated even if the country that they are from has agreed to have them back.

Considering the vast problems a stowaway will certainly cause you, and other Captains, it is understandable that some would consider the easiest option is to not to report the stowaway and to smuggle him off the ship at a convenient port, or even to take drastic action and put the stowaway over the side at sea, near the coast.

With regard to the last option, it is murder and is not what we are Captains for. Morally, no Captain can contemplate such action or allow his crew to be party to it. The man is going to cause you a lot of grief, but what has he done? He is simply seeking a better life or way of earning money for his family. When you see on your travels some of the situations that people live in, would you not do the same? This is not to condone what they do, but you should make sure that you understand why.

There is a thought at sea that, if the maritime countries and their ports are not going to keep to the UN resolutions and assist us in dealing with the problem, why should we follow their laws rather than try to get the stowaway off the ship at anchorage or at night alongside. Yes it can be done, but if you are caught, the proverbial hits the fan. Further, there are some very good reasons for not doing this. It is not your fault that there is a stowaway on board and the owner belongs to P&I clubs for this reason. So why take the risk just to save them money, someone always talks. Follow the rules and inform the port that a stowaway is onboard. Your operators, their agents and the P&I will then legally hold the problem, not you.

Many ports require that the stowaway is guarded during the vessel's stay. In some cases, they will provide a security guard rota system that will be billed to your company. In other ports, they will take him ashore and imprison him until the ship is due to sail. As a final alternative, they will want the ship to guard him. As you are unlikely to have facilities to hold him securely, and your crew are not trained as guards, I strongly advise that you organise your agent to hire a security company for this purpose.

A BBC World Service program interviewed a 26 year old man from a West African village. He was the only man in the village, all the others had stowed away to Europe. When asked why he had stayed he replied that he had attempted 6 times before and tries again next week!

If you have to provide medical treatment to the stowaway during their time onboard, get agreement to this in writing and/or on tape, in front of witnesses and before it starts. When the treatment is given, ensure an understanding of what has been given and, again, give the treatment in front of witnesses.

The whole situation of having a stowaway on board is now very complicated. No one wants them, either the ports of call or you. Yet if it is thought that in any way he or she is or has been ill treated, press and lawyers are ready to take an interest. Remember that the stowaway's story may be the thing that gets them what they want, so the truth may play little part in it. To say that you flogged them all the way across the ocean will make a far better story for the papers than one about watching videos all the way and putting on two or three kilos in weight!

19 Passengers

Passengers, breath of fresh air or a nuisance?

Personally, I have always found passengers in small numbers a pleasure to have onboard, but not so much when they are in vast crowds. Your passengers are there to enjoy themselves and you are there to work, a fact that has to be realised by your officers, especially the younger ones. In small numbers, a more personal approach is expected and there is no reason that this cannot be provided, within the restrictions of the ship. Information is more easily passed when you are on first name terms and good relationships can be developed over long voyages. The passenger you have on the average cargo ship tends to be a seasoned traveller who would not consider travelling on a cruise ship. They are paying far more and seek to be accepted into the ship. There is no reason why they should not be granted permission to go on to the bridge provided they always ask the OOW's permission when going up.

Mixing of the officers and passengers is acceptable. However, it is important that all, including yourself, realise that limits to the consumption of alcohol in their presence are observed. Always bear in mind that, should any unfortunate accident occur, the fact that 'officers were drinking' is a statement beloved by the newspapers and lawyers. Therefore, I suggest that when in the presence of passengers, you have the one drink rule.

The best time to set the ground rules for the passengers is when you can get them together to welcome them. However, rather than laying them down as rules, advise them of your requirements in their interests. Their safety must be the prime concern and this must be considered when organising trips to the engine room and other working areas of the ship.

As time goes on, especially on a voyage of several months, you will find that some passengers will believe it appropriate that they comment on the management of the ship, especially the catering. This should be discouraged, although there is nothing wrong in allowing the occasional requested item to be included, provided it is regarded as a favour and not a right. Think of your attitude as being the three 'C's - communication, calmness and courtesy. As passenger numbers increase you can become more remote from their affairs as you will now have specialist staff to deal with them and their problems. Note that I said more remote, not completely. You still have a function, even if it becomes a little more theatrical as the number grows, to appear in a social capacity and listen to those who demand to see the Captain.

Passenger accommodation must always be a priority and this should be included in your weekly inspection.

20 Ethics

Are we no longer perceived as "ship shape and Bristol fashion" then…?

You should by now have, at the very least, an idea of your ethical responsibilities. There is a growing public belief that there should be stricter ethical standards in industry and this belief strengthens with each maritime accident. The general public are not too happy with the state of affairs in the marine profession. Many at sea are also concerned and dismayed at the way their professionalism is compromised by what they perceive as a lack of integrity in ship and port management and other influencing sectors of the industry.

Dr Roger Peterson, in his paper 'Ethics and the Master', wrote:

'To most of our society, licensed mariners, particularly Captains are viewed as true professionals. If they are indeed true professionals, then it is implied that they operate under some set of strict rules for conduct and ethics'.

He then defines his interpretation of the issues a Captain should be concerned with as:

- Responsibility to society
- responsibility to his crew
- responsibility to his profession
- responsibility to himself and his professional reputation.

His remarks about our profession operating under some set of rules for conduct and ethics are interesting. There are maritime laws intended to discipline commercial and professional behaviour and, in my opinion, these are increasing in number because of our own failure to discipline ourselves. However, as many of them are not enforceable, reliance is placed on a code that seems not to exist any more. I do not know of any college that includes a discussion of this subject in their curriculum.

If professional ethics are not included during training, either ashore or at sea, the values we are left with are those of tradition and society. However, while one culture might recognise something as being relevant to professional integrity, other cultures with differing maritime traditions might not.

As an example, while 'women and children first' might not be a standard valued highly on the modern cruise ship, where everyone has assigned places and any disruption would bring chaos, there will always be someone who shouts it. The general public places more value on such traditions than we do, which is why the image of the Captain going down with his ship, preferably clutching his flag, is far preferable to him getting off without getting wet and going home!

While there are no formally supported ethical codes for a Captain to follow, there are and will be times when most of us at sea are caught up in moral dilemmas. The occurrence of these in the shipping industry is an inescapable fact. During such times we are reliant on the individual having his own moral code that guides him along the path that he has formulated to suit his own circumstances and within which he can perform his professional duties.

21 Portage Accounts, Budgets and Stores

Different responsibilities are designated by different companies. On passenger carrying vessels you will not usually have to be concerned with these problems, although you could still be responsible for the budgetary allocations. If you are fortunate enough to have a Chief Steward onboard, he will be responsible for the accounts. However, you could still be responsible for all financial accounts, including crew wages and leave balances.

There are a large number of Captains who allow themselves to get into a mess over what should be very simple mathematical procedures. I know of one Captain who, over a period of nearly twenty years, could never balance his monthly portage account. A fine Captain in all other respects I might add! The answer to doing any portage account is to keep a rough running account as you progress through the month. Cash out and cash in and make sure that the exchange rates are calculated correctly. If the ship has a budget system for all the stores, as you authorise expenditure and the receipts come in, enter these under the appropriate department heading, keeping your receipts together. If you are operating under a budgetary system, you will have far more control over what is supplied to the ship, but always keep a cash reserve for the odd unforeseen requirement. If this remains at the end of the financial year, you have the opportunity to add something to the welfare amenities.

Managing the stores can be a fine balancing act

With budgetary control you also have the freedom to choose where you purchase your items, which does free you from the tender hands of the Ship Chandlers. When odd items are required, such as working tools or electrical equipment, you can dispatch crew up the road to the nearest hardware store and usually purchase far better far cheaper. The same can apply to provisions as well. You will find that in many ports, the local supermarket is quite happy to fill your order and deliver to the ship, again with considerable savings. The local fish market can also come in very handy. By controlling the supplier of the provisions you tend to avoid finding that a considerable quantity of the fresh food is about to pass the sell by date. One benefit of smaller crews is that you can consider this kind of purchasing for the ship because far less bulk buying is necessary. Of course, if you are storing for months at a time, the Chandler will be the obvious main supplier.

If you have time, before sending a large order in, carry out an inventory check. You will be surprised at how few times this happens and it could be that some years have passed on your ship since the last correct one was completed. Regardless of what you tell the company, it is important that *you* know the true state of affairs. In most cases, you will find more stores than stated.

If you are submitting a stores order to the company, by all means keep a little reserve. You will probably order more than you actually require on the principle that they will cut your order anyway. This is nonsense of course, but all ships do it. Every so often, someone tries to be sensible and asks only for what is needed, and very occasionally the office does not reduce the order.

When you add up the cost of dry stores, especially tools, it comes to a considerable number. You must always remember that, as the company's representative, it is your job to look after the costs as well.

22   Ocean Routeing

The routeing decision debate

Your vessel could already be ocean routed, or you may be given the option of being ocean routed. This could either be because of the charterer's requirements, or because your owners are not too confident of their Captain's abilities.

When ocean routeing first got underway, I visited a major centre. I was impressed by the array of machines, computers and people dedicated to helping me and my ship cross the ocean and so I agreed to try their services for several voyages. Based on these voyages, I made the following observations:

- The route recommended was, in almost every instance, the route that we would have selected ourselves
- the information given during the voyages was, in every case, later than that received by the ship from our own sources
- the accuracy of the information given was generally about 50%
- advice regarding wave height was always underestimated
- once en-route, the diversions advised were not very effective on an average speed vessel.

While using the service, I began to feel that if anything did go wrong, I could point my finger at the ocean routeing company. Because of this I felt more and more that I should be following their ideas, regardless of my own professional instincts. That is why I stopped the service. It was becoming a 'comfort zone' that was too easy to follow, losing my own judgements and ability.

If you are not ocean routed, what have you lost? You have the same information coming in via satellite through weather facsimile and computer internet services. You have the same knowledge of weather in the oceans that their personnel have and probably have more practical experience. Personally, I think that the professional satisfaction, the continued interest and increase in your knowledge and the confidence in your abilities far outweigh the benefits of the systematic routine of being ocean routed.

Passage planning should start some days ahead by studying and correlating all of the information available for the route, including the excellent routeing charts available. Details of past weather should provide a base for your route plan.

On sailing, while constantly watching the weather data as it comes in, you still hold your options open for the first day before finally settling on your decided route. I used to have the positions of the various fronts and lows plotted on the main navigation chart and have all the officers and cadets join in the fun. We were a weather reporting ship as well, so my officers were very conversant with the subject.

As you may well know, deep lows in the oceans tend to cover many thousands of miles and are not easily avoided once you have set off on your track. Often all you can do is put the ship on a more settled course until they sweep through. Hurricanes tend to be far smaller and you can play the chess game but again, using the past routeing charts and the mass of information coming in regarding a hurricane, there is not much that the routeing company can tell you that you can't tell yourself. They certainly cannot tell you about the rogue wave!

There are still areas of the world where the weather reporting is poor or non existent, in winter or hurricane seasons or for ships that have a difficult task or cargo I do believe that ocean routeing has a place, but not as a service to be used by all ships in all seasons. However, it could be that you are chartered to Charterers who insist that you be ocean routed.

This happened to me in the early nineties and, after three voyages during which I studied their advice, using it occasionally but more often going my own way, I wrote to the charterers with the following facts:

In their weather forecasting they achieved an accuracy of 12% whereas the shore stations and other sources we were taking information from had an accuracy of 47%.

The records they gave to the chatterer, who kindly sent them to me for evaluation, showed that their claimed figures for distance saved, average speeds and fuel were all wrong and written in their favour.

When our charterers sent them back our corrected figures and showed that we had bettered their distances and speeds, they agreed but said that I had endangered my ship to obtain them. Of course, we had no record of damage to either the ship or cargo over a period of 6 months. I am pleased to say that the charterer dispensed with their services because clearly there are routeing companies and routeing companies.

In correspondence with the President of one of the largest ocean routeing companies, I was very pleased with his statement that:

'We have never varied in our conviction that the Master of the vessel is the Master of the vessel. The situation is that simple and we have no ambitions to change this

status quo. Our role is one of assistance and advice. There are times when our tools are of tremendous value, but these same tools can be of questionable value if taken too literally. We do not expect Masters to blindly follow our recommendations, and make this clear to charterers at every opportunity.'

A sensible man and a very pleasing statement. So it is all clarified, advice only and you are still the man who decides. Or are you?

Every mainstream time charter form contains the term that states the Master is under the orders of the charterer with regard to the employment of the ship, while remaining within the bounds of safety of his ship, crew and cargo. But what about navigation? Is routeing a matter of employment or of navigation? To me, it is obvious that it is navigation, but to others?

In the recent case of MV HILL HARMONY, which was time chartered, the charter contained the usual employment clauses but no special routeing clauses. The time charterers, on the advice of an ocean routeing company, ordered the ship to proceed from Vancouver to Japan by the northerly Great Circle route. The Master had experienced heavy weather on a similar voyage some months before. He disregarded the charterers' orders and insisted on taking the longer southerly rhumb line route. The charterers claimed for the extra time and bunkers consumed.

The arbitrators held that the routeing instructions were 'employment orders', which the Master should have followed, and that his refusal was unjustified. Note the word refusal. How can you refuse advice only? The owners appealed. Both the High Court and Court of Appeal found in the owners' favour but the case was finally referred to the House of Lords. The highest English appeal court changed the decision in favour of the charterers.

The British House of Lords on appeal ruled that a routeing order is an employment order

The House of Lords ruled that an order about routeing is an employment order. Time charterers are therefore entitled to give routeing orders to the Master which, unless they compromise the safety of the ship, must be followed. In addition, it was held that the Master must follow the shortest and quickest route unless there are navigational reasons for not doing so.

This appears to mean that the navigation of the ship and the safety of those onboard are still the Master's responsibility, so he can take such action as he deems necessary to preserve that safety. The same applies to ports that he deems to be unsafe. The charterer cannot order a ship to take a route that is unsafe. In this case the Master had previously encountered heavy weather and altered the route but was found against, so who can judge that the charterer's ordered route is unsafe, and in the very quick time required before the ship sets forth?

Navigation is still the Master's responsibility and he is at liberty to change course for safety reasons. He can refuse to enter a port that he considers to be unsafe and can leave a port if it becomes unsafe. The HILL HARMONY decision does not alter these principles. Neither does it give the time charterers the right to order the ship to take any route, however unsafe. The time charterers have the right to use the ship in a commercially advantageous way and can determine the route the ship takes as a matter of employment. However, they cannot place the ship, her cargo and crew in danger.

I suggest that, as Captains, we are still responsible for the navigation and can deviate from the ocean routeing advice employed by the charterers, but we must show that their recommended route was unsafe and we might have to get another opinion on that apart from our own. Possibly insane, legally correct, but certainly not the interpretation the President of the largest ocean routeing company had put on the use of its services.

The best advice I can offer is that, should you be under charterers ocean routeing and you disagree with the recommendations, contact your operators and the charterers direct with your views and suggested options. If you believe that by carrying on with the routeing directions you could be standing into danger you must tell them so and have a copy of your disagreement in writing. Should they not agree with your opinions and order you to continue with your recommended route, if anything does happen your relatives will have an interesting case to put back before their Lordships.

Always remember that if it is you that wants to be ocean routed, the confidentiality of your voyage that existed between you and your owner is now shared with a third party.

23 Weather Conditions and Ship Handling

Picking up the Pilot

23.1 Poor Visibility

Which would you prefer, bad weather or poor visibility? I know my own answer, bad weather provided that it is not storm conditions. Really I would prefer neither.

I think that the reason behind my answer is that in bad weather I feel I have some control because, unless I am in hurricane conditions, I can at least see some distance. In fog I am entirely dependant on radar. I know that radar is very good and that some ships prudently have 3 cm and 10 cm, but not all do and these exceptions are not uncommon. Only recently, with newly fitted twin ARPA radars, we had a case of a medium size ship not displaying any echo. There was no reason for this either. No blind spots or weather conditions that could interfere with the picture, just a blank spot where the ship should have been. This was not a singular occurrence as it has happened on other occasions. With that at the back of my mind, I am always uneasy about pushing on in fog.

It is a difficult subject for discussion as we know what should be done and we know what we would like to do, but we also know what is practice and expected of us. I am well aware of the collision regulations and the rules of low visibility. But in poor visibility, when you cannot see the forecastle, are all the ships stopped? If you decide to stop, what about the chap coming up astern? In fog you always have the predicament of keeping going, with all the consequences if you bang into someone.

Even in the Pacific Ocean, where you can have fog for weeks on end, you find yourself frequently drawn to the bridge to stand there looking out at nothing and worrying. In poor visibility you must take the standard precautions, ensuring that your engines are on instant response, reduction to a reasonable speed, and watch your radars carefully and while remembering that not all ships show all the time, particularly small vessels. I believe that the denser the traffic conditions, the slower you must go. If you find yourself with small craft around, remember that some of these may not have radar so stop your ship until they are clear.

I remember approaching San Francisco on a Sunday morning one summer. We were a container vessel and operating on a tight schedule. We had the berth arranged and the gangs standing by for our arrival when, one hour out from the Pilot, down came the fog. A Sunday morning in summer off San Francisco is a yachtsman's delight and we had a multitude of targets on our radar. It was obvious from their direction and speeds that they did not have radar so we had to stop and sound frequent signals. Even so, several boats came out of the fog to sheer away at the last minute on sighting the slab side of our hull. Naturally, I advised the local office of our charterer but all they were interested in was in me going full speed because of the costs of the gangs on a Sunday. In such situations there is only one course of action, apart from putting the phone down, and that is to follow the rules.

And then the fog came down…

23.2 Weather

How you handle your ship in heavy weather depends on the type of ship, ie if it is long and lean or short and fat, its draught and how the ship behaves in bad weather. Every ship has its own idiosyncrasies to learn about as you progress. Damage to ships in bad weather often occurs because Captains fail to recognise the power of the sea and the limitations of their own ships in coping with it.

Heavy lift cargoes (patrol boats and helicopters)

When I was a Chief Officer we were speeding south off Namibia, heading for the Cape on an express heavy lift cargo ship at about 23 knots. As the weather closed in, and with the seas and wind directly on the bow, I asked the Captain if we should reduce speed, but this idea was rejected. The weather became steadily worse until it was eventually blowing a full force 9 with our ship still at full speed. The inevitable happened and as we went down into a large dip in the sea we were going too fast to ride up the other side. Instead we went straight into green sea, right over the forward part of the ship. We stopped at this point and, leading the work party forward, we found the forecastle coaming bent inwards, the windlass moved from its deck plate several feet across the deck, the foremast at an angle and some other sundry damage. All the deck cargo of chemicals in drums was broken adrift, some still floating around on the decks and others over the side. These took a long time to secure, with some risk to the crew. The Captain's proud boast was that he didn't slow down for man, beast or the sea. His premature retirement slowed him down though!

The moral of this tale is that no schedule is worth damaging your ship for. Look at the seas, feel your ship, consider the forecasts if you are bunking down for the night and adjust your RPM accordingly. Ensure that your officers know they have the flexibility to adjust the RPM, calling you when necessary. A few revs can make a considerable difference to the motion of the ship, especially if the props are racing, but very little difference in time.

23.3 Seas

The breaking wave provides the biggest problem to a ship. The normal wave, or swell, produces an up and down effect on the ship as you pass over it or it passes under you. This can be broken by the force of the ship when at speed, forcing the water at you in a mostly horizontal direction. In general, the pattern and time interval of waves are regular, which is why the word linear is often applied to them. I do not like that term myself because it implies a constant wave system that does not exist. Within the pattern of waves, there is sometimes a build up to double the normal height with a similar decline but, at other times, one particularly large one can develop very quickly and with little warning.

In areas where the waves are coming from deeper water into shallow water, a confused sea can build up and short choppy waves can develop, which although of not too much consequence to larger ships, can be a problem for smaller vessels. With the sea and waves, it is the breaking wave that does the damage.

23.4 Taking Water

Have you considered the encounter period between waves?

There are types of ship, such as bulk carriers and tankers, that can accept water on deck as a matter of course and there are other ships that wish to avoid this. The amount of water the ship takes on her decks depends on the amount of pitch or roll, coupled with the stability, freeboard and the speed. A ship's roll varies with the degree of stability, with a stiff ship rolling more quickly than a tender ship and a light ship pitching more than a laden one.

If we look at a situation where the ship is heading into the sea, the water the ship takes on deck will vary with the distance between the waves, which is known as the period of encounter. A ship heading into a sea with a short period of encounter will pitch less and take less water on deck than the ship heading into a sea with a long period of encounter that tends to bury the head into the oncoming wave, causing water over the bow. The same applies to a beam sea, so if the period of roll is less than the period of encounter, again you will ship less seas. If the period of roll is more than the period of encounter, as the ship rolls she will come against the next wave and the clash of this against the hull will cause water on the decks.

23.5 Heading Into the Sea

Every hull form has its own handling characteristics

Ship's bows are designed to point into the sea, which is why they tend to be sharper than the stern. The problem is that many modern cargo carriers have become broader and broader as the block co-efficient has increased, until many ships resemble large powered barges. This has turned the cut into the sea into a smash. Both the fine and broad bow types can give problems when running at speed into seas. The fine bow cuts into the sea and, instead of rising, can try to cut through the wave, leading to green seas over the bow and very wet decks forward. The ship with the broad bow will thump into the wave, pushing the seas aside with the flare, and the bow will rise and fall heavily. The finer the bow the more speed you can achieve, but you really do not want to bury your nose into the seas. The trim of the ship can assist considerably with the pitching. Trimming by the bow will push your bow further down into the sea while too much trim by the stern will make it more difficult to keep your head into the sea. The answer to heading into the sea in heavy weather is to have the ship slightly trimmed by the stern and not push your ship too hard. Every ship performs differently and you will soon know how your ship is dealing with the weather. Your schedule is not as important as the care of your ship and so you should consider a reduction in speed if your ship is pounding hard or has green over the bow.

23.6 Running Before the Sea

Whenever I discuss this with others, someone inevitably raises the subject of pooping. Yes this is possible and must always be considered but the prospect of broaching is far more dangerous.

Recently, while crossing the Atlantic in winter in a small vessel, I was overtaken by a hurricane. It was one of those occasions when there was little you could do to get out of the way. It was not an excessive storm, with only a maximum wind of 70 knots, and we successfully ran before the seas for the duration, altering course when required to keep the seas on our stern, which was quite broad. As I only had a few feet of freeboard, I certainly did not want to go beam on. By setting the speed to just below the oncoming waves, we surfed quite well for several days and, apart from the odd sea breaking over our stern, had no problems.

I have read advice about putting the sea on the quarter to avoid pooping but it is my experience that, unless you have ample power up your sleeve, this is not a good idea. In a low power vessel, and most of us drive around in vessels that are low in power in relation to the size of the ship, in really bad weather it is too easy to broach your ship. If you are running before the sea and your ship is steering well, set your speed to just below that of the approaching waves and keep the seas directly astern. A surprising number of ships can do this without too many problems. Should you experience difficulty with the steering or you take excessive water over your stern, and this is causing or could cause damage, rather than trying to adjust the seas to a different direction, come round and head into the sea. This should be done sooner rather than later.

23.7 Turning the Ship

It is particularly important to study the pattern of the waves if you want to turn your ship to put the sea on your stern. To put the sea on your stern, watch the waves form then, after a particularly large wave, wait for a few more and turn. Run your engines up to full speed and hard-over the wheel, preferably without too much initial headway on the ship.

To put your head to the sea after running with the sea astern, again watch the seas carefully. Wait until you see the waves rising and then, as the large wave approaches, put the wheel over with engines full ahead before it gets to you. I recommend that you have a little speed on the ship for this manoeuvre as ships are more reluctant to steer with the sea astern. By the time the ship has the sea on the beam it should be on the decline again

23.8 Heaving To

There is nothing wrong with doing this if you consider that the weather conditions are such that you are taking too much water onboard, that you are pitching and rolling too violently or that damage to ship might be the result of pressing on. In normal seas in storms, it is speed not the sea that causes most damage, both to the ship and to the cargo. Containers stacked high on the forward hatches, timber lashed high on the decks and shifting cargoes below must all be cared for as well. Advice is given to heave to with seas off the bow and, in one publication I read, it recommended allowing up to 45 degrees off! Certainly not something I would try in a low powered vessel. What you are looking for is enough power on the engine to maintain steerage way and to avoid falling off the seas. The wind will generally be in the same direction as the seas and you can see this from the appearance of the sea. When hove to and in extreme weather, I believe that the best place for the sea is directly on the bow unless you have a high powered vessel and you wish to try to ease the pitch, in which case you can try the ship with the wind slightly off the bow, but not much more than 10 degrees.

When to consider heaving to?

If you fall off the wind you have two choices to get back. The first is to increase power with the wheel amidships to build up a little speed, then put the wheel hard-over. Depending on the power available to you, this might work. The other way is to accept that you cannot claw back and put the wheel over the opposite way, increase to full power and take the ship right round.

Many years ago in Japan in winter, as a young and inexperienced Captain, I allowed myself to be persuaded to sail direct from drydock in light ballast condition (do not try this at home), and naturally ran right into a severe storm while fighting to get out of the bay. The ship fell off the wind during the night and when I came on the bridge the OOW was fighting to get her back, but all that was happening was that the ship was heading for the rocks at full speed. I reversed the wheel and the ship came round just in time and set back on course again with the wind right ahead. I did not bother about heaving to. Full speed regardless as long as it took me away from land!

Should you not be able to get back with the wind ahead you have two alternatives provided you have the sea room. The first is that you accept that you cannot get back so you stop your engine. The ship will then find its own angle to the seas and wind and will drift. You will experience severe rolling but you will have no speed and that will help with the seas. If you do this, the rule of thumb to use for your drift is around 2 knots. Add another knot for a safety margin and you will see from the proximity of land whether this course of action is safe to carry out. If you cannot or if the rolling is too severe for your ship, you will have to come about and put the ship on a course with the wind astern or on the quarter, steering the best course to take you clear of land or other shipping and on which your ship is best steered on. If you have the seas on your stern or quarter, try to have only enough power to make you just a little faster than the advancing waves.

A great deal of advice has been written on handling ships. Inevitably, the way to handle your ship will depend on the ship as well as the conditions at the time, as each ship acts in a different way. However, it is surprising what a ship can do and survive provided she is not forced against the sea. Apart from the circumstance of rogue waves, I personally feel that many of the ships that are at sea are lost as a result of poor ship handling.

23.9 Severe Weather in Port

When in port, we often tend to relax our guard a little. While this is normal, you must remember that the weather can catch up here, in the same way as at sea. It is a problem that we do not watch our weather forecasts with the same diligence as when we are afloat and the port very rarely advises ships of the approach of extreme weather unless it is of hurricane dimensions. To be fair to them, they probably do broadcast on the VHF but who is listening in port unless there is VHF in the cargo office on the port channel? Quite often you notice the change in weather, mention it to the foreman and when they say that there is bad weather approaching, only then do you get contact the port. Sometimes one of the crew is watching TV and you find out that way. Either way it is pretty informal.

In the case of bad but not extreme weather there are certain precautions to take.

Is a change in the weather brewing?

23.10 Precautions

Cranes and loaders that are not in use should be moved clear of the vessel if lines should part and the ship surges ahead or astern, damage could result to the equipment and the ship. It is quite normal that in many ports there are limits for operating cargo loading and discharging equipment in wind.

Ensure that all mooring lines have equal strain and that the lines are properly secured to bollards, not on the tension winches. Tension winches are not really designed for holding the ship alongside in wind conditions.

Put out additional lines. You can always take them in again but, if you do not, as the weather worsens you will wish you had.

Additional fendering should be secured in place. If the ship is not against Yokohama fenders or well sprung permanently fixed fendering, it will do no harm to put out any fendering you have onboard as an additional precaution.

The outboard anchor should be lowered to the bottom. Should the forward lines go, and these seem to be the ones that go first if you have the wind blowing you off the jetty, this will help stop the bow swinging out into the harbour.

The gangway should be manned and tended. Hoist it if the shore workers have stopped work. Strong winds in enclosed water way can cause strong rises and falls of the tide in addition to the surging of the ship, causing the gangway to come into contact with jetty obstructions such as bollards.

Have your engines on immediate readiness, together with thrusters if you have them.

Make sure that you have the VHF channel of the tugs at hand on the bridge.

Don't forget to have your flags hauled down as it is a shame to have them ruined.

23.11 Cold Weather Conditions

Ice accretion in the North Sea

If there is a chance of your ship operating in cold weather areas where freezing conditions may occur there are precautions that you should be aware of, particularly if your ship is not ice class.

The danger of icebergs and ice must be considered and, while this is not intended as a book on navigation, there are some standard signs of drifting ice to look for. The principal ones are:

- Ice blink, where there is a reflection of light in the sky from a large mass of ice. This can also be seen on a clear night
- small blocks of ice in the water, called calf floes. These can indicate that bigger bergs are around
- sea life, such as flocks of birds and seals, well away from land
- if the wind is blowing, and there is little swell or waves, it could indicate that there is ice in the direction from which the wind is blowing.

You cannot depend on radar to provide an indication of ice in the area. While I would expect large bergs to appear on the radar, especially in the Antarctic where you tend to get large tabular bergs with faces like cliffs that provide a good radar echo, this cannot be relied upon. The rule is that if you consider that you are in the vicinity of bergs or ice, you should proceed with caution and watch your ice forecasts. However, I have twice sent in reports of previously unreported bergs and subsequently seen no reports of them in later broadcasts.

The average berg has seven tenths of its mass below the water and this can project out for a considerable distance beyond the visible portion. Sightseeing is not a good idea! Always give the berg a wide berth and, if you have not received any reports about it, send an ice report message giving the position, estimated size and, if you can, the rate of drift and direction. Also send an 'all ships' navigation warning by VHF and on 2182.

Should you not see an iceberg until the last moment and it is ahead of you, do not try to go hard-over with the wheel. Instead put the engines full astern. It might not stop you hitting the berg but at least all your damage will be on the bow and hopefully your collision bulkheads will hold. Going to port or starboard could rip your ship down the side, causing a very quick capsize (think Titanic).

Ice berg right ahead! Think what happened to "Titanic" and go astern!

Snow, especially blizzards, is also a problem when navigation is in enclosed waters. Both conditions severely affect your radar picture, particularly blizzards as they can produce a complete blotting out of the screen. Your visual visibility is completely affected as well so you could find yourself sailing on DR for a while, which is not a good idea. If possible, in blizzard conditions in restricted waters, anchor your ship and wait until it clears.

If you are in freezing conditions, drain the fresh water tanks in your lifeboats to 75 % full. Fresh water freezes at 0°C and seawater freezes at -2°C. If you are to have a prolonged stay in freezing conditions, reducing your ballast tank water and draining the fire lines should also be considered. Make sure you have anti-freeze in your lifeboat engines, anti-freeze sprays for your bridge windows, plenty of bags of sand and salt for your decks, warm clothing for the crew and a few shovels for the snow.

You do not have to be in ice conditions to have freezing spray coming onboard and this can build up very quickly. If you are heading for the sun it should eventually melt off, but if you are going the other way and it is building up to the extent that it will interfere with your moorings on the forecastle or will stop you opening your hatches, you should slow down and/or alter course to try to stop the water coming onto the decks.

If you do have a problem with the hatches, it is likely that the port you are heading to will have companies that specialise in removing the ice and getting your hatches open, so this is a good time to contact your operations department

If you are a new Captain of an ice class vessel you should already have experience of ice as Chief Officer. If not, then you have some serious reading to do very quickly!

23.12 Extreme Weather

With global warming, 100 year storms are paying a visit more regularly

By extreme weather I mean hurricanes, typhoons, cyclones and anything of force 12 plus. You will be warned of their approach and will have an important choice to make. Do you stay or do you go? Personally, I have always preferred to ride out the weather at sea, but no one can tell you the decision to make under such circumstances. Here are a few points that might help you take one.

How far are you from the sea? Meaning, how long will it take you to stop any cargo operations, close the ship up ready for sea, get the departure organised and get out to a safe position, preferably away from the approaching weather system, but away from land if that is the best that you can do? Plot the system, allow for the possible variations of course, and then work out the time of your departure against the track of the storm. If there is a good possibility that you can be caught either during the departure or when you are not yet a safe distance from land, the question is answered for you. It is too late to go and you must take whatever precautions you can where you are. If you can go then it is up to you, although in many ports they take that decision for you and hustle you out as fast as possible.

What is your position in the harbour? Is your berth sheltered or exposed? Are you close to other shipping? These factors could also influence your decision.

If you are caught in port consider:

- On smaller vessels placing the inboard anchor cable, if it is light enough, onto the shore and putting around a mooring bollard. This may sound like a problem but, by taking a lead around the bollard with a mooring line or wire, you can pull the cable ashore relatively easily provided that it is paid out enough for the chain to be slack
- if yours is an old ship it may still have insurance cable or storm lines onboard. If not, some port authorities, especially in areas subject to severe weather conditions, will provide heavy storm moorings. Check if these are available
- all lines should be out and doubled up where possible
- ensure that all loose gear on the decks is cleared away and stowed, including any cargo residue
- stop all shore leave. You are going to need your crew at stations fore and aft, standing by your mooring lines
- if the wind is blowing from a direction where it will blow you off the berth, consider having a tug standby by the ship for the duration of the extreme weather, if one will come. Because of the cost of this you might first check with your operators
- if you are a light ship and there is enough draught, ballast down as much as possible.

23.13 Extreme Weather at Sea

Extreme weather at sea can occur quite suddenly in many parts of the world. Naturally we all try our best to avoid them, but there are occasions where intense lows develop, travelling extremely quickly and with a widening diameter. When these are encountered it is not always possible to get out of their way. The hurricane I mentioned earlier in the Atlantic was a low that came hurtling out of Canada, passing just south of the Newfoundland Bank and intensifying all the way after leaving land, travelling at a speed of 40knots.

MV "Suilven" off New Zealand

The handling of the ship is no different than for severe weather, except that the very force of the seas might make it difficult to carry out your intentions and you may instead have to settle for what you can get the ship to actually do.

I have just been reading a report I made in 1989 in the Bering Sea in winter where we recorded a wind speed of 110 knots, which was as far as the anemometer would go. The ship was 41,000dwt with an engine of 13,000Hp.

We estimated the highest seas to be around 20 metres. The ice field to the north and the height and speed of the waves running through precluded any attempt to run before the seas so we came round into the wind as much as possible. The eventual heading was with the wind and seas 30 to 40 degrees on the port bow, with maximum engine power and wheel hard-over to hold this.

In my report of sea state, I said that the winds tended to flatten out the sea, leaving areas of high waves with no pattern. This caused the ship to lurch severely with the lurch ending abruptly as the ship crashed into another wave peak, causing it to shudder and begin to move in the opposite direction. At the same time, the whole ship was being lifted out of the water and then set violently down again. The wind was not constant, but gusting sent the needle of the anemometer swinging against the stop. It was of such force that the tops of the waves were torn off and the air was white with spray. Visibility fluctuated from nil to about 100 yards with the rain and spray, and it was not possible to leave the wheelhouse as the water was driven into your face with such force that you could not open your eyes. Finally, the radar scanners both ceased to turn against the force of the wind. This has only happened to me once before, again in another hurricane. It was then that I found out that most radar scanners are only guaranteed to turn in wind of up to 70 knots.

It was much better reading about it all years later than it was being in it!

What it does show is that, regardless of what you know about handling, weather, and all the rest, when you get into such conditions your actions are severely limited by the ship type, engine power, the force of the weather and the proximity of land or dangers such as other ships.

23.14 The Rogue Wave

Rogue wave – 1933 Bay of Biscay

The rogue wave did not officially exist before 1995, no matter how many were reported. Shore authorities refused to accept that wave heights could be more than 12 metres, even though ships disappeared with no other logical explanation.

This denial continued in the face of continuing reports and ship losses until 1st January 1995, when the Draupner rig in the North Sea was hit by an 80 foot wave that was recorded on a wave height recording instrument. This caused a complete change of thinking, although it was thought that they were caused by a force created by current and wind opposing each other. This was mainly because of the frequency of damage experienced by ships in the Agulhas current around the South African coast and in Norway, although this did not explain the waves in the North Pacific, Atlantic and other parts of the world. Views changed again when two cruise ships in the South Atlantic were hit.

After this event, a satellite-based programme was set up to search for rogue waves. This found waves of up to 30 metres in many sea areas of the world and it is now recognised that they can develop in any storm. Their characteristics are completely different from the normal smooth sloping linear wave and the view is that they are caused by waves becoming unstable and taking the power from the wave in front and the wave behind. This deepens the trough in front, which increases as the wave grows. The wave then assumes the aspect of a breaking wave with a wall of water bearing down, rather than a slope up which a ship can ride.

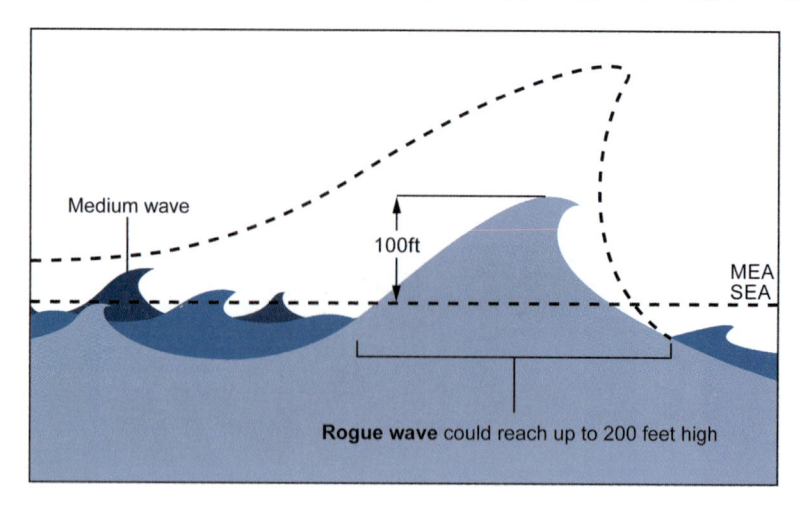

Creation of a rogue wave

As yet no one knows why waves become unstable. However, I must admit I find it strange that anyone talks of a normal linear wave in the first place as, in bad weather, I have always found that waves are different. Each roller that comes in has different heights along its length. It breaks in some parts but not in others. Each wave is a different height and every now and then a wave considerably larger than the others comes along. The direction of the waves can vary as well, which is why when you have your head into the sea you will suddenly take a large roll as a wave comes in at an angle on the bow. During my last few years on a rescue ship in the North Sea, where force 8 and 9 is normal in winter and winds over 55 knots are not uncommon, we tended to carefully study waves, especially as our ships were small. I would agree that, in bad weather, 12 metres seems to be the average but we get many larger and every winter the number of ships with their bridge windows smashed supports that fact.

In the late seventies, I met my rogue wave when crossing the North Pacific from Yokohama to Seattle in a large container vessel in winter. We were in gale force 8/9 and rolling and pitching quite severely, but nothing that we could not handle. We were at reduced RPM making way and waiting for the storm to pass through when, at 1630 hrs, a huge wave appeared on the port bow. It was not one of the really gigantic waves that are around, but it was big enough to knock us over 40 degrees one way and then the same roll the other, breaking loose two holds of containers. Our estimate was that the height of the wave from the bottom of the trough to the top of the wave was around 50 ft, but the damage was done by the hole in the sea in front of it that we went down into before facing the wall of sea. When we limped into Seattle and faced the US courts for damage assessment and costs of around $20,000,000, they refused to recognise a wave as the cause of the damage, being only interested in the wind force.

Obviously there are areas where this type of wave is more prevalent, such as around the coast of South Africa in the Agulhas current and in Norway, where current and wind can oppose each other during storms. These areas are to be avoided during such conditions but there is not very much any of us can do in the other parts of the world, where these waves may suddenly appear.

Damage to ship by rogue wave off South Africa

Ships are designed to survive an impact of 15 tons per square metre. An average 3 metre wave strikes the ship with a force of 1.5 tons per square metre, a 12 metre wave at 6 tons. So far, so good. Even if a wave strikes the ship at 30 tons per square metre it will dent rather than break the hull. However, a rogue wave of 30 metres height, measured from the bottom of the trough to the top of the wave, will hit your ship at 100 tons per square metre, and no ship is currently designed to withstand this.

It would seem that, until it can be found out why these waves occur and if there is any way for warnings of development to be given, when or where you are going to encounter them is a bit of a lottery. The wave is not constant as it can develop from part of a larger wave, grow and then break, with only a ship in the local area of that development being affected. Evidence points to there being a correlation between wind and opposing current, causing generation of such waves in certain areas, so it would be prudent in such circumstances to be especially alert in severe weather. Similarly, there is also a view that these waves frequent areas in front of weather fronts and lows, where in daylight you might have time to see it coming and at least put the bow into it, but at night there is not much you can do. It certainly emphasises the need to ensure that all deck openings are always kept secured and watertight, no matter what the conditions are. It should also make you more ready to put on your deadlights in bad weather. Many modern ships with high bridges no longer have these, on the basis that no seas could reach that height. I would suggest that if any ship is hit by a 30 metre high wave the bridge certainly will be flooded so, without these deadlights, all your electronic instruments are gone. This is what happened to the two cruise ships in the South Atlantic. One ship unfortunately lost the main engine as well, although it did manage to recover and make its way to port.

Cruise liner, Antarctic Ocean

As part of the MaxWave project, a team at the Technical University of Berlin worked on simulating their production. Using computer modelling the team found rogue waves appear to be formed when slow-moving waves are caught up by a succession of faster waves, moving at more than twice their speed, merging together.

The sobering evidence of the rogue waves was identified during a three week period of study of the ocean waves by a special satellite system. The MaxWave team, who undertook this study, identified more than ten individual giant waves around the globe, all above 25 metres in height.

I like prefer the fisherman's description of a rough sea as being 'lumpy', as that is my experience. There is a rule of thumb that I had quoted at me as a younger officer, which was that if the wind had been blowing for a length of time then half the wind force in knots would be the height of the large waves in feet. It has even worked on occasion!

24 Drydock

How much makes it past the company's red pen?

At last, you are the customer! It makes a change to go to a port where they are anxious to please rather than one that regards you as a necessary evil. Prior to the drydocking, you will have already prepared the itemised list of repairs, sent this in to the company and received the much shorter list of repairs that are to be actually done in return. As the docking nears, you should have been advised of the draught required, both at the repair berth and in the drydock, in order that the Chief Officer can prepare his ballasting program.

Prior to arrival at the drydock port you should be sent an outline plan for the stay, with information such as where the ship is to berth on arrival, when the ship will be drydocking, how long for, where the ship will be berthed for ballasting for sea and when the sea trials will take place.

It is worthwhile bearing in mind that on arrival you will be quite light. Take this into consideration when planning your arrival and harbour passage. Also ensure that your sanitary tanks are pumped out prior to arrival, unless you want to go tripping along the dock at three in the morning in your dressing gown.

It is wise to have a drydock meeting onboard to discuss the following:

24.1 Responsibilities

In normal situations the responsibilities on a well run ship are clearly defined but in the drydock there are additional problems and areas where responsibilities can cross over. In addition, it is quite normal for the engineering department to be working flat out, while the deck department will have more time on their hands. This is not to say they will not be busy but, for example, it could be that while the Chief Engineer is normally responsible for pollution control, this might be passed to the Chief Officer. Who will be responsible for deciding on times of blackouts? Who will provide the work sheets for entry into enclosed spaces and who will provide the crew for guard duties of spaces with men inside? Who will be in charge of ventilation control and opening up tanks? Most importantly, who is designated as Drydock Safety Officer? If the Safety Officer is normally the Chief Officer or another deck Officer, there could be no reason to change this, but what if he is the Chief Engineer? Is he really going to have time to do this properly? The company's ISM may well designate who the Safety Officer is and what the various officers' responsibilities are but this is not engraved in stone and the temporary designation of a Drydock Safety Officer would not be conflicting with the ISM code.

World Vale (bulk carrier) in drydock

24.2 Safety

Whoever is going to be Safety Officer will have to distribute the drydock safety orders to the crew and prepare the ship for the drydock staff. These should be the same as the safety requirements for those boarding the ship from the shore, but with the addition of hot work permits, enclosed space entry, etc. It is worth sending the ship's regulations ahead to the drydock, requesting a meeting with the drydock Safety Officer on arrival. Most drydocks are fairly safety conscious these days, so no more bamboo scaffolding collapsing with the screams upsetting your afternoon nap!

You must also consider safety in the yard. The yard could well have regulations regarding walking areas, workshop areas, out of bounds and traffic control, especially if you are riding around in cars or bikes. The yard will generally have their own first aid post and instant communication with the local emergency services, so should you have any emergency onboard one call to the yard will initiate the reaction of the service required.

With regard to hot work and entry to enclosed spaces, the yards are pretty professional these days. For hot work they will provide their own watch service and have a fire extinguisher standing by, but it is the ship's staff's duty to first check the area and adjoining compartments and give the go-ahead if all is in order and, when finished, check the area again to ensure that all is well. The hot work list should be given to the ship each morning at the daily meeting before the start of work. This should be placed prominently on a work board in the ship's office with the times of start, completion and who has signed off the work.

The same goes for entry into enclosed spaces. The list should show the tank lids that are off, when ventilation was started and completed and whether oxygen and/or gas tests have been completed and verified safe. It is also important to ensure that the open tank accesses have a guard rail and notice.

It is essential that the ship has a watchman on duty through the night and that, apart from his normal duties, he also checks the hot work areas that were worked on through the day and any night work that is going on.

24.3 Security

It is good practice to have your own night watchman check any areas where hot work was conducted during the day

Even if the yard is a secure area, your Security Officer will have to make contact with the yard security and co-ordinate on this.

The yard security may affect the ship's personnel going ashore. It is likely that the gate will want to have an up-to-date crew list and your ship's company might wish to have ship identification. It is a good idea to get a batch of plastic holders and put in the name of the ship, name of the crew member and his rank or rating so that all can clip these to their boiler-suits or shore gear when going ashore.

Ship ID tags are a good idea

Drydocks are notorious places for theft so ensure that all your lockers are secured and relocked after entry. Cabins should also be locked and any shore worker found in the accommodation areas removed, with their name taken and a report made to the Repair Manager. Tools should not be left out after use or they are unlikely to be there in the morning.

24.4 Pollution

Because of the politics of pollution, if the yard has nothing else organised, you can be sure that this will be. Generally, no pumping of tanks will be allowed while in the dock and it is essential that your pollution equipment is at hand ready for use and not stuffed in the usual locker. It does no harm to organise a pollution drill before docking, based on the plan you intend to use there. The dock will have an emergency number to call in the event of pollution.

24.5 Fire Control

You might have to make a new temporary fire station list based on the requirements of the yard and the ship. In the event of fire many yards will want everyone not directly concerned to evacuate the ship and be accounted for in an area away from the immediate scene of operations. Consider the alarm you intend to use for a fire emergency onboard. If you are using internal alarm bells these might not be heard by personnel, both on ship and shore, working on the decks or on the hull in the dock. If you still have air to the ship's whistle, this could be used as a signal provided all have been advised about it.

24.6 Shipboard Management

With all the different demands put upon personnel, the number of shore workers around, the visiting company superintendents and the class, P&I, Flag State and other inspections going on, it is easy for a ship to descend into chaos in a drydock environment. But, by pre-planning and with everyone's co-operation, it can be managed.

In a well managed company, the Drydock Superintendent from the technical department will be in attendance, sometimes with an assistant. On large vessels, there may also be a hull or steel man and there may be an accountant to watch the cash. They should be onboard on arrival at the lay by berth and have the latest plan of action, as well as (hopefully) the crew mail and newspapers. Find out from the Superintendent what he wants and what time he wants the daily meeting in the morning. Who do you require at the meeting and where it should be held? Remember, you are the Captain. This is your ship and, while listening to the Superintendent's requirements and doing what you can to co-operate, you also have your own need to manage and run the ship. You can, with courtesy, declare this as it is better said now than later. You might also require essential stores, such as additional Personal Protective Equipment (PPE), boiler-suits, lighting, rolls of kraft paper for alley way protection, etc. Have the list ready and the logical reasons why they are required.

When deciding where the morning meetings are to be held, think of the numbers attending. Apart from who you want from your staff and the Superintendents, there will be drydock representatives from the paint shop, the steel shop, the ship manager, the Engineer and tool shops and anyone else who thinks that they have a place there. The larger the ship, the larger the numbers. Ensure that wherever you choose has ample seating. If you are to make space for the Superintendent's office as well, ensure that you have the ship's general arrangement plan pinned up on a bulkhead for easy reference, and have other useful plans such as hull, tank diagrams, etc, ready for use. Get in a good supply of plastic cups and lots of coffee and tea and then everyone can make their own. This saves your catering staff from running around.

The Superintendents will want a spare cabin for changing. If you have an old ship this will be no problem as there will be lots of spare cabins around. However, on a newer vessel this may not be the case. As a thought, if you really have no spare cabins, try the bridge. That is usually a quiet place in drydock unless you are having new equipment fitted.

One of the great problems to manage in drydock is where everyone is. You can guarantee that, if you are not organised, every man and his dog wanting someone or something will immediately head for your office or cabin. The prevailing idea in all ports is that the Captain is the one with a magic ball, who always knows where the Chief Engineer is or what the Chief Officer is doing.

Try organising your OOW system to have one officer on duty in the ship's office each day. On the gangway, a large notice requiring visitors to report there and to this officer will hopefully point them in the right direction or pass them to you if it is you they wish to see. Give the duty officer a walkie-talkie and make sure that the Chief Engineer, the Superintendent and the Chief Officer have one. At the end of the working day, the OOW can collect them in and recharge them for the next day. This officer can also issue the work permits, check that the job evaluations have been done and keep the port log. The Superintendent is a very busy man and, to save him running around on small matters its worth considering giving him a junior officer or cadet to act as his runner.

Next lay down your rules for shore workers in the accommodation. All too often you find them creeping into the seamen's mess and although the crew might not speak out about it, it is very irritating for them. This is still their home, not the drydock canteen. Stamp on this one from the very beginning.

In Drydock, like any other port – watch out for prowlers

24.7 Catering

During the drydock, you will be expected to arrange catering for all of the Superintendents and visiting inspectors. This means that you will have to arrange messing times, especially if the duty mess room is small. I suggest that you arrange the ship's officers to mess first, then the shore visitors. Where possible, have the deck officers change and use the officers' mess. Do not under any circumstances allow boiler-suits or work shoes in the officers' mess.

Keep a strict check on all meals over and above those for the ship's crew. At the end of the drydock you can present the Superintendent with a list of extra meals, the cost of which should not come out of your messing allowances.

24.8 Crew Welfare

For many ships, the drydock is a time when, after work, the crew have a rare chance to go ashore and relax. Discuss this with the Repair Manager, find out the transportation the yard provides and get maps and any information about the surrounding area. If families are onboard try to arrange something for them, as living onboard a ship in dock is not very pleasant if you are not busy working. If the ship has been in dock for a period arrange to get customs down again for a bond issue.

Drydock offers a chance to properly relax and wind down

24.9 Completion

The prudent Captain has the odd bottle of scotch and a few cartons of cigarettes stashed away on arrival. This is international ship currency around the world and it is surprising how many small jobs that you want done can be completed with a little oiling of the wheels. Having now established your management and with a well run machine in operation, you should not be needed. If that is the case then you have done your job.

Be careful when signing off the work list at the end of the dock. Make sure that you have time to go over the list with your officers to see that they are satisfied with the work, rather that have the list shoved in your hands for signature a few minutes before the Superintendent disappears down the gangway. If you are not satisfied with an item, then don't sign.

There was a time when all the plugs taken out of bottom tanks were labelled and stowed in the Chief Officer's office. Prior to sailing, they were issued for putting back and if you found the odd one remaining, preferably before flooding up, you knew that all the plugs were not in. That seems to have stopped now, probably because large ships have so many tanks and so many plugs you would need a truck to put them in. However, it is essential that, regardless of whether or not the yard takes responsibility for sealing any openings in the bottom, you organise a good check around with your own staff to ensure that all is well. Once the ship is flooded up in the dock, have the ship sounded around. In addition, make sure that the Chief Engineer checks his engine room bilges.

So you exit the drydock with your tanks roughly the same, although we never seem to have exactly the same draught coming out as when we entered, and hopefully with the repairs completed. The ship will be a dirty mess, papers will be everywhere, the Cook will have thrown a fit and the Superintendent is going to report you to the Operations Manager. A normal drydocking then!

I recounted earlier the time I left drydock without ballasting and found out the hard way why this should not be done. I really do advise you to ballast up before setting out for your trials as you never know what is coming along. The story is always the same. A ship has been in the dock for a considerable time, and suddenly everyone is in a tearing hurry to get rid of you. When you do the trials make sure that you are away from other shipping, regardless of what the Pilot or the Superintendent says about getting off soon, especially if you are swinging your compass at the same time. You can always return to the pilot station to disembark your visitors.

At last, when all are satisfied, you can wave them down the gangway and depart, spending much of the time to your next port putting your ship back together again!

25 Port Entry

On your marks, get set... (Make sure the gangway has a clearly marked safe person load!)

In many countries it appears that the port bureaucracy exists to engage the ship's staff in hours of paperwork, employing the maximum number of officials with little else to do. Of course, all ports are not like that. However, having in the not too distant past visited a port where I had the pleasure of 23 officials in my cabin, disposed of 40 crew lists, anything not tied down and all the cobwebs from the bond, I feel I am not overstating the case. Those who have the added pleasures of transiting the Suez Canal, West Africa, South America or parts of India will have their own stories.

The frustrations that you will feel in dealing with ports and their officials during your time in command have been felt by us all and there are two ways of dealing with them. In the first, you use logic and fight the system. This leads to stress, further frustration and, because you will not win, eventual alienation from the port. You and the ship suffer, not the port. Bear in mind that owners or managers pay you to get the ship through the port as quickly and smoothly as possible, rather than engage in demonstrating your ability to run the port. They will not be amused.

The second is to accept that each country has differing ways and customs and that a port has the right to determine how it is managed, regardless of your opinions. Instead, use your intelligence to prepare the ship for that port, avoiding as much as possible, any problems. This way leads to long life, a prolonged career and getting ashore far quicker that you would by following the first route!

25.1   Port Planning

How you prepare your ship entirely depends on the trade, type of ship, staff you have available and the port you are visiting. A ferry trading between two ports on a daily basis will be treated entirely differently to a foreign ship that has never visited before.

Regular visits to a port allow a relationship to develop with the personnel. Couple this with familiarity with the port procedures and you should have trouble free visits.

Let us look at the worst case scenario, which is the large tanker or bulk carrier that spends long periods of time between ports, with the ports often diverse and with the time in them measured in hours rather than days.

There is a problem of perception between the ship and port. To a ship of the type described above, port arrival is a major management event. To the port, it is just another ship in a long line of them so it is not too interested in your problems. The terminal is only interested in getting the cargo in and out as quickly as possible and any other problem is a nuisance.

To achieve even organised chaos, pre-planning is essential. If we assume that you have a well managed ship, and by that I mean a ship where the Master does not try to do everything and where the officers all have some degree of responsibility, they must be consulted on their requirements and priorities established. If the port stay is short and the world and his dog are waiting for you, some form of port planning meeting should be held. During this meeting, you will produce a list of events and your officers will know what is happening, which might be a new development for some ships.

So, let us assume that such meeting has been held and that you now have a list to make up, based on modern manning and with no Chief Steward or Radio Officer, it could be as follows:

The Captain
Port formalities and paperwork
Agent
Mail in and out
Cash
Payments to various suppliers
Port victualling arrangements

Chief Officer
Cargo
Tonnage to load
Loading sequence
De-ballasting time
Fresh water requirements
Essential safety programme to complete, for example lowering lifeboats
Stores to load
Deck surveys
Essential work program in port

Chief Engineer
Bunkers to load
Essential maintenance work CSM or engine surveys
Spares to load or land
Shore technicians as required

2nd Officer
Port navigational requirements
Medical or dental treatments

To the above list must be added any special port requirements, such as rat guards, brows, communications, signals and port regulations if they are known.

It is not only the named officers who should deal with the specified items. On a well managed ship with a modern company approach, all officers should have delegated their individual responsibilities and cross department management should be in place. However, we do not always sail with officers with management ability or in companies that recognise shipboard management, and so it is not unusual for the whole list to devolve to the Master and the Chief Engineer.

Once the list of requirements for the port is established, the next phase is forward preparation.

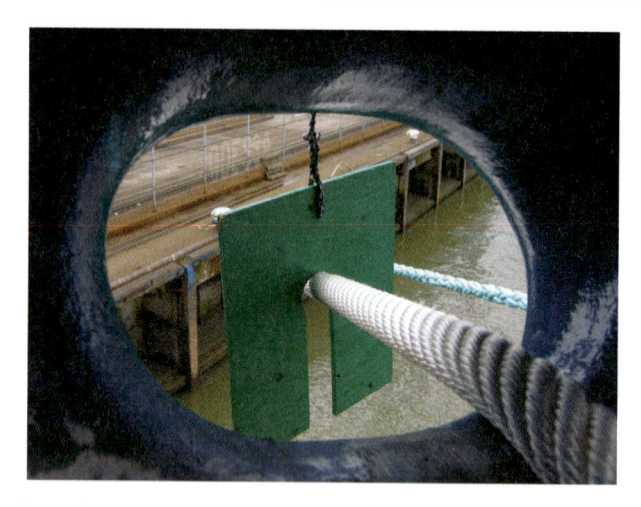

Don't forget when all fast to ask for the rat guards to be fitted

25.2 Forward Preparation

In this phase we are trying, as far as possible, to pave the way. Hopefully, the more work put in before you arrive, the less there will be to do on arrival.

25.2.1 Port Papers

The crew list should always be sent ahead. In the case of the US, a visa stamped crew list must be sent and considerable problems are caused when these lists arrive after the ship. With regard to the US, it is wise, with their ever changing security requirements, to check what is required well beforehand.

Some ports will accept computerised customs forms and crew lists in lieu of their own, but unfortunately not too many. Maybe this can all be electronically automated in the future, but for the moment port papers must be prepared by hand in advance. In many cases, when you are going to a port for which you do not have the forms, these can be requested in advance, possibly by fax or e-mail. If the port will accept forms being faxed, it all helps on the day.

Although not port papers as such, it is wise to check that the following are up-to-date and signed:

- Oil record book
- garbage disposal record book
- GMDSS log - remember this has to be signed daily, not just each page
- pilot card
- log books

- port passage plan
- hours of work
- work permits ready
- medical log.

The bridge can now become a bit manic

The bridge of a ship in port can be like a sweet shop for some officials and you never know when one is going to want to sift through your documents.

25.2.2 Cargo Documents

It is essential that the cargo stowage or discharge plans, together with the ballasting arrangements, are sent to the port as soon as possible. That way if there is any dispute, the issues can be clarified prior to the ship arriving.

If changes are requested and made, send your changed plan back again. On your final plan you might consider stating that there will be no further changes made, otherwise they will inevitably be requested within hours of arrival.

The worst case will be when, having sent your plans, there is no reply from the terminal but when you arrive they wish the whole plan changed. At least when this happens the ship cannot be blamed for any delays incurred.

25.3   The Agents

The days when the agent visited the ship are largely gone unless you are a cruise ship with a nice restaurant and female company. Now the ship will be visited by a boarding clerk whose experience can be variable and who may well have been selling shoes a few weeks before.

The agency itself may not feel it is representing you as it could be the charterer's agent that your owner or management is using. It might be worthwhile finding out if your company is paying a proportion of the agency's costs as this will then allow you to refute this belief. In other cases, the agency might be a division of the terminal that you are using, with no other agency allowed to compete.

The worse case scenario is that the agency is a division of the charterer and the charterer owns the terminal. In this circumstance they can behave as they please, with not a lot able to be done about it.

Therefore, the agency can be considered variable enough that nothing can be taken for granted. You cannot assume that they have all the information either. Communications within the port organisation can also be variable and often the terminal does not advise the agency of changes or matters that may affect your ship. Equally, the fact that you have requested your company to arrange a surveyor or technician to attend on arrival is no guarantee that it will be done. In other words, regardless of what you may think has been arranged, assume that the agency has no information.

You should advise the agent of the following:

- Your requirements regarding presentation of manifests, etc prior to discharge
- a copy of the crew list and cargo
- personnel leaving or joining
- any personnel requiring medical or dental treatment
- fresh water requirements
- any technical assistance required or technicians that have been requested to attend. It is essential that any equipment is detailed, together with the suspected problem or area of concern
- surveyors requested and what the surveys are for
- cash required, together with the denomination of the notes and exchange rates
- any stores or spares that have been sent to the port, preferably with the shipment number
- if storing, which side the crane is on. If you only have one stores crane requesting to berth that side alongside in the port
- if you do not have an appropriate chart for entering the port, arrange through the agent for the Pilot to bring it to the ship. The same applies to courtesy ensigns
- advise the agents of any bunkers ordered. Remember that you are the customer. If time allows specify when you want the bunkers to be delivered otherwise you will get them whenever the bunkering company sees fit. If the ship arrives early in the morning and is sailing early morning the next day you want the bunkers on arrival, not during the night before sailing

- any special ship peculiarities, such as unusual mooring arrangements or any malfunction of navigational equipment.

For your port emergency listings, you will require the names and phone numbers of the pollution agencies. At the same time, find out the pollution protection that the port provides.

Disposal of waste continues to be a growing problem for ships, with many ports not able or unwilling to cope with the problem. Again, advance notice is suggested.

Ask if the port regulations allow overside painting, lifeboats to be lowered and, most importantly, if there are any port regulations regarding work on the main engine involving immobilisation.

25.4 Note of Protest

In maritime terms, a 'protest' is a declaration by the Master of a vessel about any special occurrences during a voyage, such as bad weather or accidents. It deals with events that the Master has no effective control to prevent and covers damage to the cargo and /or vessel during them. The protest may be extended by up to 6 months so that the full extent of any damage can be assessed.

Because of the differing regulations in various ports and countries, if you are intending to note protest it is wise to advise the agency in advance of your arrival. In some countries the notice must be made in front of an attorney or notary, in others before a consular officer and in others it can be handed over to the agent for transmission.

The strength of the note of protest has been diluted by the requirement many charterers make for these to be tendered on arrival in a port, regardless of the voyage or lack of apparent damage.

> *I experienced this in the pulp trade to Japan where, on arrival, a swarm of young cargo surveyors would board the ship and claim for the smallest of perceived damages, even to the wrapping that was on the pulp to prevent damage! I must admit that, in all my years of tendering them, I was never advised that they did any good or served any purpose.*

There is no standard document for such a notice and, in some countries, the officials will have their own type of document that your protest is to be written in. Copies of any relevant entries in the ship's log book should be attached, regardless of whether you use your own format or theirs.

25.5 Ship Regulations

Most ports or terminals have regulations that you are asked to sign when your ship arrives. Generally these refer to safety matters and the particular terminal requirements. Normally, the Captain signs these as 'sighted only'.

There is no reason why the ship should not produce its own regulations for the terminal. Outline the requirements for PPE in the working areas of the ship, the prohibited areas to shore personnel, the method of accident reporting, etc. This should be sent ahead of the ship via the agent. Not only will this assist with the general safety and efficiency of the combined operations, but will also help remind the terminal that the ship is in port and has a factory function with its own particular problems as well.

You could find that the Chandler is your best source of information

In many cases you will find the Chandler the most useful man in the port and sometimes the only man working for you. He will know what technical assistance is available and whether your crane is suitable for the berth. Even his estimate of when you are sailing will often be more accurate than the agents!

In Command   **Port Entry**

While this is not a comprehensive list, it hopefully provides you with an insight into the normal requirements of a ship arriving at port.

26 Anchoring

I dream of a quiet roadstead, not a busy Singapore parking lot!

While ample regulations exist about how ships must conduct themselves on the high seas, and government authorities continue to add to their routeing requirements around their coastlines, it is surprising just how little attention is given to anchorages around the world.

I have not seen any statistics relating to accidents in anchorages, but suspect that more collisions occur in anchorages than anywhere else. While loss of life or the sinking of a ship is very rare in such circumstances, the risk of pollution is high, especially as anchorages are close to land. Even without this, the expense of repairs and delays can be considerable and the stress and effect on careers traumatic.

The source of the problem seems to be a question of responsibilities. The attitude of most ports to their anchorage ranges from complete disinterest about where ships anchor to designated anchorages within port areas, either on chart or by port instructed position. Regardless of the type of anchorage, when any accident occurs, all ports place the responsibility with the ship, regardless of the type of accident or how it occurred. This is based on the grounds that the Captain is responsible for the navigation of the ship and, should he feel that the anchorage is unsafe, he should not attempt to anchor his ship.

It might be an acceptable position if the wait for the berth is only a few hours and the ship has seaway where it can heave to and drift or slowly cruise around, but it is not acceptable if the waiting time is longer or if the ship has to navigate a long passage back to a safe area. In the latter situation, the problem is compounded if the ship, deciding that the anchorage is unsafe and so moved a considerable distance away to find a safe area, misses the berthing time. Where does the Captain stand at that point?

In Command | Anchoring

**The process for tendering an NOR makes you
feel that anchoring is compulsory**

There is also the problem that many ports do not accept a ship as having arrived for notice or readiness purposes until it has anchored in a defined port area anchorage, making anchorage compulsory.

26.1 Regulations

I accept that the Master is responsible for navigation in an anchorage, but it seems strange that this area of greatest potential danger, where ships gather in close quarters and are hampered in their movements, is largely ignored by the International Regulations, which require ships to conduct themselves as if they were on the open sea.

While this is workable in theory, it is hardly practical. The International Regulations allow a Port Authority to make local rules for their ports and roadsterads, but it would take a brave port management that, without compulsory pilotage for the anchorage area, to make navigational rules that conflicted with the International Regulations.

Another problem is the difficulty that an approaching ship has in recognising if another ship is at anchor, about to anchor or get under way. Vessels will, if possible, approach their anchor position into the wind and/or current so the other ships in the anchorage will present a stern aspect. However, the signal for an anchored vessel in daytime is a small black ball hoisted forward, completely out of sight of an approaching vessel. At night anchored vessels are fully lit, but there is still nothing to indicate that the vessel is about to heave anchor.

Heavy claims for accidents involving pollution have already been caused by this problem. Anchor signals designed for ships a century ago are not adequate for today's shipping. A signal such as a flashing blue strobe light to indicate that a ship was anchoring or heaving up anchor would be far more practical. However, there is nothing to prevent Captains from displaying the 'signal for a vessel restricted in her ability to manoeuvre when engaged on anchor operations', with reference to the International Regulations rule 3(g) (ii).

26.2   Manoeuvrability

A major problem affecting ships in anchorage areas is their varying limits of manoeuvrability. The general guideline is the larger the ship, the less the degree of manoeuvrability. Using the worst case scenario, a loaded VLCC or VLBC, when making a final approach, may well have its engine stopped a mile away from the selected position, with way on the ship of four knots or less. When light, especially if deballasted ready for loading, the manoeuvrability will be severely hampered by wind and current.

At up to three cables away from the anchor position and with the engines about to come astern, under no circumstances is the vessel able to manoeuvre within the context of the existing rules. However, under these rules, the ship is still required to comply with the International Regulations.

26.3   Anchorages

Anchorages can be divided into three basic types:

Open anchorage	An undefined anchorage in open waters
Defined anchorage	An anchorage in open waters with defined limits
Confined anchorage	An anchorage that is confined on more than one side by natural or man-made hazards

If the International Regulations cannot adequately cope with the navigational problems of an anchorage, the anchorage itself and the way in which it is defined and controlled is of prime importance.

26.4   Positioning

Far too many ports claim to have traffic control when their service is traffic advice, and the difference is considerable. 'Control' is when a port is capable of directing the navigation of shipping from shore based radar with trained and experienced professionals operating the service. Without this, regardless of the radar system and availability, any service offered can only be advice. Few, if any, ports exercise control or give advice covering traffic in their anchorage areas.

Far too many ports claim (or name) traffic control, when it is really only advice.

In anchorages without defined anchor positions, the problem of ships anchoring too close together often arises. The distance a Captain will anchor his ship away from other vessels depends on his own view of a safe distance, after consideration of prevailing or expected weather conditions, exposure of the anchorage, size of ship, holding ground and occasionally, engine maintenance requirements.

However, safe distance is a matter of perspective. A safe distance for a coastal vessel is too close for a VLCC. Often a situation will arise where a VLCC or VLBC will anchor at a distance of seven cables away from other vessels only to have a coastal ship anchor within two cables. Who moves? The large vessel can protest the position of the other vessel but, if the smaller ship refuses to move, the Captain of the larger ship has a duty to move on the principle that he is the one who perceives danger and it is his duty to place his ship into a safe position. Carried to an extreme conclusion, in a busy and unrestricted anchorage, the larger ship could be on the move all day or even have to move out of the anchorage altogether if there is not another safe position to anchor in.

*It could be your turn to move again,
sooner than you think*

The fact that a vessel, anchored in a safe position, can be forced out of the anchorage by another vessel might seem absurd, but it can and does happen.

26.5 Responsibilities

For open anchorages, where ships can anchor where they choose and with no restrictions except those imposed by draught and depth, it is reasonable for the port to have no responsibility, although advice on traffic movements would still be very useful. Defined and confined anchorages are a different matter.

It is the port that states the limits of a defined anchorage so it must be assumed that it has taken into account the number of ships that can be expected to anchor at the same time, as well as the variations of size and manoeuvrability of those ships. By defining an anchorage they are stating that ships must anchor within their stated limits, so the port has an obligation to provide a safe anchor position. If this is not available, the port should advise the ship to anchor outside of the port limits but still accept, for Notice of Readiness purposes, that the ship has arrived.

It is interesting to speculate on a situation where a port instructs a ship to anchor in a defined or restricted anchorage that is already full by acceptable seamanship standards, causing a collision with another vessel. Although the ship attempting to anchor must accept blame for the collision, I also would suggest that in these days of environmental concerns, blame should also fall on the port.

If we accept that International Regulations cannot adequately cover the safe navigation of ships in an anchorage, we must see a requirement for a realistic approach from port authorities, accepting that defined and restricted anchorages must have some form of traffic control or advice and ships allocated to anchor positions.

26.6 Anchorage Design

Many anchorages and their limits have remained unchanged for decades, regardless of how the commercial activities and the ships using the port have changed. Anchorages have rarely been designed. They have been developed by ships anchoring near the port and, as they increased in numbers as the port developed, someone drew a line around the area to limit further spread. As cables started to be laid again limits were drawn.

There is a need for ports to make a survey of the ships using the anchorages and plan accordingly. Anchorages should be separated by ship size, with separate anchorages for coastal, medium and large vessels. Anchorage positions within these areas should be allocated with radius based on the sizes and manoeuvring limitations of the ships assigned to them. The anchorages should be clear of through-traffic routes. The port should have a clear approach channel that extends seaward beyond the furthest limits of the anchorages and a pilotage area that is clear of the approach channel and anchorages and is restricted to vessels using the pilotage service.

A number of ports have done this but, although the number is growing, they are still comparatively few in number. Of those that have there is little agreement about which size of ship is a problem and what the safe distance apart should be for the assigned anchorages. A survey of a range of ports that have anchor positions shows a range for large vessels of three and a half cables to six cables. Most Masters who command VLCCs would say that they regard seven cables as a minimum and many require one mile, especially in weather variable areas and seasons.

Of the ports that have established anchor positions, none have yet assumed the responsibility of traffic control or advice within their anchorage areas. A busy anchorage with constant traffic movement is similar to an airport. If it is unimaginable that aircraft be allowed to move freely on the ground without any control or advice, why should ships in an anchorage?

Anti-pollution pressures are so strong that any port involved in pollution caused by an accident in an anchorage, with ships moving without any traffic advice or controls or having designated anchor positions, will find itself in serious difficulties when the inevitable questions are asked.

If you observe oil pollution drifting down on your ship at anchor notify the port control, if not notified and the port discovers the pollution in the vicinity of your ship guess who will be blamed? There is also an advantage in taking a sample of oil to protect your ship from any claims that could arise.

26.7 Anchoring Your Vessel

Before you approach the anchorage, you and the Navigating Officer should have already studied your approach courses and had a passage plan drawn up.
As you start to get a radar picture of the anchorage area it is a good idea, if there are a number of ships already anchored, to plot their position on the port area chart. This provides a far better idea of the situation than you can judge by sight and radar. Once these are plotted you will be able to see the spaces where your ship will fit and then you can check the depth of the chosen position from the chart. This is the type of scenario where ECDIS is beneficial.

You want as much distance as possible from other vessels, but for a ball park figure. If you do not know how long you are to be anchored for, go for a mile. Personally, I was never happy with anything less than five cables on very large vessels.

As you get closer, you will be able to see how the ships are lying and that should be the general direction of your approach. This way you should be able to maintain a steady course over the last mile, reduce your speed without deviating and, when you let go, fall back with the ship's head in the direction in which you want to be lying. It is not essential that you do this and there might well be reasons why you cannot, but it is the preferred direction for anchoring.

It could be that port control has given you a designated anchorage as after many years of prodding, some ports are actually coming round to the idea. If not you will have to find your own slot. Before you do this try to find out from the port if there are movements that are taking place during your approach, not just in the anchorage but also to and from the port. Small ships leaving the port will quite often take a short cut through the anchorage and, as we have discussed and regardless of your predicament at the time, the International Regulations will still apply. Having to suddenly place the wheel hard-over and put the engine full astern, just as you are on your final approach, can ruin it. If you consider that you are a restricted vessel, there is nothing to stop you displaying that signal, but many will not recognise it or see it. If any ship is heaving anchor I suggest that that you either wait until her anchor is up and she is under way or give her a wide berth.

Is there a strong current running?

By looking at the lie of the cables of the anchored vessels you will get good indications of the current. Certain ports are notorious for having strong running currents, the ports in the Agulhas current immediately coming to mind.

Once you have arrived at a point just before your position and started to come astern remember that, depending on whether your screw is right or left handed, your bow will fall off and even with variable pitch there will be some effect from this, so allow for it on your final course. When the ship is stopped, you can let go or walk back, depending on the depth of water and current. On very large ships, I always walked back as a matter of course and then took the anchor out of gear and let out the remainder of the chain on the brake to avoid stress on the windlass motor, taking care that the ship did not fall back too quickly. This avoided jerking or piling the chain in a heap on the sea bed. You can use the GPS to see when your ship is stopped and falling back but, as this quite often varies when you are nearly stopped, I always preferred to use the old rule of thumb that when the wash from the astern movement of the propeller reached two thirds of the length of the ship then let go your anchor. How many cables is again dependant on the length of stay and if it is good weather. The old rule of thumb of five times the depth of water is usually enough.

A colleague of mine went to Brazil with his ship and anchored for several days. He was then told that the berth was now ready and went alongside. However, he had forgotten to give notice that his ship was ready in all respects to load cargo. Normally this is not made a big issue of but, on this occasion, it was used by the charterers and all the costs of the several days delay went against him. The owners were not amused.

Once your ship has settled to the cable don't forget to give your position and time of anchoring to the port. Until this is done, officially you have not arrived. At the same time send off your NOR to the agent. This is very important.

Remember, it is not compulsory to anchor your ship in the prescribed anchorage or even to anchor your vessel at all. If you decide that the anchorage is so full that to try to enter and anchor would hazard your ship, then you should explain this to the port and request another anchorage position or ask if you can anchor in another area as close to the anchorage as possible. Similarly, if you decide that owing to weather it is not possible to anchor, then giving the time of arrival off the port to the port authorities and the NOR to the agent, you can stay off the port until the weather clears or you are called in.

26.8 The Anchor Watch

It is always a good idea to tell the engine room what is going on when you are manoeuvring your ship. Apart from keeping them up-to-date, it stops them from ringing the bridge to find out when you will be finished. It is also wise to remember to finish with the engines when you are satisfied that the ship is holding her position. Chief Engineers can become quite irate if, after a few hours, they come up for air to find you all round the barbeque with a cold one in your hand.

Don't forget to keep those onboard informed

It is a standard rule of the sea that, as soon as you anchor, the Chief Engineer will want to imobilise the engine. 'Only for a short time' echoes in my ears as one of the great lies of the sea. It seems that every time I relented the Pilot appeared, the weather worsened, the anchor dragged or the Chief phoned to say that we had serious engine problems. It always becomes 'we' when anyone but you has a problem, and 'we' didn't have a problem until he touched it. So, think hard before you allow this. Check the weather, check with the port and, if you have any misgivings, lie back to him and say that there is some regulation or other that prohibits this and put them on the standard 15 minutes notice! If poor weather approaches then go to instant readiness. As a young Captain off Livorno, I thought 15 minutes was acceptable and nearly ended up on the breakwater.

Make sure that you are notified of any other ship that is anchoring in your vicinity and ensure that the OOW is watching not only your position, but also those of the nearest vessels to you.

Ensure that the correct flags are displayed and that you are not caught out by the sudden appearance of the Pilot wanting to know why you are not under way ready for port entry. Watch out for small boats, especially at night, and also for the crew dropping the pilot ladder over the side for the attractive contents of the small boats. Remember that your ship has still not been cleared and some ports are very strict about customs and immigration regulations. One ship off a Brazilian port had some female visitors onboard when she suddenly got orders to sail for Argentina. They could not get their visitors off so the ship took them to Argentina and back. The Brazilian police were deluged with distressed parents looking for their missing offspring and, when the ship returned, the authorities were not amused.

27 Arrival at the Port

Bridge team for port arrival

27.1 The Port Approach

The increasing amount of port approach controls or advice is welcome, although there seems to be an unwritten agreement that port control or advice should be limited to shipping movements and should only begin when ships are about to enter the channel or are within port limits.

In the air industry it is standard procedure to advise an approaching aircraft about traffic movement and relevant weather conditions that might affect the approach. So why not ships, which can be just as affected by current and wind, especially at low speed and in light condition? A bulk carrier, at slow speed and in light condition, can require fifteen degrees of set to maintain course in strong wind and current conditions.

Ships are in contact with the port for at least one hour before arrival and so there is no reason why the port services should not advise them of current, wind and tidal conditions, in addition to local navigational and traffic warnings.

There is a considerably difficulty in telling navigation lights from shore lights, especially with so many flashing lights being shown these days. So, port approach at night is made almost entirely on radar. However, radar clutter as you approach the port is a problem, especially the identification of small craft or ships moving in the area. In addition, because of the shore light background, their navigation lights often cannot be seen. For these reasons, any port approach should be made at a sensible speed and you should slow down well before the pilot station. Build in a readiness to sheer off into your approach plan and have your last position for this marked on the chart.

Prior to arrival at this point ensure that your steering, engines and thrusters are all tested and logged as such. Finally, don't forget to have your bridge windows washed down free of salt spray.

You should have included the tide in your passage plan but remember that the tidal streams are predictions, even though they would be accurate if wind and pressure changes did not cause surges that interfere with the predicted changes in height and time.

27.2 Pilotage

Caution when picking up the Pilot, this is an area that is experiencing increased incident occurrence

The ship is responsible for advising port services of the ETA, with updates as frequently as are required. In addition, boarding arrangements must be properly prepared, safety arrangements put in place, speed adjusted and a lee made if weather conditions require it.

The pilot boarding or landing must be supervised by a responsible person. However, the requirement for officer attendance throughout is becoming more difficult for ships to comply with, often leading to a situation where the Master sends the OOW off the bridge to meet or disembark the Pilot in a busy traffic area, leaving himself as the only person apart from the QM on the bridge. I recognise that this does not fit in with the 'bridge team management' concept, but it is what happens.

The relationship between the Master and the Pilot must surely be unique. It is a relationship based on trust, founded on the assumption of professional competence between experienced seamen in the common aim of the safe navigation of the ship in confined waters.

You pass the con of the ship to the pilot yet retain overall command. It could be assumed that when the Pilot is on the bridge the Captain is also there, but as we all know this is not the case. The Captain generally assumes that the Pilot, purely because he is the pilot, is experienced and within minutes of the pilot boarding will, if the pilotage is lengthy, happily leave the bridge in his hands together with the OOW. Pilots should be flattered at such trust!

While all ports have the pilotage boarding position identified on the chart, few Pilots actually board there. Often ships are requested to approach closer or the pilot boat decides to approach the ship some distance before the ship reaches the assigned area. Both situations can cause problems.

APL Panama, not the kind of beach party we want

There are a number of ships that have grounded when proceeding closer to the pilot boarding position with scant communication with the Pilot (if any), such as the "APL Panama", a 4,000 TEU Containership that grounded in a Mexican port in December 2005 while the vessel was waiting for a Pilot that she received no communication from. The "APL Panama" was heading towards the beach and attempted to turn to parallel the beach just off the harbour entrance when she ran aground in the early evening with good visibility, light breezes and smooth seas. After numerous attempts to refloat the Panama she finally refloated in April 2006.

With the requirement for the Master to discuss the pilotage with the Pilot before commencing the approach passage, the boarding area of many ports is already too close to the approach fairway or channel to allow time for adequate discussion. When requested to board the Pilot closer, in some ports in the approach channel itself, there is no time. There is often no turn back point or room to manoeuvre, even to give the Pilot a lee to board. Be very wary of this.

The Pilot boarding before the ship reaches the pilotage area is a better situation. However, many a Master has left the pilot boat disappearing into the darkness astern, shouting for the ship to slow down as he still has three miles to go to the pilot area, at a speed of ten knots and the crew are still preparing the pilot ladder. Keep a good communication with the pilot boat about his location and, once you have identified him on radar, you can adjust your own speed in time.

The same can apply to helicopters, whose regulations vary wildly from a full scale airport requirement with ship traffic control and fire brigade on deck to a helicopter appearing out of the darkness, setting the Pilot down and leaving him standing on a hatch or containers waiting for someone to notice him. I once had a Pilot deposited on my bridge wing off Richards Bay in South Africa.

I remember in one port the Pilot saying "keep coming, keep coming", when he hadn't even finished his breakfast. At this particular port you approach directly towards the beach and then turn 90 degrees to starboard to make the entrance. I stupidly kept coming until I ran out of room and then turned into the port. The Pilot was still saying "keep coming", so I progressed up the harbour to the container berth and, just as I was turning in, a screaming Pilot hit the bridge asking why I had entered the harbour without a Pilot!

As a new Captain, you will welcome the pilot like a long lost son, especially if the voyage has been difficult and the weather poor. You have not quite reached the end of the voyage but now at least you have someone to share the problems with. I well remember my first departure in command when it seemed as if the departure channel was too narrow for my ship and that the pilot wanted to leave long before he should. After he had left I proceeded down the channel far slower than I should have, which of course made the handling of the ship more difficult and the anchor party became permanent fixtures on the forecastle until I was well and truly clear. On arrival at the next port we went through the same procedure, with me advising the pilot when he boarded that the pilot station was far too close to land and constantly telling him that the speed was too fast in the port. He accepted all my comments without a murmur and nodding wisely. After berthing, when he politely asked me how long I had been in command, I realised what a gentleman he was!

During those first years, I had the knowledge but lacked the experience and the pilotage system considerably added to it. However, remember the Pilot is not perfect, doesn't walk on water or wear a cape. Like you, he is trying to do his job properly but occasionally makes mistakes. There is nothing wrong in asking him why he is doing a particular manoeuvre or suggesting that he check his actions. This is what teamwork is all about. Bear in mind he also gets fatigued. If he is on your ship at the end of a long shift or you are making a particularly long pilotage, then take extra care with your checks. If you are on a particularly long pilotage, and the opportunity presents itself, suggest relieving him for a while.

In unfamiliar ports ships are almost totally reliant on the Pilots for their opinion about whether or not berthing is safe in the prevailing weather conditions. The relationship between the Captain and the Pilot is one of trust and mutual professional respect. When the pilot service was independent there was little question about this. However, with changes in pilotage around the world either making Pilots port employees or having separate pilotage companies competing in the same port for employment, this situation has changed, with many ports now placing pressure on Pilots to act against their professional judgment. Therefore, you must also be the judge of the weather conditions and remember that, if you are concerned, you can always order another tug if this would help in your decision.

When you have the pilot on the bridge, you have a unique opportunity to learn from him about the handling of your ship in closed waters. After the first few ports, try asking the pilot if you can unberth your ship. A good way to do this is to tell the pilot what you would do, and then he will tell you what you should do. Hopefully the two will coincide! Berthing your ship under their guidance comes later. Obviously you must pick your time and weather for doing this but many pilots will find it acceptable.

It is interesting that while the regulations require full discussion of the pilotage approach to the berth with the Pilot and need the Pilot to board in adequate time for this to take place, little has been said about a harbour Pilot who might board, taking over from the sea Pilot just off the berth. Where and when is such a discussion to take place with these gentlemen?

Finally, ensure that the Pilot is given the pilotage card whether he reads it or not. If you have any deficiencies, now is the time to tell him. Ask about the tugs being used, where they are to be placed and what lines, then inform your stations.

In Command   Arrival at the Port

You will learn a lot from Pilots

27.3 Port Navigation

Having once been towed into a jetty by an inebriated tug Master, subsequently finding that not only was I responsible for the damage to ship and jetty, but also to the tug which, still secured to the ship, had finally wrapped itself around a dolphin, it could be said that I am a little biased on this subject!

The port has a responsibility to provide adequate pilotage and tug services and, as they continue to shoehorn larger ships into smaller spaces, tugs are used to control the movement of the ship in the final approach rather than any reliance put on the ship's rudder or engine power. It should be recognised that once several tugs are secured to a large vessel for berthing, the responsibility for control of the ship is out of the hands of the Captain, especially when control of the tugs is in a foreign language.

If the ship or crew makes an error leading to an accident, the ship must accept responsibility. Why cannot the ports accept the same for port equipment and personnel? Tugs tend sometimes put dents into the hull so if you feel a particular jolt when they are pushing, remember to have a look in that area when you can. Not that you can do anything as, whatever they do, it is still your responsibility!

It is the Pilot who should control the number of tugs a vessel requires although we often have Pilots complaining about the tugs being insufficient when these have been ordered by the agent without any reference to the ship.

Exactly as on departure, it is the job of the bridge staff to advise the Pilot of any movement of other shipping that might affect your own ship and to frequently check his navigation and position.

I've had my share of incidents where errors on the part of the tug have unstuck me

28   In the Port

World Vale alongside Vancouver. First impressions work in port too!

I have no doubt that how the ship is treated depends considerably on first impressions. Clean, well prepared gangways, clean accommodation and uniformed officers show a well ordered and disciplined ship that the port will like. The fact that all the documentation is prepared further enhances the image of the ship. In many countries the officials are in uniform so if you are as well you have an equal presence of authority.

With the reduced personnel of the modern manned ship, many of the niceties of old can no longer be offered. However, there is always room for courtesy and it is essential that politeness and courtesy are maintained, especially with those who can assist the smooth passage of the ship through the port formalities.

It is important that all the required documents are correctly filled in and ready for the official's arrival and that personnel are standing by to assist with the port entry formalities. You know that customs must inspect the bond so make sure someone is ready for this. Port health may wish to see the galley and store rooms so the Cook should be ready.

Immigration may want the passports or seamen's documentation. If these are ready, the port procedures will be over quickly and you can begin the ship's business. All too often, advice about the documentation that is required by the port is wrong or out-of-date. It is generally wise to have most forms ready, and a typical list of port documentation required follows:

28.1.1 Port Documentation

Last Port Clearance — If any certificate is going to be mislaid it is this one, mostly because it is brought by the agent at the last minute and left around in the ship's or Captain's office for days, or because it was difficult to determine what it was, especially when written in a foreign language so got thrown away. There are unscrupulous ones amongst us who would say that when this occurs, it is what photocopiers, tippex, or even an old laundry receipt from Somalia are for and a good reason to keep old forms! Of course this is not correct, but if this form is missing, have a copy faxed from the agent of the previous port.

Crew Lists — Whatever you think the number of crew lists required is, double it. Also remember that if there is any change of crew this list will have to be changed for departure.

Passenger Lists — The definition of a passenger is often a problem. Some ports want the supernumeraries listed as crew, others will want them on a separate passenger list. Check ahead with the agent.

Customs Forms — Read the requirements with care. Most ports find the entry 'personal effects' quite acceptable, but there are those that require every single item belonging to the crew to be listed. This can be quite a racket in some places, you make up the list of everything you can think of and then they find a paperclip not on the list. A large fine is imposed, which means another trip to the bond.

Health Forms — Few ports have their own form and so any health form is generally acceptable.

Vaccination Lists — Very few ports insist on these any more. Generally, you must make your own list.

Arms or Ammunition — List or state none. Make your own list.

General Stores Declaration — This is a peculiar form that in some cases seems to go back a couple of centuries, as you are still required to list the cordage and tar carried onboard. When this is required, each country will have its own list for completion.

List of Previous Ports — Make your own list. This can be required for a period of up to three previous months.

Drug List — Make your own and state where they are held.

**Stores or Spares
to be Landed** List ready for the agent and customs.

Ship's Certificates These are the statutory trading certificates, such as the Safety Certificate and Registry. In some ports they will be inspected in situ by a number of agencies, in others the agent will take the certificates ashore. Ensure a receipt is obtained for these.

This list is not comprehensive, but it should cover the majority of forms required by most ports.

28.2 Official Visitors

We didn't think we needed an appointment? (Courtesy USCG)

In the normal world of business it is customary to make appointments before visiting. Not so with a ship. The assumption is that everyone onboard is instantly ready to deal with anyone who appears. Therefore, Port State, Customs, Coast Guard and any other inspectorate body have a habit of just turning up, usually at the worst times. They do not contact the agents or even the terminal. However, it does no harm to ask the agent if any of these organisations intend to visit the ship and then request that their visit is planned for a convenient time.

If there really is no one readily available to assist whoever has just appeared, then explain the problem and ask for their patience. On the grounds of safety alone, they should not be allowed to wander around the ship unaccompanied.

Visitors to the ship should be 'signed in' to a Visitors Book. They should also sign an indemnity form, especially if they are spending time in the working areas of the ship.

When dealing with the port, which can be a difficult relationship, think of the three C's, communication, calmness and courtesy, as a guiding theme.

No port is the same and each country has regulations specific to that country and government. In some you will treated with courtesy, in others an up-market AB.

Either way, your job is the same, to have the ship entered in and cargo work commenced as soon as possible and to respect that country's laws and comply with the port regulations during your ship's stay. If you can do this, then you have done your job as Captain.

28.3 The Port

Your job is to ensure a smooth stay in the port

With time in ports continually declining and with an increase in port requirements and inspections, the need for efficient ship management and port liaison has never been greater. Regrettably, the decline in professional competency and experience, both on the ship and in the port, has lead to situations where the ship and port are in conflict rather than harmony.

The first problem area that the ship encounters in the modern port is that of the establishment of responsibilities. Some ports have a Harbour Master, others a Port Captain, others a Port Manager, Port Directors and Harbour General Managers. The ship could immediately relate to the Harbour Master or Port Captain, who would be in charge of all port related matters, but today this is not necessarily the case. Some ports have Harbour Masters who are only responsible for marine matters, while the port will have a Port Manager who is responsible for the berths and possibly others responsible for financial matters, with a General Manager in overall charge. To this might be added Terminal Managers with their own sectors of responsibility.

To a ship arriving in an unfamiliar port, with a length of stay measured in hours, the division of responsibility is confusing. Often there is a lack of practical knowledge, with little shipping experience and little interest in visiting the ships. Unfortunately, when a Captain tries to meet port management, they are often told that they are 'not available'.

This all seems to stem from a belief that all such contacts should be via the agent, even though many agents have little or no interest in such representation. It is the Master who represents the owners of the ship, not the agents, so it is important that the ship has a port reference guide that explains the responsibilities of the port management and, more importantly, how to contact them.

28.4   Cargo Management

Cargo management and authority ashore would be appreciated

Cargo must be discharged or loaded as efficiently and safely as possible. This is the prime aim and I am sure would be recognised by both ship and port as such. However, efficient management of this is not enhanced by the non-existence of any form of berth or terminal management for discussion of cargo related problems. Often the ship is faced with a foreman with no management authority.

The ship must prepare and agree with the berth or terminal the cargo load or discharge programme. It is then the obligation of the berth to follow that, with any changes owing to equipment failure agreed by the ship. In the past it was accepted practice that the ship was loaded to the Captain's requirements and many Charter-Parties stated this. However, there are many terminals or berths where this is reversed so the ship must load to their instructions.

The ship is in a difficult position in these circumstances. It must either agree to load as the port or berth requires or risk the port refusing to berth the ship or blacklisting the ship or Captain on future occasions. On the other hand, the Captain has an obligation to place the safety of his vessel and crew before all other interests. For example, a common problem is a dispute regarding bulk carrier loading rates, with some ports wishing to constantly increase them, regardless of the age or state of the ship. Although there have not been any conclusive findings on the effect of this rate of loading on the steelwork and stresses on the vessel, you should assume the worst and err on the side of safety.

A shipping loss alongside where high loading of bulk cargoes was being conducted didn't have as much industry impact as we'd hope!
(MV "Trade Daring", 145,000 GRT, Ponta de Madeira, Brazil 1994)

28.5 Ship Management

The ship, as a 'factory', must carry on with the normal maintenance, repairs, office management and safety regulations. With the lengthening time between drydocks, the reduction of skilled personnel, increased port inspection services and the time and paperwork associated with safety enhanced by the ISM requirements, management in port is essential for these tasks to be completed.

It is not unusual for a ship with 24 hours in port to have a programme of engine repairs, surveys, bunkering, storing, crew changing or medical treatment while dealing with ISM items. If an unscheduled visit by Port State, the Coast Guard or other inspection parties is added to this, any attempt at management can easily break down.

The meetings in port can begin to have the air of needing an orderly queue (Courtesy USCG)

It is crucial that there is co-operation from the berth and port, both in recognition of the busy schedule of the ship and assistance in completing the various tasks.

28.6 Personnel

The personnel and catering functions of the ship must carry on because the ship is still the home of the ship's company. This is often a forgotten function as there is, in most cases, very little regard for ship personnel within the port management structure. However, to the ship this is extremely important. Seamen who are harried from one job to another with interrupted mealtimes because of unscheduled port requirements, who have to struggle over railway lines on filthy berths with stores unable to be delivered to the ship's side, who are told that they cannot go ashore without ordering a taxi and that they cannot have their family or visitors aboard because it is the berth or port regulation, are not going to be your most co-operative workers. It is not easy trying to fit these types of problems into your management schedule but the crew must have some kind of consideration if the ship is to function efficiently while all the distractions are taking place.

28.7 Port Services

When port services are discussed, there is again a division of responsibility between the terminal or berth and the port. Because of the differences in the way in which various ports are managed, it is impossible to say who is responsible for what service.

28.8 Pollution Control

One of shipping's aims is not to pollute. However, if such a thing should occur, it is to be expected that the port will provide immediate assistance. But it is surprising that, with all the concern and publicity surrounding the pollution problem, there are many ports that do not provide oil booms around the ship when bunkering or that do not have any pollution service on standby.

Oil sludge barges have been a requirement for provision by ports for a long time yet many ports still do not have such a facility or any intention of providing them. When bunkering, apart from all the required shipboard requirements, it does no harm to advise the port and ask if there is a pollution boom provided for the operation.

28.9 The Berth

World Vale berthing at Robert Bank

In many ports the berths are both Port Authority owned and private. There seems to be the belief that if a berth or terminal is private, then the port has no responsibility whatsoever for the conditions at that berth. But is this correct? After all, the ship pays the port dues and so has a right to expect the basic services to be provided, regardless of who owns the terminal.

As the port sends the Port State inspection service and port health to inspect the ship at any berth, private or port owned, it would seem sensible to make it a mandatory requirement that essential services are provided at all berths within the port, extending their inspection to include the berths whether they are private or public.

28.10 Berth Preparation

When the ship arrives off the berth, the following can be reasonably expected:

- The berthing position should be clear of other vessels and barges with cranes or gantry arms lifted and moved out of the way of the berthing area
- the bridge position, or the position along the berth where the ship is required, should be clearly marked
- there should be adequate bollards for lines to be made fast to and sufficient linesmen to handle the lines
- the depth of water at the berth must be the depth or greater than that shown on the chart
- the berth should be well fendered.

28.11 The Gangway

The gangway can be quite a tug of war

This is a constant source of problems in many ports. If the fendering arrangements stop the ship's gangways being safely used the berth must provide safe access on and off the ship at all times. It is pointless to continue claiming that this is the ship's responsibility when the ship can do nothing about a three metre gap between the end of the gangway and the shore and a large rise and fall of tide. Equally, if the midships gangway is used on large vessels, it must be protected from the falling cargo debris that so often happens on bulk carriers.

The port should require that all ships berthed within it have a telephone service, either by land line or cellular, irrespective of the ship having a satellite link.

There should be garbage disposal facilities at every berth, with the cost included in the port fees. If we continue with the policies of many ports, that there is no service available or that the ship must order and pay for this service, the ports will continue to have the garbage from ships washed up on their beaches after they sail.

Fresh water must be available at all berths.

There should be access to the ship side for service and stores vehicles. The port has to recognise that they have a responsibility to assist in safely loading the essential ship supplies necessary to keep the ships running safely and adequately. If the berth fending facilities preclude the use of ship's cranes in reaching the shore, then the berth has a responsibility to provide a crane or a boat service when required.

The berth must be well lit and clear of garbage or cargo residue. This particularly applies to bulk terminals.

The ship's company and their visitors must have safe access to and from the shore. If the berth considers that an individual walking within the port or terminal area is unsafe, the berth has a responsibility to provide free transportation to the exit from their property.

28.12 The Watch in Port

It is important that the OOW knows what's expected of him

The OOW in port has plenty to look after apart from the cargo work that is meant to be his prime responsibility. It is important that, just like at sea, the OOW knows what is expected of him and what his authority is. The Chief Officer is in charge of the deck and watches in port, but is generally immersed in the problems of cargo and immediate deck work so their nightly orders are written with these problems in mind. For this reason, I suggest that you establish permanent standing orders for port, in which you can itemise what you expect and want from the OOW.

Here is an example of a set of standing orders for port use.

28.12.1 Port Standing Orders

Issue separate standing orders for port

These orders are intended to complement those of the Chief Officer. The OOW, in addition to cargo duties, is responsible for the safety and security of the ship and those onboard. To assist in this, the following will apply:

- The OOW will ensure that the ship is tight alongside and that the mooring lines are adjusted with the rise and fall of the ship
- in the event of the weather deteriorating, the OOW should not hesitate to order additional moorings to be put out to ensure the ship is secured. If required, the outboard anchor may be walked out to the bottom. Should there be a danger of the ship coming off the berth, the VHF should be used to contact the port and tugs ordered to keep the vessel alongside
- the OOW will ensure that the gangway is kept at the correct height to avoid damage, with special regard for passing vessels and that it is safe, well lit and secure at all times
- when ships are passing it is important to ensure that all the mooring lines are tight. Should any damage to ship or lines occur during the passing of a vessel, the time and name of the ship should immediately be entered in the Port Log, and the port authorities advised of the occurrence by the VHF. A damage report should be filed

- safety equipment is to be worn by all personnel, both ship and shore, when on the decks
- in the event of any oil spill, the ship's emergency response plan is to be followed
- it is important that any oil in the water near the ship is investigated immediately. The ER should be checked and any pumping that is taking place stopped until the source of the oil is established. If it is from the ship, then order 6 applies and the harbour authorities are to be immediately advised. If it is not from the ship, the terminal operators are to be advised and the agents notified. An immediate entry is to be made in the Port Log, together with the names of those notified
- any deposits of oil or grease on the decks must be immediately cleared and the area secured until safe for use
- during the hours of darkness, all gangway and deck lights must be switched on and working
- should an accident occur onboard it is imperative that, if required, shore assistance is obtained as soon as possible. If there is no immediate contact or telephone available, then the port authorities should be contacted on the VHF. The following information should be given:
    - name of ship
    - position in the port
    - nature of the problem and the services required
    - an officer should be stationed at the gangway to ensure that, on the arrival of the requested services, they can be immediately directed to the accident area
- in the event of injury to any person, shore or crew, it is essential that the facts of the accident are recorded as soon as possible. The following are required:
    - nature of injury
    - treatment given, if any
    - place and time
    - lighting conditions
    - safety equipment worn by the injured person
    - any suspicion of drug or alcohol
    - statements and names of witnesses
    - the company accident form is to be completed
- in the event of any damage occurring to the ship or equipment, a damage report is to be filed, signed by the required personnel and an entry made in the Port Log
- no shore worker is to enter the accommodation except on official business. Any shore worker found in the accommodation must be challenged and either conducted to the person they wish to see or requested to leave

- if at any time the OOW observes a shore worker behaving in an erratic manner or suspects that they might be under the influence of alcohol or drugs, or that they are working in such a manner that they might cause injury or damage to others or to the ship, then their supervisor is to be informed. This is to be entered in the Port Log. Should their behaviour continue, then the OOW is to request their removal from the ship

- each morning, the deck area in the way of the gangway and accommodation entrance is to be washed down and the main deck alleyway cleaned

- flags will be hoisted at 0800 and lowered at sunset

- the bridge equipment check list must be completed when testing gear prior to departure

- the bridge wings and coamings must be washed down prior to departure and the bridge windows cleaned

- should the OOW have difficulties at any time, if any accident occurs, or there are difficulties with shore personnel, then he will consult with his head of department or myself if onboard. I am to be advised immediately of any accident, damage or pollution incident. In dealing with any member of the ship's company or shore personnel, the OOW is acting on my behalf and with my authority and, provided that he has acted in a responsible manner, will always have my support. I expect that all visitors to the ship are dealt with in a courteous manner regardless of who or what they are

- the gangway board must state clearly the date and time of departure and the time the crew must be onboard. This must be put on the board at least 24 hours prior to the ship's ETD

- no smoking signs are to be displayed and enforced where relevant

- no alcohol is to be brought onto the ship by any crew member or shore worker

- during bunkering, the pollution equipment will be placed out on deck at the bunkering position ready for immediate use and the appropriate signal is to be hoisted. The bunkering check list MUST be completed prior to bunkering operations

- the Ship Security Plan is to be complied with dependant on the Security State the vessel is at. Normally this will be State 1. Any persons onboard who are not identified as bona fide workers are to be challenged and identified

- the OOW will obtain, each morning in port, the weather forecast and bring any change in the weather conditions to the attention of the Chief Officer and myself.

If all the above is complied with, you are not only a lucky man, but you should be able to proceed ashore without too much worry about your absence. One suggestion I would make is that in your deck office there is always a ship's camera ready for use. In fact it is not a bad idea if the OOW gets used to carrying this around with him. He will then be in a position to photograph the scene of any accident or incident that occurs during his watch. If he is too busy he can give the camera to a crew member to do this but, whoever takes the photographs, the ship will have vital evidence of the accident or incident site.

When going ashore you should notify the Duty Officer and the Senior Officer onboard of your departure and provide an estimate of time back. In addition, if you have a mobile phone signal where you are, your phone number should be made available to them and the agent.

29   You and the Law

You never seem to be far from the shadow of the law as Captain

The legal position of the captain has been touched upon in many sections of this book. This is because an understanding of that position has become increasingly important and it is not difficult to imagine the day when cruise ships recruit legal officers to sail as assistants to the Captain.

The current fashion for arresting ship's officers is growing and is unlikely to go away. The anti pollution lobby and the political gain its support provides to government agencies is one of the main drivers of this fashion. However, it sometimes feels that we have reached the stage where, when a ship appears from over the horizon, the first thought is 'what can we arrest them for', especially if the flag is of some minor marine administration and the crew is mixed. It is a moot point whether or not any flag provides protection any more.

There are Laws in existence regarding the right to arrest, detain or impose fines on Seamen. The United Nations Convention on the Law of the Sea (UNCLOS) is the encompassing umbrella for the laws of the Sea. According to article 230, only monetary penalties can be imposed for violations of national or international laws for the prevention and control of pollution when the violation is committed by a foreign vessel, except where the violation is a *'willful and serious act in territorial waters'*. Articles 73 and 292 contain the regulations against the unreasonable detention of seafarers and for their release against the provision of a suitable bond.

Three other clauses that are extremely important to us are found in Article 97:

- In the event of a collision, or any other incident of navigation concerning a ship on the high seas, involving the penal or disciplinary responsibility of the Master or of any other person in the service of the ship, no penal or disciplinary proceedings may be instituted against such a person except before the judicial or administrative authorities of either the Flag State or the State of which such person is a national

- in disciplinary matters, the State which has issued a master's certificate or a certificate of competence or license shall alone be competent, after due legal process, to pronounce the withdrawal of such certificates, even if the holder is not a national of the State which issued them

- no arrest or detention of the ship, even as a measure of investigation, shall be ordered by any authorities other than those of the flag State

Finally, the IMO resolution A.987(24), adopted on 1st December 2005, on the fair treatment of Seafarers in the event of a maritime accident:

- Urge all states to respect the basic human rights of seafarers involved in maritime accidents

- urges all states to expeditiously to investigate maritime accidents to avoid any unfair treatment of seafarers

- urges further all states to adopt procedures to allow the prompt repatriation or re-embarkation of seafarers following maritime accidents.

So it does seem that there is legal support for fair treatment within the framework of international law.

However, looking at some examples, we find that fair treatment to be often missing:

In 2002, the Captain of the MV Prestige experienced catastrophic hull failure off of the west coast of Spain. He requested port of refuge in Spain to shelter his ship and crew and hopefully discharge the cargo. This was refused. He then, as was his duty, ensured the safety of his crew by evacuating everyone but himself and the two others onboard who were needed to support the salvage operation. Owing to the continuing severe weather, on the 19th of November the ship broke in two and sank.

This Captain, who had carried out his duties in an exemplary manner, saved his crew and continued to try to save his ship, was imprisoned by the Spanish Authorities, without trial, and refused any legal aid or contact. Eventually, he was allowed back to Greece on a bond that he return for trial

The Erika suffered a catastrophic hull failure in the Bay of Biscay in December 1999. The captain closed in to the French coast to abandon ship, which with the use of helicopters and a lifeboat he succeeded in doing with no loss of life before the vessel sank.

He was imprisoned for two weeks before being released to detention in Paris. He was eventually allowed to return to India in February 2000. Another case where the Captain did all he could and by his actions saved the life of his crew.

In both of these cases, class have not been called for trial and, in the Erika case, the class society RINA placed the blame on the Master, even though the weather, at around force 9, was not excessive.

The final and most disturbing case, and most disturbing is that of the Virgo which, in international waters in 2001, was allegedly involved in a collision with a US fishing vessel, with loss of life on the fishing vessel. The vessel was arrested and held in a Canadian port at the request of the US government, completely contravening UNCLOS article 97. The Captain was imprisoned by the Canadian authorities, together with the OOW and the lookout. The Master was eventually released but detained in Canada for a further 18 months before being released on a $US100,000 bond pending extradition charges.

It would seem that the words of the United Nations have had little effect on maritime states, who impose their own laws on seamen as they think fit. The latest fad is in cases where the operator of the ship goes bankrupt and abandons his ship. The Captain, apart from the financial loss he probably has suffered, is now 'detained' until all bills are settled on behalf of the bankrupted owner.

Case after case shows that, far from there being any desire to comply with the Laws of the Sea, there is now flagrant disregard for them. New national laws are constantly formulated to further criminalise seamen.

Even more worryingly, the humanitarian aspect that we could always rely on is itself now in question. Take the case of the Delta Pride, whose owner went bankrupt while the ship was in Mexico. The Mexicans confiscated the ship's documents and passports.

With no owner, and increasingly desperate, the master sailed for Brownsville in Texas, hoping for proper legal proceedings to be followed. Instead they were left without food and water for several weeks, existing on the fish that they caught and rainwater. The court in Brownsville sold the ship for well below its worth. The internationally accepted procedure of the crew having first lien on the money was abandoned and instead they were taken into a detention centre and kept there for 6 months. Where i the humanity and justice in such actions?

Are they all the same?
The benefits conferred by flag appear to be reducing

At the present time, regardless of where we are from, the flag our ships fly or the countries we are sailing between, apart from the actions and support of the owners, operators, unions or associations to which we belong, there seems to be very little our own governments are doing about these arrests and detentions. If we are working for a ship management company or for an owner who is only a name plate on some island hideaway, that leaves only the unions. If you do not belong to a master's association or union, as many Captains do not, then you could well be on your own.

If your company is operating from somewhere like this you'll need to have your own parachutes in place

Even for those who have support it is a harrowing experience, creating the possibility of a criminal record for something that was absolutely nothing to do with you, or at least something that was unavoidable.

30 The Final Word

The Last Phase: Retirement

Command will often be lonely but hold on to your dreams

Your command is yours not mine and it is not my intention to tell you how to run your ship. Each ship will add to your confidence and each incident, for there will be a few, will add to your experience. I hope that the events described and my suggestions for coping with problems have made you think. If they help you with any problem the book has served its purpose.

The sea is constantly teaching us new lessons. There are many excellent books that will go deeper into the subjects raised and I recommend that your seamanship library grows with your knowledge.

As a Captain you will not have friends onboard and if you think you do, wait until something goes seriously wrong. Command is a lonely place. It is privilege that comes at a high price. Those who have never experienced it will not understand it.

You will learn to catnap during brief periods to catch up on sleep. If you stay long enough at sea in command, you will wake to the slightest change in the engine or change of movement of the ship and you will develop a sixth sense that will draw you to the bridge for no other reason than you think that you should be there. You will be called 'old man' before you are old, cautious when you are prudent and old fashioned when you require professionalism. You will eventually know the ways across the oceans during the different seasons, the port approaches and the rivers of the world. You will be able to look at the seas and weather and from that, together with the way of the ship, feel what is coming and even begin to regard hurricanes in the area as an interesting challenge to your tactical ability! All that is ahead of you.

One of the most difficult problems that you will have to face is the change within yourself. You will, if you are doing the job right, become more authoritative and decisive. As you progress you will become confident in your abilities and less tolerant of the frailties of others and be able to speak your views on any number of subjects, some of which you know little about but there are not who will correct you!

All this is fine while you are Captain of the ship, but there are times when you leave your seagoing environment and step ashore. Welcome to Mars. You are not a Captain here or, if you are, no one cares. When you visit the office, your blunt speaking ways, regardless of how honestly you are trying to express yourself, will not be appreciated. Authority and decisiveness are not such admired qualities ashore, except at election time. Regard the shore now as visiting a different country where different rules prevail and, if only out of courtesy, you must follow them. They really much less interested in hearing your tales of 'derring do' than you are in telling them, except for some of the better yarns that you tell in the pub. The cat having kittens is more relevant than a storm that just sank three ships. Keep it that way. Learn to take off your stripes and oak leaves as you leave the gangway. Tell them about the mermaids or anything that keeps them happy and enjoy the relaxation of being off of your ship and free from responsibilities. They will return soon enough.

As a last rejoinder, never admit you do not know what to do, especially on your ship. While you may ask for opinions never ask what to do from your staff even if you do not know. Always show confidence. The tougher a situation gets the more confidence you must display. This will hold your ship's company together.

But I will think the real final word must go to someone who unfortunately did not have the opportunity of learning through experience:

'When anyone asks me how I can best describe my experience in nearly forty years at sea, I merely say, uneventful. Of course there have been winter gales, and storms and fog and the like. But in all my experience, I have never been in any accident... or any sort worth speaking about. I have seen but one vessel in distress in all my years at sea. I never saw a wreck and never have been wrecked nor was I ever in any predicament that threatened to end in disaster of any sort'.

E. J. Smith, 1907, Captain, RMS Titanic

In Command	The Final Word

The Apostleship of the Sea (AOS), traditionally known as the 'Stella Maris', provides practical and pastoral care to seafarers. Present in over 90 countries, their port chaplains and pastoral workers offer friendship to all seafarers regardless of religion, gender or race.

In larger ports they work from seafarers' centres. Recognising the pressure of turnaround times, they bring their services to seafarers in the docks and onboard. These include communications facilities, transport and a sympathetic ear. When seafarers remain in port, for example through illness, pastoral workers offer practical help and friendship.

Although part of the Catholic Church, they never impose their beliefs. They encourage seafarers to maintain their own moral values and self-respect and know that, after weeks onboard, seafarers may need comfort and social contact when ashore and their Seafarers' centres are safe places for socialising and relaxing.

In Great Britain, AOS is active in 57 ports and berthing facilities with 26 port chaplains and over 100 volunteers offering welfare services, welcome and pastoral support. Find us through our international online directory at **www.stellamaris.net**

Apostleship of the Sea Great Britain is a wholly independent Registered Charity No. 1069833 (registered with the Charity Commission) and a Company Limited by Guarantee No. 3320318 (registered in England).
Website: **www.apostleshipofthesea.org.uk**

AOS GB would like to thank Witherby Seamanship International for their generous support

The good work of the Apostleship of the Sea was brought to our attention by David Savage of OCIMF, who is a trustee of the Charity. In 2007 David undertook a sponsored cycle ride over the length of the UK to raise money for the charity. WSIL is delighted to be able to support the Apostleship of the Sea through sales of this book.

Recommended Reading
view more products at www.witherbyseamanship.com

Peril at Sea & Salvage: A Guide for Masters 5th Ed.

The object of this guide is to provide information to assist masters in making decisions when confronted with a perilous situation. Prepared principally with oil tankers and gas carriers in mind, but much of the advice is appropriate to other ships.

£30 , Eur 42, USD 60

A Master's Guide to Berthing

Ship handling is an art rather than a science. However, a ship handler who knows a little of the science will be better at his art.

A ship handler needs to understand what is happening to his ship and, more importantly, what will happen a short time into the future. This knowledge is essential in a port environment when a ship encounters close quaters situations, narrow channels and the effects of cross-winds and currents. The purpose of this guide is to provide some insight into what can go wrong and why. Why ships are designed the way they are. Why they handle the way they do and how to berth them.

£35, Eur 49, USD 70

Drug Trafficking & Drug Abuse 2nd Ed.

A high proportion of drug trafficking is undertaken by sea because of the opportunities for high volume movements from producing to consuming countries. Shipping is vulnerable to drug trafficking on two fronts. Firstly, the threat of drugs being concealed on vessels means that the enforcement efforts of Customs authorities can result in delays to ships and cargoes. Secondly, the possible involvement of crew members in drug abuse threatens the safety of the vessel.

£18, Eur 25, USD 36

Anchors and Anchorwork

When you consider anchors there is a large number of ocean going ships to consider. This pdf covers the anchors in use on merchant vessels, their associated equipment, anchorages, anchoring and the problems of anchorages and manoeuvring in such a close confine which is too often an often underestimated hazard.

£15, Eur 21, USD 30

Ship Manoeuvring Principles and Pilotage

This book is an excellent addition to the pool of knowledge on the subject. The text is easy to read and often delivered in an anecdotal style. For experienced pilots it will often ring draw to mind half forgotten night watches and sticky manoeuvres while, for the aspiring pilot, it provides first class advice. The book mixes practice with theory and will find a welcome place in any pilot station.

£25, Eur 35, USD 50

Bridge Procedures Guide 4th Ed

This 4th Ed of the (ICS) Bridge Procedures Guide is intended to reflect best navigational practice on merchant ships operating today, in all sectors and trades.

The Guide brings together the good practice of seafarers with the aim of improving navigational safety and protection of the marine environment. The need to ensure the maintenance of a safe navigational watch at all times, supported by safe manning levels on the ship, is also a fundamental principle adhered to in this Guide.

£60, Eur 84, USD 120